P9-AQK-598

A Tretise of Miraclis Pleyinge

A Tretise of Miraclis Pleyinge

Edited by
Clifford Davidson

With Commentary on the Dialect
by Paul A. Johnston, Jr.

EARLY DRAMA, ART, AND MUSIC
MONOGRAPH SERIES, 19

Medieval Institute Publications
WESTERN MICHIGAN UNIVERSITY
Kalamazoo, Michigan
1993

Revised, corrected, and expanded edition
© 1993 by the Board of the Medieval Institute

Originally published as *A Middle English Treatise on the Playing of Miracles*
by the University Press of America in 1981

Printed in the United States of America

Cover Design by Linda K. Judy

ISBN 1-879288-31-1
ISBN 1-879288-32-x (Pbk.)

Contents

PLATES

Acknowledgements

The present edition of *A Tretise of Miraclis Pleyinge* is based on a provisional text which was published from typescript in 1981 under the title *A Middle English Treatise on the Playing of Miracles*. At that time the study of medieval English drama was at the beginning stage of an exciting period with the recent founding of the Records of Early English Drama and Early Drama, Art, and Music projects, and it seemed crucial that a more accessible and more accurate edition of the *Tretise* than the outdated nineteenth-century texts of Halliwell and Mätzner should be quickly available to students and scholars. In spite of its shortcomings, my provisional text has been widely used and cited. However, a new edition is clearly called for, and I have in the present volume attempted to fulfill the need for a transcription of the *Tretise* according to the same principles as previously but providing a freshly edited text and expanded introduction and apparatus that will take into account more recent research. I have also had the advantage of having more than a decade to think about the *Tretise*, and I hope that my own interpretations have matured during this time.

Once again I am grateful to Professor (now Emeritus) Robert Palmatier for his advice toward developing the principles of transcription initially, and to Nicholas Davis, whose Cambridge University dissertation remains a most useful source of information about the *Tretise*. And I am again indebted to previous editors, especially Anne Hudson, whose *Selections from English Wycliffite Writings* includes a well-edited selection from the first part of the *Tretise*.

Three persons in particular have been of substantial assistance in the preparation of the present edition. Ann Eljenholm Nichols kindly read the entire manuscript and made useful suggestions, and John Wasson, whose expertise in paleography far surpasses my own, has generously checked my transcription. Paul A. Johnston, Jr., agreed to study the dialect of the *Tretise* and to provide an essay entitled "The Dialect of *A Tretise of Miraclis Pleyinge*," which I have included in the present volume with considerable enthusiasm since it raises some basic questions about the text and gives some very welcome answers. His presentation of his methodology will also be useful to future researchers. A number of other scholars also kindly answered my queries about various details. However, whatever blemishes remain in the present book are entirely my own responsibility.

My transcriptions and the photographic facsimiles are presented by courtesy of the British Library, which has been invaluable for my research in other ways as well. The Western Michigan University Library and the University of Michigan Graduate Library were also crucial for my work, but I also benefitted very considerably from the library of the University of Chicago, the Cambridge University Library, the Warburg Institute Library, the libraries of University of Minnesota, and the Bodleian Library.

I need with gratitude to acknowledge fellowships and research grants from Western Michigan University, most recently a generous grant from the Faculty Research and Creative Activities Support Fund to cover travel expenses for examination of the manuscript in the British Library as well for photographs of the pages which contain the *Tretise*. Finally, this edition of the *Tretise* probably would not have been completed except for the encouragement of Thomas Seiler of Medieval Institute Publications who insisted that it merited inclusion in the Early Drama, Art, and Music Monograph Series.

Introduction

A Tretise of Miraclis Pleyinge, which is contained in a single manuscript (British Library MS. Add. 24,202, fols. 14^{r}-21^{r}) copied in the early fifteenth century, is the longest and most significant piece of dramatic criticism in Middle English. Most often identified as the product of a hostile Wycliffite (or Lollard) author or authors and usually believed to have been written at some time between 1380 and 1425,[1] this tract directs its polemic against the playing of "miraclis." According to Jonas Barish, the *Tretise* is the "chief surviving antitheatrical document from the Middle Ages,"[2] but it also uniquely serves as an useful source for revealing some important aspects of the theatrical aesthetics of the late Middle Ages. There are, however, some very serious difficulties of interpretation to be encountered. Most prominently, the term 'miraclis' which is central to the *Tretise* is ambiguous; it seems to cover a fairly broad range of dramatic representation and related activity, though religious drama—especially the playing of the Passion—is specifically singled out as utterly reprehensible. The difficulty of defining the term 'miracle' was noted as long ago as 1916 by George R. Coffman,[3] and recent scholarly investigation by Lawrence Clopper focused on Latin and Middle English usage of the term has affirmed its ambiguity.[4]

'Miracle' apparently may not originally have necessarily signified a religious play, for it seems to have included a type universally condemned by ecclesiastical authorities, who objected to the participation in such plays by the clergy. Thus in 1293 at Lanchester, Durham, clergy from the collegiate church were forbidden to attend "such spectacles or sightes, which ar comonly called *Myracles*."[5] Clopper has argued that the source of the word 'miracle' is the Latin term *miraculum*, used in the Vulgate to designate "horror," as in *Jeremiah* 44.11-12.[6] Based on evidence from medieval legislation and commentary, *miracula*, according to Clopper, are therefore to be understood as entertainments which mix truth and falsehood, jest and earnest; they were hence "derisive" and "jest with or mock the truth of God's word."[7] It is not impossible that a spectacle of this type was presented on the eve of the feast of St. Peter ad Vincula in 1345 at Carlisle; clerics produced this *miraculum* in the market place, and afterward there was an affray which was serious enough to be recorded in extant legal documents. The information that we have, however, does not allow us to speculate about the content of the spectacle or play.[8] It is possible that the "pleyes of miracles" attended by Chaucer's Wife of Bath were of this type,[9] but even here we cannot achieve certainty. In the early twelfth century a saint play of St. Catherine ("ludum de Sancta Katerina, quem 'miracula' vulgariter appellamus") had been rehearsed and probably presented at Dunstable—a drama hardly likely to be either secular or derisive.[10]

If there were a "precise" meaning of the term 'miraclis,' however, it was not used in the *Tretise* in any exact way but instead seems to have been intended as a broad category that would link the word "miraclis" with a spectrum of dramatic activity ranging from the staging of religious scenes to representions on feast days and seasons such as Christmas.[11] In any case, Nicholas Davis still appears correct in asserting that careful attention to "some of the more knotted passages in the text" of the Wycliffite or Lollard treatise suggests reference "to more than one kind of play, and to a particular economic institution which made possible the proliferation of large-scale public drama."[12] Though at no point in the treatise are the great civic Corpus Christi cycles mentioned, such dramatic spectacles were already in existence by the late fourteenth century. The dramatic records of such cities as Coventry and York verify that a very large monetary outlay was required for these plays, which also had economic motives; further, dialect evidence places the manuscript of the *Tretise* in the Midlands—i.e., in a region accessible to Coventry where the Corpus Christi plays coincided with one of the greatest fairs of medieval England.[13] Though the available evidence does not give a full picture of Lollard attitudes toward playing, such conditions of dramatic production were inevitably condemned by some (but certainly not all) Lollards, who would have seen the money spent on the plays to involve draining resources that should have been spent on charity. One of the most successfully argued points in the *Tretise* is precisely that people complain much less about money spent on the production of miracles than about giving to the poor and needy. This argument has a high degree of credibility since examination of the dialect of the *Tretise* (see below, pp. 53–84) suggests locations in Huntingdonshire (for Part I) and Northamptonshire (for Part II). Northampton is possibly associated with an extant play text of Abraham and Isaac and probably had other plays as well since, according to post-Reformation records, its pageant wagons had been stored in St. George's Hall on Abingdon Street in c.1542,[14] and Coventry, which drew widely from the surrounding regions for audiences for its famous plays, was lavish in expenditure on its play cycle to the point where it was a serious drain on the local economy during times of economic depression. A letter of Coventry's mayor, William Coton, to Cromwell in 1539 calls attention to the "decay and povertie of the said Citie" and specifically identifies the Corpus Christi "playes and pagyontes" as so costly that the citizens "fare the worse all the yeire after."[15]

In the midst of its attack on the stage, the *Tretise of Miraclis Pleyinge* presents a set of propositions that may in combination be regarded as providing a fairly coherent argument in the defense of religious plays and of the recreative experience associated with the theater. This argument, set forth in the *Tretise* only as a false defense of the stage to be put down, has been focus of most previous critical attention given to the work. Rosemary Woolf even suggests that the author may have been "replying to some corresponding Latin treatise in defence of mystery plays" much in the manner of the attack, contained in another tract included in the same manuscript (fols. 26^r-28^v), upon arguments like those presented in Walter Hilton's Latin treatise defending images.[16] Whether or not such a defense of the plays ever existed, the evidence of *A Tretise of Miraclis Pleyinge* nevertheless establishes the existence of an aesthetic basis for the religious stage of the late Middle Ages. Thus V. A. Kolve is correct in questioning the long-accepted view that these religious plays were naive and lacking in "theory."[17] On account of the portion which summarizes a *defense* of religious drama, the importance of the treatise can hardly be overestimated, for it contains a view of the religious stage that helps to make sense of other available evidence concerning the presentation of late medieval vernacular plays. But the treatise's arguments *against* the stage also have considerable interest for us since they help to chart the pattern of religious hostility to the theater that originated in the early Church and culminated in the suppression of the religious stage in England during the late sixteenth century[18] and then eventually also in the closing of the secular playhouses in 1642.

The *Tretise of Miraclis Pleyinge* is in two parts (in the present edition, the first part ends at line 385, followed by the second part, lines 386–749), each apparently written by a different author; however, neither author was the Mertonian Nicholas Hereford—a candidate put forward by Nicholas Davis[19]—since the dialect evidence presented by Paul A. Johnston, Jr., below, contradicts this identification and establishes both writers as native to the East Central Midlands. The first part, in spite of the harshness of its rhetoric directed against the theater, has marks of being written by a priest who was not demonstrably heterodox, while the second part, which differs in tone and is much more characteristic of Wycliffite writings, added further arguments addressed to a specific individual, presumably a Lollard or Wycliffite who to this writer's dismay approved of religious plays and supported them.[20]

The first part of the *Tretise* summarizes six points in favor of dramatic presentation of scenes of a religious and/or recreative nature:

1. Plays function to assist in the service and worship of God.

2. Dramatic presentation allows men to visualize the result of sin and thereby encourages their conversion.

3. Representation of the Passion of Christ brings people of both sexes to tears; such tears are in all seriousness a sign of piety that requires to be distinguished from mockery.

4. The only way to attract some men and thus to convert them is through "gamen and pley" or entertainment.

5. Recreation is a human need, and the playing of miracles represents the best type of recreative activity.

6. The wonderful deeds of Christ and his saints may be represented in painting; thus it should also be appropriate to represent such deeds in theatrical display, especially since these are more lively and hence more easily imprinted on the memory than any representation in the visual arts can be.[21]

The last of these points represents the culminating argument in favor of visual representation by living actors, who are able to assist spectators to remember various scenes from sacred history with greater clarity than would be possible in the case of static pictures.[22] But the principal purpose of the first section of the treatise is to refute such arguments in favor of playing religious drama, while in the second part both the tone and the method of argumentation change as the second writer opens a shrill attack on the opinions of someone who shares his "bileve" though he nevertheless sees value from a didactic, mnemonic, and pedagogical standpoint in plays on sacred subjects. There is throughout a strong antagonism to the act of viewing plays because such activity is allegedly to be regarded as idle behavior without positive value—empty signs lacking the substance of truth.[23]

Both parts of the Lollard or Wycliffite treatise are thus broadly opposed to the practice of the medieval theater, including its efforts to set forth events from sacred history within the context of religious festivals. In the *Tretise* the true miracles of Christ and his apostles are contrasted with the pretense of theatrical "miraclis"; the first were done in "ernest," the second merely in "pley" and "bourde." Significantly, the *Tretise*'s attitude toward *play*, particularly when religious matters are involved, remains throughout harsh and lacking in sympathy. The view of life which is implied is rigidly ascetic and puritan, and looks forward to the total rejection of the stage by the more zealous Protestants of the sixteenth and seventeenth centuries. It is of a piece with the Protestant and Humanist attack on religious drama in the Reformation period—an attack that suppressed first the liturgical drama—never very strong in England except for the quasi-dramatic *Depositio crucis* and *Elevatio crucis* for Good Friday and Easter—and then the vernacular plays, including the great civic cycle drama at Coventry and elsewhere.[24]

Hostility to drama of course had been a characteristic of the Christian Church during the Patristic era, for which Tertullian perhaps spoke most forcefully in his *De Spectaculis*. For Tertullian stage spectacles were devil-inspired,[25] an idea that returns in the *Tretise of Miraclis Pleyinge*. To *see* stage plays is self-indulgence in wicked sights which cannot be viewed without harm to the soul, for the eyes thus necessarily become the vehicles by which evil is communicated to the person. Christians, says Tertullian,

> are bidden to put away from us all impurity. By this command we are cut off once for all from the theatre, the proper home of all impurity, where nothing wins approval but what elsewhere has no approval.[26]

Tertullian describes the stage as ultimately "so much honey dropping from a poisoned bit of pastry."[27] For the late medieval *Tretise*, however, the most horrifying spectacle was to see sacred events mimicked on stage allegedly for religious edification; the presentation of secular scenes, albeit at times "japing" which was less than edifying, would be far less reprehensible. Hence the playing of miracles is said to be "worse than though they pleyiden pure vaniteis"; further, the argument is presented that it is normally less wicked "to pleyin rebaudye than to pleyin siche miraclis."

The early Christian attitude toward theatrical spectacle as associated with sexual immorality is not far beneath the surface of the *Tretise*, which charges that "miraclis pleyinge is of the lustis of the fleyssh and mirthe of the body." Isidore of Seville had associated the theater with prostitution—an association that was still to be reckoned with in Shakespeare's time.[28] Isidore's comments are, as Mary Marshall and Joseph R. Jones have shown, repeated through the Middle Ages; Chaucer's statement in translating Boethius—"thise comune strompettis of swich a place that men clepen the theatre"—may be taken as typical.[29] Ovidian treatises on the art of love from the Middle Ages include plays among those places where young lovers are most likely to make "progress" with ladies.[30] Later, in 1493, the woodcut showing the theater in the edition of Terence printed by Trechsel at Lyons also shows activities in the lower part of the illustration that are appropriate to a brothel.[31]

Medieval antagonism to drama, even to liturgical drama and quasi-dramatic forms, has often been surveyed. Well known is the condemnation after his conversion by Gerhoh of Reichersberg of the practices of the monks of Augsburg, who he said needed the inducement of a representation of such a scene as the Slaughter of the Innocents if they were to sup in the refectory. In c.1117-20 he himself had been in charge of dramatic productions at Augsburg Cathedral, but thereafter these plays and spectacles were to be roundly condemned by him.[32] Gerhoh suggested in his later *De Investigatione Antichristi* (c.1161) that clerics who transform the church into a theater are themselves doing the work of the same Anti-Christ whose works are the subject of the spectacle being presented.[33] Plays are said to be false and empty vanities, for they give precise form to sacred events in ways that deserve only condemnation. It is the *illusion* that is being rejected here—the same principle that was similarly controversial in the visual arts of Gerhoh's time. The tendency toward verisimilitude or realism was particularly distrusted, both in drama and the pictorial arts. Additionally, the element of *game* was found particularly noxious, for Gerhoh, like the later writers responsible for *A Tretise of Miraclis Pleyinge*, saw stage spectacle as presenting an illicit form of *pleasurable* experience.

Thus Herrad of Landsberg, in a frequently cited passage, also laments the abuses of the presentation of the *Stella* in the twelfth century:

> But what nowadays happens in many churches? Not a custumary ritual, not an act of reverence, but one of irreligion and extravagance conducted with all the license of youth. The priests having changed their clothes go forth as a troop of warriors; there is no distinction between priest and warrior to be marked. At an unfitting gathering of priests and laymen the church is desecrated by feasting and drinking, buffoonery, unbecoming jokes, play, the clang of weapons, the presence of shameless wenches, the vanities of the world, and all sorts of disorder.[34]

All of this is said to stand in contrast to the decorum of the ritual forms established for the Epiphany by the Church Fathers, whose care was for the strengthening of belief and the attracting of unbelievers rather than for mere entertainment.[35] As in the view of the Lollard or Wycliffite writers, the harmful elements in drama include mimicry, comedy, play, and lack of seriousness.

In twelfth-century England, Aelred of Rievaulx complained of the theatricality of the liturgy, since in his eyes it had become more of a spectacle than a service of prayer. The gestures and emotional effects were, he felt, "suitable not to the house of prayer, but to the theater, not to praying, but to viewing."[36] Aelred, a Cistercian abbot during the early history of the Order, naturally shared the ideals of the Cistercian movement, which aimed at simplicity in the adornment of their churches and at a rejection of ostentatious decoration. In the windows of their churches they therefore adopted plain grisaille glass, which avoided the lavish pictorial display so familiar elsewhere. Examples of this kind of glass remain, most splendidly in the Five Sisters window in York Minster. For a reform movement such as the Cistercian Order, therefore, a strong rejection of actual visual representations either in the visual arts or by the living performers would seem to have been the rule. For example, the staging of the liturgical *Visitatio Sepulchri* on Easter was mainly associated with the Benedictine liturgy or with cathedral practice, not with the Cistercian reforms. Cistercian service books normally contain no liturgical drama. Yet it is significant that Aelred, following St. Bernard of Clairvaux, admitted the important role of *mental* images in devotion; addressing a novice, he wrote:

> I feel my son, I feel the same, how familiarly, how affectionately, with what tears, you seek after Jesus Himself in your holy prayers, when this sweet image of this sweet Boy appears before the eyes of your heart [oculos cordis], when you paint this most lovely face with, as it were, a spiritual imagination, when you feel His most lovely and at the same time mild eyes radiate sweetly at you.[37]

To *play* such a scene with living actors, however, would have been inconsistent with Cistercian ideals and practice.

Prohibitions and restrictions against verifiably secular entertainments or indeed the majority of theatrical representations were deeply imbedded in ecclesiastical law and tradition from Patristic times. The very early *Treatise on the Apostolic Tradition* of St. Hippolytus specifies that participants in games at the circus or in wild-beast shows in the amphitheater, gladiators, actors, and playwrights or theatrical directors must give up their craft or be rejected for instruction in the faith and baptism,[38] while the Emperor Justinian decreed that actors are not to put on the "holy robes" of monastics of either sex in order to impersonate them in a comedy on stage.[39] The Second Council of Nicaea in 787 still proclaimed that the life of an actor was unrighteous,[40] and in 789, for example, an episcopal edict indicated corporal punishment as appropriate for those actors (*histriones*) who put on the clothing of priests, nuns, or monks.[41] The Anglo-Saxon King Edgar in 969 accusingly noted that "a house of clergy is known . . . as a meeting place for actors [histrionum] . . . where mimes [mimi] sing and dance."[42] Such performances had been (and continued to be) forbidden,[43] yet it is known that in England they are recorded up to the dissolution of the monasteries. Through the twelfth and thirteenth centuries sacred drama was not exempt from prohibitions against playing, though it is often difficult to know exactly the type of drama that is being proscribed. Such was the case with the statutes issued by Robert Grosseteste, Bishop of Lincoln, in 1236-44 to prohibit certain types of involvement in performance by his clergy; here secular entertainments are lumped together with the celebration of the feast of fools and plays, specifically "ludos quos vocant miracula."[44] The prohibitions of Pope Innocent III in 1207 likewise are not entirely without ambiguity:

> From time to time theatrical games are produced in certain churches. Not only are imitations of devils introduced in parody; in truth, in certain festivals of the year that immediately follow Christ's birth, deacons, presbyters, and subdeacons in turn present mad parodies with obscene gestures in the sight of the people. They thus tarnish the honor of the clergy who ought better, at that time, to be delighting people by preaching the word of God. The house of God mocks us and the reproaches seem to fall on us. Brothers, we command you to root out these customary parodies and commend the observance of divine and holy orders in your churches. . . .[45]

As Marianne Briscoe indicates, Innocent's condemnation seems to be indicative of a contemporary tension between Church and theatrical practice. On the other hand, there is proof of considerable clerical acceptance at this time of plays that were sufficiently devotional in character.[46]

In spite of the Church Fathers' insistence on the contrast between the false spectacles of the stage and the true spectacle of the Mass, however, Honorius of Autun about the year 1000 had nevertheless felt justified in comparing the sacred rites of the Church to the playing of tragedies. The celebrant is a "tragedian" who "re-presents" Christ's Passion as well as his victory over death to those who look on. When in prayer he extends "his hands he delineates the stretching out of Christ on the cross," for example. Thus also the Preface signifies "the cry of Christ hanging on the cross," while the secret prayers of the Canon represent in some sense the "silence of the Sabbath" or Holy Saturday. Finally, according to Honorius, the giving of "peace and communion" to the congregation by the priest is possible "because, when our accuser has been overthrown by our champion in the conflict, peace is announced by the judge to the people, [and] they are invited to a feast."[47] Honorius was a disciple of Amalarius of Metz, whose importance for modern dramatic criticism has been argued by O. B. Hardison, Jr.[48]

That mimesis in religious plays[49] was coming more and more by the twelfth century to be accepted is, however, indicated not only by extant dramatic texts such as the Anglo-Norman *Adam* and *La Seinte Resureccion* but also by other evidence of the kind presented in William Fitzstephen's comment on the religious plays of London. In Fitzstephen's *Life of Thomas of Canterbury*, he praises the city of London for its sacred spectacles, which were set forth on feast days in order to show miracles and martyrdoms.[50] Except in the case of extant texts, there is no way of ascertaining how such dramatic forms during this period departed from ritual; nevertheless, evidence concerning their transitional nature is convincing. That there was in the twelfth century a resurgence of interest in the theater is also indicated by the revival of theatrical metaphors at that time.[51]

The understanding of religious drama as properly *devotional* rather than merely entertaining or recreational is established by the Anglo-Norman writer William of Waddington in his *Manuel des Péchés* of the late thirteenth century. William rejects open-air theatricals as distinguished from liturgical drama, and especially denounces the use of masks, which may be connected with the "imitations of devils" in Pope Innocent's decree of 1207.[52] John Bromyard, in a passage noted by Clopper, specifically distinguishes masks as distinctive to miracles: "players in the play which is commonly called *miracula* use masks [larvis], beneath which the persons of the actors are concealed. Thus do the demons, whose game is to destroy souls and lure them by sin: in which play, masks are used, that is, curious adornments, and dancing is used, in which the feet run to evil."[53] Nevertheless, for William dramatic forms that are not actually detached from ritual are allowed and serve a devotional purpose.

In his English adaptation of the *Manuel des Péchés*, Robert Mannyng of Brunne, while reducing the idea of *devotion* to the more narrow *inspiring of belief* as a major purpose of the drama, otherwise accepts on the whole William's argument. His adaptation of William's text is as follows:

> Hit is forbode him in the decre,
> Miraclis for to make or se.
> For miracles yif thou byginne,
> Hit is a gadering, a sight of sinne.
> He may in the cherche thurgh this resun
> Pleye the resurrecciun,
> That is to seye, how God ros,
> God and man in might and los,
> To make men be in beleve gode,
> That he ros with flessh and blode.
> And he may pleye with outen plight
> How God was bore in yole night,
> To make men beleve stedfastly

That he lighte in the virgine Mary.
Yif thou do hit in weyys or grevys,
A sighte of sinne trewely hit semys.
Seint Isidre I take to witnes,
For he hit seith that soth hit es.
Thus hit seith in his boke:
They forsake that they toke,
God and here cristendam,
That make swiche pleyys to any man
As miracles and bourdys,
Or tournamentes of gret pris.[54]

Harsh on what he believes to be unauthorized theatricals, he nevertheless approves the *playing* of the Resurrection (probably the *Visitatio Sepulchri*, dramatizing the visit of the three Marys to the tomb) and Incarnation (probably the *Stella* or Magi play) within the church. For his condemnation of churchyard playing and games (often presented or participated in on the north or devil's side of the church building) he calls upon the authority of Isidore of Seville. His attempt at making distinctions is indicative of the fact that through the later Middle Ages the Latin liturgical plays continued to be played in monastic and cathedral settings, while, usually appearing in very different locations, the vernacular religious drama had also emerged. As early as c.1220 at Beverley a production in the summer on the north side of the church by actors wearing masks (*larvatorum*), "as usual," had presented a representation (*repraesentatio*) of the Resurrection with spoken dialogue and gestures; the crowd, gathered around in a ring (*corona*), was said to be motivated "by delight or curiosity or devotion."[55]

The vernacular plays are, of course, no longer today seen as the result of an evolutionary process by which they were supposed to have grown out of the liturgical drama; rather, their source appears to have been quite separate though as yet not fully understood. In some instances religious processions with *tableaux vivants* or royal entries may have been an influence, and some scholars believe that these festival presentations provide an explanation of the origin of the pageant wagon stages used in certain regions, including Northampton and Coventry.[56] In any case, the vernacular plays seem to stand in closer proximity to the iconographic tableaux of the visual arts than to the ritualized liturgical music-drama or related ceremonies such as the *Depositio crucis* on Good Friday. This close relationship with the visual arts seems confirmed by the *Tretise* when the writer notes the argument that the plays are a more lively kind of visual display than a mere painting, whether on wall or glass window or other surface. It is hence important to look at these vernacular plays, particularly those included in the great cycles that developed at Coventry, York, and Chester, through the concept of *devotion* which, derived from popular urban piety, provided their principal animating force.[57] Yet it is a concept that, as Robert Mannyng's text suggests, tended to become obscured among English-speaking people. Thus the *Tretise of Miraclis Pleyinge* argues that the stated purpose of the plays was to bring people around to belief and to sustain them in that belief. In Lollard or Wycliffite terms, the plays were to "convert" people to the faith. Unfortunately, according to the Lollard or Wycliffite text, the playing of miracles is spiritually subversive, a practice that instead undermines faith and inverts the values to be found in true religion.

It seems clear that by the time that the Lollard or Wycliffite treatise was written much of the early Christian hostility toward vernacular drama had dissipated, though certain varieties of theatrical practice would never for very good reason achieve acceptance everywhere. Briscoe notes that the *Destructorium Viciorum* of Alexander Carpenter, produced in approximately 1425, continues to identify both acceptable and unacceptable games and plays[58]—a reminder also that the same term, *ludus*, was used to signify both theatrical event and game.[59] There are those which are socially acceptable and serve well to refresh the soul; included in this type of approved play will be found a related type of performance—King David's harping.[60] Not approved are games and acting identified under the rubric of *perverse illusionis* as well as those kinds which involve lascivious dancing or "plays of the theater" done in locations normally used for theatrical display.[61] These plays seem, however, to be entirely secular in character, though admittedly Carpenter's descriptions lack explicitness which would determine their exact nature.

But by the early fifteenth century there appears to have been considerable dramatic activity in such locations as York, Chester, and East Anglia that was of the approved sort of vernacular play—a vernacular drama that had the support of civic leaders, guildsmen, and clergy alike. In the Midlands, the Corpus Christi play at Coventry seems to have been established in some form by 1392.[62] Productions of these plays very likely involved close collaboration between citizens and clerics, particularly those associated with urban churches, as presumably in the instance of the previously noted Resurrection play in c.1220 at Beverley.[63] In 1426, the Franciscan preacher William Melton came to the city of York where "he commended the said [Corpus Christi] play in several of his sermons by affirming that it was good in itself and most laudable," though the festival atmosphere which accompanied the staging of the sacred scenes in the Creation to Doom cycle in this city also encouraged some unruliness among those in attendance. There were persons, both strangers and residents, who came "not only to the play . . . but also greatly to feastings, drunkenness, clamours, gossipings, and other wantonness";[64] nevertheless, such behavior need not cause us to doubt that devotion was one of the principal factors bringing people together to see the plays, while it would also be hard to deny that the other reasons noted as motives for attendance at the play two hundred years before at Beverley—i.e., the motives of delight and curiosity—would have been involved. Because the Register of the York cycle is extant,[65] we are able to see from the text of the plays that a major purpose must in fact have been devotional, though its inherent dramatic interest also would inspire delight and its dramatic form would draw forth curiosity. Performed on a major feast day, Corpus Christi, by guilds under the surveillance of a city corporation motivated by piety and a desire to advance the honor (and the economic interests) of York,[66] these plays, like similar dramas elsewhere, involved a serious religious function under the façade of play and game. At Chester, the cycle plays were reported to have carried the additional benefit of indulgences for "every person resorting in pecible manner with gode devocion to here and see the . . . [plays]."[67]

In spite of the sneer in the *Tretise* about the weeping of spectators watching a play of the Passion, such empathy with the hero of Christian drama was in fact a mark of Northern piety in the late Middle Ages.[68] The author's reference to weeping is therefore an important piece of evidence concerning the reception of the vernacular religious theater in England. Margery Kempe's uncontrollable weeping in response to the sight of an Our Lady of Pity was different in degree only and not in kind from what was considered acceptable behavior during this period.[69] Emotionalism was widely encouraged, and was believed to signify a healthy inward reaction to the sight of images which themselves carried the reality of the divine story into one's consciousness through the senses. The model for the individual's reaction to the Passion was, after all, the Virgin Mother herself—a powerful argument which the Lollard or Wycliffite text is at pains to counter. The Blessed Virgin was a figure appearing prominently in a pose of sorrow in the work of the Flemish painters, who were zealous to characterize her response to the suffering of her Son. Such is the case in the famous triptych by Roger van der Weyden in the Gemäldegalerie, Vienna, from c.1440; this painting shows the Virgin at the foot of the cross and weeping profusely. Joining the Virgin, though clearly separated from her by space representing temporal distance, are the unidentified donors, a husband and wife who with hands in late medieval positions of prayer seem to be meditating on the scene with the purpose of *feeling* the agony of the event.[70] Perhaps, as Nicholas Davis has suggested, the Lollard or Wycliffite writer objected to the emotionalism expressed by members of the audience at religious plays at least in part because it was unreflective and intellectually shallow,[71] but in late medieval civic piety it was considered very important indeed not only that the very scenes of sacred history be remembered and imagined but also that they should be *felt* on the level of the heart. J. W. Robinson has observed that modern audiences watching the scenes of the Passion in a production of a medieval play may still be moved at the sight of the Crucifixion.[72] The *Tretise* thus in fact serves as a witness to the powerful emotional effect of religious drama—an emotional effect which may still be experienced by audiences several hundred years later.

The emotionalism of late medieval Christianity which was so prominent in private meditation and so much in evidence in the religious drama owes a very great deal to some rather important theological changes that are too complex to describe fully here.[73] The shift has been identified with the change in medieval Christianity from emphasis on the Resurrection to emphasis on the Crucifixion, from Christ's victory over death to his sacrificial death upon the cross. Franciscan theology in particular laid great stress upon the close identification of the self with the suffering Christ; ultimately this tendency was very widespread and is reflected in the vast difference between the static crucifixes of the earlier period and the agonized postures of the representations in art that appear after the twelfth century.[74] The sources of this new *affective theology* have been located in twelfth-century theological currents, particularly in the writings of St. Anselm and the early Cistercians whose emotionalism is well illustrated in the passage in defense of mental images quoted from Aelred of Rievaulx above. In art as well as in drama, the new theology provides the basis for understanding forgiveness of one's sins and reconciliation to God in terms of personal identification with the sufferings felt by Christ as a *human*. Thus Walter Hilton wrote of the contemplation of Christ's Passion as follows:

> For it is an opening of the ghostly eye into Christ's manhood. And it may be called the fleshly love of God, as Saint Bernard calleth it, in as mickle as it is set in the fleshly kind of Christ. And it is right good, and a great

> help in destroying of great sins, and a good way for to come to virtues. And so after to contemplation of the Godhead. For a man shall not come to ghostly delight in contemplation of Christ's Godhead, but he come first in imagination by bitterness and by compassion and by steadfast thinking of his manhood.[75]

This sort of argument, however, seems to be particularly offensive to the writers of the *Tretise of Miraclis Pleyinge*, for this text objects especially to the placing of the divine on the same level as the human. An *exemplum* noted by Siegfried Wenzel in a Good Friday sermon notes, to be sure, some problems that can occur when human actors play the roles of Christ and of those who torment him:

> I knew where there once was a play in summertime [somergame]. One person was Christ, another Peter, another Andrew, some were tormentors, and some the devils. Christ was stretched out, crucified, and beaten, mocked, and held a fool; . . . no one gave him anything but strokes and scorn. And whoever knew how to torment and scorn him was reckoned to play the best. When the game was over, all the players talked among themselves and considered playing again; and one of them said, "Who shall be Christ?" The others said, "He who played today, since he played well." This player then said to them: "I was Christ and was crucified, beaten, mocked, held to be a fool; I was hungry and thirsty, and nobody gave me anything. I looked down below and saw tormentors and demons in great joy. . . . And therefore I tell you for sure that if I must play again, I do not want to be Christ nor an apostle but a tormentor or demon."[76]

In this *exemplum*, one of the other actors then reminds the speaker that Christ fares "badly . . . while the play goes on," but at the end of the play he "shall be well off." And so too it will be at the Day of Doom.[77]

But the *Tretise of Miraclis Pleyinge* analyzes the problem of role-playing involving Christ more specifically in terms of class distinctions. By playing, the *Tretise* charges, the master and the servant are confused, and class distinctions are broken down to an intolerable degree. The awful power of God expressed through Christ is thus challenged. But quite normally in orthodox circles of thought during this period Christ was approached precisely on the level of his humanity, which was regarded as an appropriate gateway to proper contemplation of his divinity. Indeed, for a man to come to terms with Christ's divinity, it was often demanded that the approach must be first to his humanity. This position, which on one level was to be sure supported by the theological nominalism that stressed the awful power of God, was strongly identified with the Franciscans, who remained under the influence of their founder, St. Francis of Assisi, himself the recipient of the gift of the stigmata as a sign of his close identification with the sufferings of Christ. It is surely no accident that the Wycliffites and Lollards, who objected so strongly to seeing Christ in just such terms, should have targeted the Franciscans as their most bitter opponents, though there were also other issues (such as the practice of mendicancy itself) that were involved.[78]

Dominican theology also came to support the theater in those cases in which drama was turned to the service of good or was presented without evil intent for recreative entertainment. St. Thomas Aquinas defends recreative enjoyment and makes reference to a story that was told of "Blessed John the Evangelist" who provided defense of such activity through an analogy: like a bow, "man's mind would break if the tension were never relaxed." Not surprisingly, he insists that pleasure is never to "be sought in indecent or injurious deeds or words."[79] But pleasure itself is not more wicked than sleep, a function that likewise disengages man's reason.[80] Drama is therefore not to be judged evil if it provides recreation without licentiousness, nor are actors themselves members of an illicit vocation. "The occupation of play-actors, the object of which is to cheer the heart of man, is not unlawful in itself; nor are they in a state of sin provided that their playing be moderated, namely that they use no unlawful words or deeds to amuse, and that they do not introduce play into undue matters and seasons."[81] Such a view of plays and players is, of course, completely the reverse of the insistence upon total seriousness that characterizes *A Tretise of Miraclis Pleyinge*, which implicitly rejects Aquinas' position in favor of the sternest medieval asceticism. The *Tretise* ridicules the idea that "summe recreacioun men moten han, and bettere it is (or lesse yvele) that they han theire recreacioun by pleyinge of miraclis than by pleyinge of other japis." For the writers of the *Tretise*, "al holinesse is in ful ernest." In this way the *Tretise* stands in direct opposition to the view encountered elsewhere that recreation is not inconsistent with holiness and that it is also useful in maintaining health of mind and body.[82]

The attack on the stage represented by the *Tretise* coincides with the apparent widespread popularity of vernacular drama in the same period of time in which most Wycliffite and Lollard writings were produced—i.e., 1380 to 1425. As among more strictly orthodox writings, Lollard and Wycliffite tracts might raise objections to activities related to playing seen as pernicious; one such tract, attributed by Margaret Deanesly to John Purvey, sneered: "Let us live as our fathers did, and then good enough; for they were well loved of cheters, wrestlers, buckler-players, of dancers and singers."[83] Yet there is no indication that either the followers of Wyclif or the members of the popular Lollard movement were widely obsessed by any unique hatred of playing or the stage,[84] and indeed the accusation directed against recreation quoted above could as well have been made by the most orthodox of churchmen. Nevertheless, another document which has been identified as a poetic attack on Franciscan iconography, and also most likely on their involvement in theatrical presentation, has been plausibly attributed to a Lollard or Wycliffite writer.[85] The poem, "On the Minorite Friars" from Cotton MS. Cleopatra B.ii, fol. 65^{v}, attacks Franciscan practices and beliefs on grounds that have been said to be heterodox. Its satire does seem precisely directed against the scenes of drama or *tableaux vivants* as these were associated with the activities of the friars:

Of thes frer minours me thenkes moch wonder,
That waxen are thus hauteyn, that som time weren under.
Among men of holy chirch, thay maken mochel blonder:
Nou he that sites us above, make ham sone to sonder.
With an O and an I, thay praisen not Seint Poule,
Thay lyen on Sein Fraunceys, by my fader soule.

First thay gabben on God that all men may se,
When thay hangen him on hegh on a grene tre
With leves and with blossemes that bright are of ble;
That was never Goddes Son, by my leute.
With an O and an I, men wenen that thay wede,
To carpe so of clergy that can not thair crede.

Thay have done him on a croys fer up in the skye
And festned in him wyenges, as he shuld flie;
This fals feined byleve shal thay soure bye,
On that lovelich Lord, so forto lye.
With an O and an I, one said ful still,
Armachan distroy ham, if it is Goddes will.

Ther comes one out of the skye in a grey goun
As it were an hog-hyerd hyand to toun.
Thay have mo goddes then we, I say by Mahoun,
All men under ham, that ever beres croun.
With an O and an I, why shuld thay not be shent,
Ther wantes noght bot a fire that thay nere all brent.

Went I forther on my way in that same tide,
Ther I saw a frere blede in middes of his side,
Bothe in hondes and in fete had he woundes wide,
To serve to that same frer, the pope mot abide.
With an O and an I, I wonder of these dedes,
To se a pope holde a dische whil the frer bledes.

A cart was made al of fire, as it shuld be;
A gray frer I sawe ther-inne, that best liked me.
Wele I wote thay shal be brent, by my leaute—

God graunt me that grace that I may it se.
With an O and an I, brent be thay all,
And all that helpes therto faire mot byfall.

Thay preche all of povert, bot that love thay noght,
For gode mete to thair mouthe the toun is thurgh soght.
Wide are thair wonninges and wonderfully wroght;
Murdre and horedome ful dere has it boght.
With an O and an I, ffor sixe pens, er thay faile,
Sle thy fadre and rape thy modre, and thay wil the assoile.[86]

In spite of the confusion evident in this poem—its author (deliberately, out of pretended ignorance?) does not recognize the nature of the scenes from the life of St. Francis but apparently mistakes, for example, such tableaux as those showing the Seraphim as the crucified one appearing to the saint (stanza 3), the figure of the saint with stigmata miraculously appearing to Pope Gregory IX (stanza 5), and the miraculous appearance of the same saint to his followers at Rivo Torto[87]—it not only seems to verify the acting of biblical and saint plays but also suggests a clear connection with the activities of the Franciscan Order.[88] In a statement added in the Middle English redaction of Wyclif's *De Officio Pastorali* it is claimed that "freris han taught in Englond the Paternoster in Engliyesh tunge, as men seyen in the pleye of York. . . ."[89] The poem "On the Minorite Friars" additionally, like the *Tretise of Miraclis Pleyinge*, appears to imply that theatrical activity is simply one more sign of the decadence of the visible Church, which spends its energies in activities that are said to falsify religion rather than to spread the true faith—a decadence regarded as a sign also that the end of history is approaching. Nicholas Davis has argued for the influence of the new understanding of motion developed by the Oxford Calculators, whose thinking was drawn upon in the *Tretise* to support (1) its confidence in the acceleration of religious and moral change in the face of such decadence as well as (2) its apocalypticism.[90] But if there is ample evidence that all suspicion could not by the fifteenth century be laid to rest with regard to the appropriateness of playing religious scenes,[91] such activity definitely had very strong support from many in the Church and from civic leaders and guild members in cities such as Coventry, York, and Chester during this century and in the next, with civic support continuing for some time after the Reformation.

As has been recognized,[92] the capstone argument of the defense of drama as reported by the *Tretise* involved the analogy between theatrical representation and the visual arts: if painting of religious figures and scenes is approved, then the staging of lively depictions of the same in drama must be valued even more highly, for painting by itself "is a deed bok" while dramatic expression gives life. The defense of drama at this point curiously depends upon the Lollard insistence upon images as "dead" and therefore not properly the objects of devotion,[93] while the reference to "bok" is a reminder of the centrality of the Western Church's understanding of pictures as making the scriptures and sacred stories available for the poor and illiterate—a stance that represented the official Western view of religious pictures until the Reformation.[94] This official view, to be sure, lacks completeness as an explanation of the popular valuing and use of the religious image among the people in the late Middle Ages. However, the suspicion with which iconomachs like the authors of the *Tretise* viewed the *visible forms* presented on stage actually provides a very important clue to the aesthetic of medieval vernacular religious drama and its relationship to the devotional image. Indeed, pictures and plays appealed to the same sense of sight. Both were inspired, if we read the evidence correctly, by the motive of raising devotion in the viewers, though of course this was not the only function of the dramatic scene.

Some additional connections between the purpose of examples of the visual arts in the late Middle Ages and the reception of the vernacular drama need, however, to be explored. The movement toward verisimilitude in both art and drama has been widely recognized, and we may see some linkage between this trend in artistic practice and the philosophical thought of the period, though again there are complexities which must remain outside the perimeters of this discussion. In Franciscan thought as in Thomist philosophy, perception and therefore the senses were of prime importance for cognition—the acquiring of knowledge and the apprehending of aesthetic objects.[95] Additionally, the tendency toward nominalism, along with other aspects of mendicant thinking and devotional practice, helped to create a climate in which details from the sacred story as *imagined* could function to direct the soul toward the deepest religious experience. If the religious image is no longer the icon through which the devout may make contact with the reality of the person or persons represented,[96] it nevertheless can function as a mnemonic device which existentially brings the soul into tune with the reality of the scene. *Appearances* in such art and/or drama become more important than the *reality* in which the image participates.[97] The universal and transcendent, previously visualized in forms which tended to eliminate unnecessary specific details, appear often to be put aside in favor of attention to exactly such details, which to be sure are yet often highly symbolic as in the instance of the symbolism of the architecture denoting the old and new orders in the well-known "Friedsam" Annunciation attributed to Hubert van Eyck in the Metropolitan Museum, New York.[98] The new style of handling subjects and details has been directly associated by Erwin Panofsky with nominalism,[99] and hence the following statement by Meyrick H. Carré is worth noting carefully: "One tendency of the new school of thinkers was the inclination to seek for reality in the individual thing in preference to the universal entity. Associated with this trend there appeared increased emphasis upon intuition or sensory apprehension in knowledge."[100] Granted such a stance, drama would indeed be likely to be considered superior in some sense to mere painting, which can approximate the forms of life only in a spatial and not in a temporal way in spite of attempts among pre-fifteenth-century artists to illustrate a sequence of movements in order to represent narrative. Painting hence might accurately be regarded as less "lively" than theatrical presentation, which would for this reason have been understood to impress itself more efficiently on the memory.[101] It is important to recognize that the iconography of religious scenes cannot be simply frozen within such a living art as drama, even if there were a conscious attempt to display devotional scenes with special attention to detail at the center of a drama or pageant presentation—"sights" in which the action seemingly becomes fixed in devotional tableaux.[102]

In the drama, therefore, the "sight" central to a scene contains details which are embued with meaning, and it is placed against a definite background, either an architectural setting or a setting in nature. This is technically quite different from the Byzantine practice of providing depth in front of the scene in the picture instead of behind.[103] The assertion of *temporality*, as opposed to the abstract timelessness of earlier Western and Byzantine art, marks late medieval visual presentations of religious scenes as also consistent with the new theological emphasis upon the experience of empathy toward and identification with the humanity of Christ. From the standpoint of such a practical theological position, what better direction could the visual arts take than to overflow into a different form—drama—which in its temporality might more fully recall and express the human feelings and actions of the Savior of men?

The position which has been described immediately above is, of course, quite radically different from the one taken in *A Tretise of Miraclis Pleyinge*. Though the *Tretise* does not totally condemn the mnemonic function of religious art, it clearly has no sympathy for its role in devotion. With regard to drama and to the devotional function of art, its authors are in fact more extreme followers of Wyclif, for they maintain a strongly *realist* (as opposed to *nominalist*) position. Images in their devotional function and plays alike provide "sensible" signs that are allegedly lacking in substance and therefore return to the inadequate ways of seeing prevalent in pre-Christian time, according to many Wycliffites and Lollards.[104] The *Tretise* not surprisingly therefore designates signs and "feignyd tokenes" as demonic, especially when great expense is involved in their making.[105] The use of images may prove attractive to the friars, but many followers of Wyclif and Lollards tended to emphasize the falseness of images, in particular when these were regarded as anything more than mnemonic aids—i.e., as books for unlettered lay people.[106] God, who is everywhere present, can hardly be approached more efficiently in an image or through an actor. Hence the concept of the divine *Logos* as potentially communicated through the sense of sight, a concept more familiar perhaps in Byzantine iconophile thinking, is rejected in favor of communication through language alone whenever possible.[107] Nicholas Davis thus is able to describe a major theme of the *Tretise* as "the radical insufficiency of the image."[108] Such an attitude toward the religious image and to religious art in general of course foreshadowed the iconoclastic element in the Protestant Reformation. Responsible for the radical way in which this attitude is presented in the *Tretise* is the rigidity of Wyclif's philosophical position. Serious in tone and deterministic, Wyclif insisted upon reducing knowledge to exclude anything tentative or imaginative. Gordon Leff notes that his realism was so extreme "that he believed in the self-subsistence of all universal concepts, such as goodness, man and so on, only stopping short of Plato—who had made them autonomous—to locate them eternally in God."[109] Biblical scenes for him were to be understood literally and outside the scheme of time;[110] any attempt to give substance in time to such scenes was to be regarded as vain—an exercise in futility and an affront to the pure understanding of the *Logos*.

Another Lollard tract, written by a man more antagonistic toward representations in the visual arts than the authors of *A Tretise of Miraclis Pleyinge*, is the treatise against images and pilgrimages also contained in British Library MS. Add. 24,202. This writer makes a bitter attack upon representations of the Trinity (a favorite target of Lollard polemic[111]) and certain other images which are held to be contrary to scriptural commandment—a disciplinary rather than theological objection. Though he grudgingly is willing to allow men to have a "pore crucifix" since—and here he echoes the orthodox position in defense of such images—Christ had truly become a man, he insists that normally such representations quickly become the occasion for vain displays of jewels and precious metals.[112] With the one exception—i.e., the plain crucifix noted above—images are otherwise therefore thoroughly condemned since "the rude puple tristus utterly in thes deade imagis" and thus are encouraged to be lax in their duties to God.[113] The visual arts provide a distraction that is decidedly seductive in encouraging love of self rather than the performance of charitable acts.[114] Though *A Tretise of Miraclis Pleyinge* seems not so restrictive with regard to the kinds of images allowed, it likewise condemns richly adorned devotional images and, of course, applies iconoclastic arguments to the scenes of drama. Here the *Tretise*'s arguments seem clearly related to Wyclif's realist position. Its objection consists of seeing "miraclis pleyinge" as "verrey leesing" since the drama presents only "signis withoute dede" for the purpose of seducing viewers out of motives that are as hollowly hypocritical as those of a practiced "lecchour" who "sechith signes of verrey love but no dedis of verrey love." That the *sign* is detached from the "dede" surely is the most serious charge that can be hurled at theatrical representation which presents images and movement that allegedly pretend to be something they are not. In his most serious tone, one of the writers of the *Tretise* states that "not he that pleyith the wille of God worschipith him, but onely he that doith his wille in deede worschipith him." Therefore, "by siche feinyd miraclis men bygilen hemsilf and dispisen God" in the same manner that Christ's tormentors did when they insisted that he join in their game (see, for example, *Matthew* 26.67-68). The writer identifies their game as the one elsewhere also called "*the bobbid* game,"[115] and specifically associates play-acting with the cruel sport of the torturers "that bobbiden Christ."

As external signs without substance, the scenes of drama are regarded by the Wycliffite or Lollard writers to be lacking in reality; hence they are to be understood as false.[116] For those who regarded the plays highly, however, signs were on the contrary felt to be practical guides toward a proper devotional state of mind. The plays were also viewed as useful for confirmation of belief, as in the instance of the priest in *The Hundred Merry Tales* who, when expounding the Creed, facetiously advised: "And if you beleve not me, then for more suerte and sufficient auctorite go your way to Coventre and there ye shall se them all playd in Corpus Cristi playe."[117] But on a very basic level the religious plays for which we have the most reliable information were intended to be mnemonic and devotional, with the scenes informed by a desire to bring to life in an imaginative way precisely those scenes from biblical history or the lives of the saints which were felt to touch most closely the feelings and thoughts of the individual spectators. As signs, the plays were thus regarded as highly efficient in that they appeal directly to basic aesthetic experience in a way that spontaneously stimulates enjoyment; by this process, the senses become for the audience the gateway through which the soul may receive enlightenment. In *Dives and Pauper*, a treatise written c.1405-10, we may read that there is a crucial religious value in dramas that "arn done principaly for devocioun and honest merthe to teche men to love God the more"—in contrast, of course, to the "ribaudye" which takes men away from the proper service of God.[118]

The passage cited immediately above from *Dives and Pauper* is in its entirety, as Kolve has noted, "among contemporary notices of the drama . . . second in length only to the Wycliffite sermon"—i.e., the *Tretise of Miraclis Pleyinge*.[119] In contrast to the Wycliffite or Lollard work, it provides a strong defense of playing as an expression of devotion, mirth, and recreation. There is, as expected, some nervousness about not only "ribaudye" but also "errour" and "pleyys agens the feith of holy chirche" or its "statys" as well as "good livinge," and the speaker, who is Pauper, insists that such plays "arn defendyd [i.e., forbidden[120]] both in haliday and warke day." But specifically approved as "leful and comendable" is the representation "in pleyinge at Cristemesse Heroudis and the thre kingis and other proces of the gospel both in than and at Estryn and in othir times also." Thereupon Dives asks, "Than it semyth be thin speche that in halidayys men mon lefully makyn merthe?" and

Pauper responds, "God forbede ellis."[121]

The author of *Dives and Pauper* is aware of the objections of the Church Fathers to theatrical activity. Following the quoting of Psalm 117.24 ("This is the day that God made; make we now merye and be we glade"), Dives says, "Contra. Sent Austin seith that it were lesse wicke to gon at the plow and at the carte and cardyn and spinnyn in the Sonday than to ledyn dauncis," which are grouped together here with plays. Pauper's response is significant:

> Sent Austin spekyth of swyche dauncis and pleyys as wern usyd in his time whan Cristene peple was muchil medelyd with hethene peple and be old custom and example of hethene peple usyd unhonest dauncis and pleyys that be eld time wern ordeinyd to steryn folc to lecherie and to othir sinnys. And so if daunsing and pleyying now on halidayes steryn men and wymmen to pride, to lecchery, glotonye, and slouthe, to over-longe waking on nightys and to idilschip on the werkedayes and other sinnes, as it is right likly that they done in oure dayes, than ar they unleful bothe on the haliday and on the werke day, and agens alle swyche spak Sent Austin. But agenys honest dauncis and honest pleyys don in dew time and in good maner in the haliday spak never Sent Austin.[122]

Hereupon, Dives objects further that the biblical account demands solemnity and mourning on the Sabbath, but again Pauper turns the argument aside and proves that, except in certain seasons, people should experience mirth and engage in recreation rather than sorrowful exercises on Sundays and feast days.[123]

But for the *Tretise* and the ascetic tradition the presentation of plays with religious content is not useful recreation but instead is "maumetrie"—i.e., the worship of idols, after "Mohomet." "Maumetrie" is apparently a principal concern in Lollard writings.[124] The distinctions which had long set pagan idols apart from Christian images thus are collapsed in such writings in a manner that must have puzzled and angered many a churchman and layman of the time—and that certainly did lead to legal action against those who held to such allegedly heterodox views.[125] However, this kind of thinking was eventually to become dominant in the more radical English Protestantism that insisted upon the suppression of religious images and of stage actions in the sixteenth and seventeenth centuries—a suppression of visible forms that I have elsewhere grouped under the term 'anti-visual prejudice.'[126] For the orthodox churchman and for the practitioner of popular religion in the late Middle Ages, however, religious images were indeed normally associated with divine power which might be available to those who approached them correctly.[127] As channels between the worshipper and the transcendent reality, images since the late Patristic period had been crucial to Christian devotion. This perspective on the devotional image had been a factor which informed the spirituality of the liturgical drama, and further developments, as we have seen, had been introduced in the late Middle Ages which altered the devotional response to both images and vernacular plays. Nevertheless, the bond of emotion that was established between audience and the character represented by the actor was intended to be an authentic religious experience. The common view is described in the *Tretise*: "ofte sithis by siche miraclis pleyinge men and wymmen, seinge the passioun of Crist and of his seintis, ben movyd to compassion and devocion, wepinge bitere teris, thanne they ben not scorninge of God but worschiping." Durandus had much earlier insisted that pictures move the soul more directly than words,[128] and the *Tretise* cites those, as we have seen, who feel that the lively images of drama are even more likely to present an emotional impact on the soul.

But from the point of view of the Wycliffite or Lollard writers, the playing of scenes, since they are in their opinion false, must substitute *jest* for the *earnestness* with which the realities perceived by a religious person ought to be approached. A play is a *game*, an activity that rearranges the social and cosmic realities according to seemingly arbitrary rules by which the players must abide. Holiness, on the other hand, is "in ful ernest," while *playing* involves that which will provoke laughter or even derision.[129] Laughter, rather than a healthy response to drama, was seen to be disturbing, for the *Tretise* insists, following the precedent of St. John Chrysostom, that Christ never laughed.[130] The humorless authors were able to see no excuse whatsoever for levity in things sacred. Yet, if we are to take the words of the *Tretise* as evidence that is also corroborated from other sources, people ordinarily in fact had by then come to see drama in terms of game—a characteristic which set the vernacular play off from the liturgical drama that would have been understood in terms of *rite*. Corroboration for thus understanding the late medieval vernacular religious stage hence comes from linguistic evidence as well as from the *Tretise*. In normal circumstances, therefore, those who produced and watched the late medieval vernacular religious plays seem to have seen nothing harmful about seeing a drama as *play* or recreation, which would not need to interfere with its devotional function and indeed might enhance that dimension of the theatrical scene. Such playing, however, needs to be understood in terms appropriate to its own time; post-modern literary theory, which has a reputation for distorting the past to fit current presuppositions and prejudices, will not be very helpful. *Playing* is in the vernacular plays something to be displayed—i.e., something to be seen by members of an audience, who are encouraged to engage themselves imaginatively in the scenes that are represented before their eyes. The *purpose* is in the end thus something more than mere recreation, though the recreative element is not by any means denied. Playing is often in fact intended to lead toward the enlightenment of the audience and to its improvement in the life of the spirit. This is possible because, as modern phenomenological study has demonstrated, the play may result not only in the recovery of a collective past necessary to the understanding of salvation history but also (if we may use Heidegger's terminology in this case) in the *deconcealment of Being*.[131] If the late medieval sponsors of such plays had not thought thus, they would never have consented to the huge expenditures of money that are recorded for the production of civic drama in such centers as Coventry and York. At the latter city the Corpus Christi play was presented "especially for the honour and reverence of our Lord Jesus Christ and for the profit of the . . . citizens."[132] Judging from the Abraham and Isaac play that has been associated with Northampton, that community also may have pursued civic drama energetically for similar reasons.

As indicated above, it is important to recognize that the authors of the *Tretise* had in mind more than one kind of local vernacular drama—drama of which we have insufficient evidence—and that much of this drama might well have been less well controlled and hence less decorous than the major cycle plays at Coventry or York. We can be certain, I believe, that the livelier handling of sacred themes in the plays in the Towneley manuscript would have offended them; such scenes as the sacrifice of Cain in the *Mactacio Abel* in which the wicked son of Adam and Eve refuses to sacrifice properly and reviles both God and the Church also suggest the presence of much drama, now lost, that might have been fully as offensive to sensitive viewers of the type implied in the text of the *Tretise.*

The Manuscript. The Tenison Manuscript (British Library MS. Add. 24,202), which contains *A Tretise of Miraclis Pleyinge*, is a collection of Lollard or Wycliffite and other writings copied at the beginning of the fifteenth century.[133] Previous research has been unable to locate the manuscript any more precisely than in the Midlands[134] where the Lollard movement was strong; however, study of the dialect by Paul A. Johnston, Jr. (see below, pp. 53–84) identifies the manuscript of the *Tretise* with Huntingdonshire and Northamptonshire. Internal evidence suggests that the authors must have lived in or near a region which gave strong support to various kinds of drama, especially religious plays which dramatized the martyrdom of saints and the Passion story; they seem to have been familiar with civic drama of the kind that was sponsored by the city of Coventry[135] and may also have been presented in Northampton.[136] While the identity of the writers must remain unknown to us, it is attractive and plausible to believe that they would have had the Coventry plays in mind as the focus of his anti-theatrical polemic.[137] The second part of the *Tretise*, correctly regarded as the more radical and specifically Wycliffite, speaks quite directly to a friend who apparently shares the writer's views but favors plays, presumably religious drama with devotional, mnemonic, and recreative functions that are seen by him as legitimate. This friend very likely was someone immediately involved with civic support for such plays as the Coventry pageants. In contrast, the first part of the *Tretise*, though it expresses Lollard concerns, not only seems to be an outgrowth of the tradition of anti-theatrical writing inherited from the early Church but also accepts the orthodox view of the role of the priesthood and the sacraments.

The transcription of the *Tretise* which follows is, like the provisional edition prepared more than a decade ago under the title *A Middle English Treatise on the Playing of Miracles*, designed to make the text available in a form accessible to students of medieval drama specifically and also others with a broader range of interests in dramatic theory and theater history. The object has been to present a text more faithful to the original than the somewhat inaccurate editions of Halliwell (also reprinted by Hazlitt) and Mätzner which were subject to the erratic methods of the nineteenth-century copyists who served as intermediaries between manuscript and printer. Nevertheless, because the aim has also been to produce a more readable text that will be accessible to students of the drama who are less conversant with Middle English, certain elements of orthography have been regularized. The thorn and yogh have been replaced by modern equivalents, while the letters j, i, y, u, and v have been regularized as much as possible to conform with modern usage. Capital letters have been supplied where appropriate, abbreviations have been silently expanded, and punctuation has been partially modernized though in a manner consistent with the indications in the manuscript. Some paragraphing has also been added in the interests of readability. I have felt comfortable providing this kind of text because I have been able to include a photographic facsimile of the relevant pages of the original manuscript so that scholars interested in such matters as orthography and language will be able to have before them those details that in fact no modern transcription is able to transmit very well.

NOTES

1. In his Cambridge University dissertation ("The Playing of Miracles in England between c.1350 and the Reformation," unpublished Ph.D. diss. [1977]), Nicholas Davis suggested a date of c.1400–09. More recently, in his article "The *Tretise of Miraclis Pleyinge*: On Milieu and Authorship," *Medieval English Theatre*, 12 (1990), 124–51, Davis has revised his opinion to date the *Tretise* in the 1380's (p. 144). He bases his new dating in part on the optimism expressed in this text—an optimism that he connects with philosophical trends at Merton College, Oxford, among Wyclif and his associates. His speculation concerning date, however, is also dependent to some extent on further conjecture concerning authorship—conjecture which seems unlikely in the light of careful study of the dialect of the manuscript; see below, pp. 53–84. Any date after 1414, on the other hand, is certainly too late. The author of at least the first part of the *Tretise* must have been a clergyman, and, as Davis noted in his dissertation, such a person's authorship would have been unlikely after the Oldcastle uprising in 1414 ("The Playing of Miracles," pp. 106, 107n). On the difficulty of dating Lollard and Wycliffite tracts, see Anne Hudson, *The Premature Reformation: Wycliffite Texts and Lollard History* (Oxford: Clarendon Press, 1988), p. 11, and of course there is the additional problem of distinguishing between the academic followers of Wyclif and the writers who sympathized with or were involved in the popular Lollard movement. But even the attribution of the *Tretise* to a Wycliffite or Lollard has been questioned; Hudson, for example, cautiously notes: "whether the text that has come to be known as 'The Lollard Tract Against Miracle Plays' is really a product of Wycliffism seems to me doubtful, but its attitude to the plays is assimilable to Wycliffite thought as that is expressed elsewhere" (*The Premature Reformation*, p. 387). Davis' recent research attempts to link the *Tretise* rather directly to Wyclif's academic followers in the universities; cf. Joseph Dahmus' review of Anne Hudson's edition of *Selections from Eng-*

lish Wycliffite Writings, in *Manuscripta*, 23 (1979), 52–53.

2. Jonas Barish, *The Antitheatrical Prejudice* (Berkeley and Los Angeles: Univ. of California Press, 1981), p. 67.

3. George R. Coffman, "The Miracle Play in England—Nomenclature," *PMLA*, 31 (1916), 448–65.

4. Lawrence Clopper, "*Miracula* and *The Tretise of Miraclis Pleyinge*," *Speculum*, 65 (1990), 878–905; for a useful list of occurrences in Middle English of the terms *miracula* and 'miracles,' see ibid., pp. 904–05, but see also Davis, "The Playing of Miracles," pp. 40–55, and Erwin Wolff, "Die Terminologie des mittelalterlichen Dramas in bedeutungsgeschichtlicher Sicht," *Anglia*, 78 (1960), 18–21. Clopper's concern is to identify a core meaning of 'miraclis'; it seems to me necessary to keep in mind the signification clearly identified or implied by the text of the *Tretise of Miraclis Pleyinge*, though admittedly this tract is itself not unambiguous about the types of play and entertainment intended by the term.

5. Ian Lancaster, *Dramatic Texts and Records of Britain: A Chronological Topography to 1558* (Toronto: Univ. of Toronto Press, 1984), No. 822, citing Robert Surtees, *History and Antiquities of the County Palatine of Durham*, II (1820), 309.

6. The Wycliffite version of the Bible translates *Jeremiah* 44.11-12 as follows: "I shal sette my face in you into evel, and destroyen al Juda, and take the remnauns of Juda, that setteden ther faces, that they shulden go into the lond of Egypt, and dwelle there; and they shul be wastid alle in the lond of Egypt, and they shul falle in swerd, and in hunger shul be wastid, fro the leste unto the meste, in swerd and in hunger they shul die, and they shul be into right of swering, and into *miracle*, and into cursing, and into repref" (*The Holy Bible . . . Made from the Latin Vulgate by John Wycliffe and his Followers*, ed. John Forshall and Frederic Madden [Oxford: Oxford Univ. Press, 1850]; italics mine).

7. Clopper, "*Miracula* and *The Tretise of Miraclis Pleyinge*," p. 890.

8. *Cumberland, Westmorland, and Gloucestershire*, ed. Audrey Douglas and Peter Greenfield, Records of Early English Drama (Toronto: Univ. of Toronto Press, 1986), pp. 63–64; for translation, see ibid., pp. 147–48.

9. "The Wife of Bath's Prologue," l. 558, in *The Riverside Chaucer*, 3rd ed., gen. ed. Larry D. Benson (Boston: Houghton Mifflin, 1987), p. 112; this text also makes reference to a "someres game" (l. 648), which may be interchangeable with the term 'miracle.'

10. C. B. C. Thomas, "The Miracle Play at Dunstable," *Modern Language Notes*, 32 (1917), 337–44.

11. For a different conclusion concerning the range of activity condemned by the *Tretise*, see Clopper, "*Miracula* and *The Tretise of Miraclis Pleyinge*," pp. 894–902.

12. Nicholas Davis, "Another View of the *Tretise of Miraclis Pleyinge*," *Medieval English Theatre*, 4 (1982), 53.

13. *Coventry*, ed. R. W. Ingram, Records of Early English Drama (Toronto: Univ. of Toronto Press, 1981), *passim*; *York*, ed. Alexandra F. Johnston and Margaret Rogerson, Records of Early English Drama (Toronto: Univ. of Toronto Press, 1979), *passim*. The great Coventry Corpus Christi fair lasted eight days and, along with the Coventry plays, attracted peopled from all over England. For the extant pageants (dating from 1535, when they were rewritten by Robert Crow) from the Coventry cycle, see *Two Coventry Corpus Christi Plays*, 2nd ed., ed. Hardin Craig, EETS, e.s. 70 (1957), and for discussion of another (now lost) play in the cycle, see Clifford Davidson, "The Lost Coventry Drapers' Play of Doomsday and Its Iconographic Context," *Leeds Studies in English*, 17 (1986), 141–58. See also Charles Phythian-Adams, "Ceremony and the Citizen: The Communal Year at Coventry 1450–1550," in *Crisis and Order in English Towns 1500–1700*, ed. Peter Clark and Paul Slack (Toronto: Univ. of Toronto Press, 1972), pp. 57–85, and, for a relevant review of social and economic conditions at the end of the Middle Ages, the same author's *Desolation of a City: Coventry and the Urban Crisis of the Late Middle Ages* (Cambridge: Cambridge Univ. Press, 1979).

14. *Non-Cycle Plays and Fragments*, ed. Norman Davis, EETS, s.s. 1 (London, 1970), pp. 32–42; J. Charles Cox, *The Records of the Borough of Northampton* (Northampton: Corporation of the County Borough of Northampton, 1898), II, 183–84.

15. *Coventry*, ed. Ingram, pp. 148–49.

16. Rosemary Woolf, *The English Mystery Plays* (Berkeley and Los Angeles: Univ. of California Press, 1972), p. 85; see *Selections from English Wycliffite Writings*, ed. Anne Hudson (Cambridge: Cambridge Univ. Press, 1978), pp. 83-88, for the Wycliffite treatise against images and pilgrimages.

17. V. A. Kolve, *The Play Called Corpus Christi* (Stanford: Stanford Univ. Press, 1966), p. 11; for the argument that "this drama had no theory and aimed consciously at no dramatic effects," see Hardin Craig, *English Religious Drama of the Middle Ages* (Oxford: Clarendon Press, 1955), p. 9.

18. See Harold Gardiner, *Mysteries' End: An Investigation into the Last Days of the Medieval Religious Stage*, Yale Studies in English, 103 (1946; rpt. Hamden, Conn.: Archon Books, 1967), *passim.*

19. Davis, "The *Tretise of Miraclis Pleyinge*: On Milieu and Authorship," pp. 139–46. On Hereford, see also A. B. Emden, *A Biographical Register of the University of Oxford to A.D. 1500* (Oxford: Clarendon Press, 1958), II, 913–15. Hereford would be an attractive candidate if there were evidence of his dialect and vocaculary in the *Tretise*. On the difficulty of assigning authorship to Wycliffite works, see Hudson, *The Premature Reformation*, p. 10.

20. Davis suggests ("The *Tretise of Miraclis Pleyinge*: On Milieu and Authorship," p. 145) that the friend may have been Sir William Neville, who rescued Hereford in 1387 from the Nottingham municipal jail and kept him in protective custody at Nottingham Castle for a time; see also Emden, *A Biographical Register*, II, 914.

21. For a similar summary, see Woolf, *The English Mystery Plays*, p. 85.

22. On the *Tretise* as a source for the study of mnemonic theory as applied to theatrical event, see Nicholas M. Davis, "The English Mystery Plays and 'Ciceronian' Mnemonics," in *Atti del IV Colloquio della Société Internationale pour l'Etude du Théâtre Médiéval*, ed. M. Chiabò, F. Doglio, and M. Maymone (Viterbo: Centro Studi sul Teatro Medioevale e Rinascimentale, 1983), pp. 75–84, and "The Art of Memory and Medieval Dramatic Theory," *EDAM Newsletter*, 6, No. 1 (Fall 1983), 1–3. For a full discussion of memory theory, see Frances A. Yates, *The Art of Memory* (Chicago: Univ. of Chicago Press, 1966).

23. According to a traditional view quoted by Wyclif from Augustine, a player who plays a role is a model of hypocrisy, and the key to such behavior is the separation of the sign from the thing signified; see John Wyclif, *Opus Evangelicum*, ed. Johann Loserth, Wyclif Soc. (London: Trübner, 1895), II, 248–49. Attention is called to this passage by Nicholas Davis ("Allusions to Medieval Drama in Britain: A Findings List [3]," *Medieval English Theatre*, 5 [1983], 85), who quotes Wyclif's commentary and cites this same commentary as it is included in the Lollard *Floretum* in Harley MS. 401, fol. 156.

24. Pamela Sheingorn, "'No Sepulchre on Good Friday'," in *Iconoclasm vs. Art and Drama*, ed. Clifford Davidson and Ann Eljenholm Nichols, Early Drama, Art, and Music, Monograph Ser., 11 (Kalamazoo: Medieval Institute Publications, 1989), pp. 145–63; Gardiner, *Mysteries' End, passim*; R. W. Ingram, "Fifteen Seventy-Nine and the Decline of Civic Religious Drama in Coventry," in *The Elizabethan Theatre VIII*, ed. G. R. Hibbard (Port Credit, Ontario: P. D. Meany, 1982), pp. 114–28.

25. Tertullian, *De Spectaculis*, ed. and trans. T. R. Glover, Loeb Classical Library (Cambridge: Harvard Univ. Press, 1931), pp. 260–61.

26. Ibid., pp. 274–75.

27. Ibid., pp. 292–93.

28. Isidore of Seville, *Etymologiarum*, ed. W. M. Lindsay (Oxford: Clarendon Press, 1911), II, Book XVIII.xlii; Ann Jennalie Cook, *The Privileged Playgoers of Shakespeare's London* (Princeton: Princeton Univ. Press, 1981), pp. 202–04.

29. Mary H. Marshall, "Theatre in the Middle Ages: Evidence from Dictionaries and Glosses," *Symposium*, 4 (1950), 8–9, 39, 375–76; Joseph R. Jones, "Isidore and the Theater," *Comparative Drama*, 16 (1982), 26–49. The quotation from Chaucer is from *The Riverside Chaucer*, p. 398 (ll. 49–50).

30. Marshall, "Theatre in the Middle Ages," p. 372.

31. Terentius, [*Comedies*] (Lyon: Johannes Trechsel, 1493), sig. a4^{v}. For a convenient reproduction of this illustration, see Douglas Percy Bliss, *A History of Wood Engraving* (1928; rpt. London: Spring Books, 1964), p. 53.

32. Karl F. Morrison, "The Church as Play: Gerhoch of Reichersberg's Call for Reform," in *Popes, Teachers, and Canon Law in the Middle Ages*, ed. James Ross Sweeney and Stanley Chodorow (Ithaca: Cornell Univ. Press, 1989), p. 135n.

33. E. K. Chambers, *The Mediaeval Stage* (London: Oxford Univ. Press, 1903), II, 98–99.

34. Ibid., II, 98n.

35. Ibid.

36. Aelred of Rievaulx, *Speculum Charitatis* ii.33, as quoted in translation by Herbert M. Schueller, *The Idea of Music: An Introduction to Musical Aesthetics in Antiquity and the Middle Ages*, Early Drama, Art, and Music, Monograph Ser., 9 (Kalamazoo: Medieval Institute Publications, 1988), p. 355; for the Latin text, see Karl Young, *The Drama of the Medieval Church* (Oxford: Clarendon Press, 1933), I, 548.

37. Aelred of Rievaulx, *Tractatus de Jesu puero duodenni*, as quoted in translation by Sixten Ringbom, *Icon to Narrative*, Acta Academiae Aboensis, ser. A, 31, No. 2 (Åbo: Åbo Akademi, 1965), p. 16.

38. *The Treatise on the Apostolic Tradition of St Hippolytus of Rome*, ed. and trans. Gregory Dix (London: SPCK, 1968), pp. 25–26.

39. Justinian, *Novella* 123.44, as cited by Peter Brown, *The Body and Society: Men, Women and Sexual Renunciation in Early Christianity* (New York: Columbia Univ. Press, 1988), p. 429.

40. Allardyce Nicoll, *Masks, Mimes, and Miracles* (London: George G. Harrap, 1931), p. 146.

41. Mansi, *Concilia*, XVII Supplementum, Capitulare Tertium Anni 789, as cited by J. D. A. Ogilvy, "*Mimi, Scurrae, Histriones*: Entertainers of the Early Middle Ages," *Speculum*, 38 (1963), 608–09.

42. Richard Axton, *European Drama of the Early Middle Ages* (London: Hutchinson, 1974), p. 19; Chambers, *Mediaeval Stage*, I, 32n, quoting from *Oratio Edgari Regis*, in *Concilia Magnae Britanniae et Hiberniae, 446–1717*, ed. Wilkins (1737), I, 246.

43. Nicoll, *Masks, Mimes, and Miracles*, p. 147.

44. *Records of Plays and Players in Lincolnshire, 1300-1585*, ed. Stanley Kahrl, Malone Soc. Collections, 8 (Oxford, 1974), p. 99; Chambers, *Mediaeval Stage*, I, 91. Another instance of such legislation (at Lanchester) has been noted above; see n. 5.

45. *Decretum Magistri Gratiani*, ed. Emil Friedberg (Graz: Akademische Druck, 1959), II, 452, as quoted in translation by Marianne Briscoe, "Some Clerical Notions of Dramatic Decorum," *Comparative Drama*, 19 (1985), 1.

46. Ibid., pp. 1, 9.

47. *Gemma animae* I.lxxxiii, as quoted in translation by David Bevington, *Medieval Drama* (Boston: Houghton Mifflin, 1975), p. 9; see also Young, *The Drama of the Medieval Church*, I, 83.

48. O. B. Hardison, Jr., *Christian Rite and Christian Drama in the Middle Ages* (Baltimore: Johns Hopkins Press, 1965), pp. 45–77. See also Christine Catharina Schnusenberg, *The Relationship between the Church and the Theatre Exemplified by Selected Writings of the Church Fathers and by Liturgical Texts until Amalarius of Metz* (Lanham, Maryland: Univ. Press of America, 1988).

49. For comment on earlier forms, see C. Clifford Flanigan, "The Roman Rite and the Origins of the Liturgical Drama," *University of Toronto Quarterly*, 43 (1974), 263–84.

50. Chambers, *Mediaeval Stage*, II, 379–80; Woolf, *The English Mystery Plays*, pp. 29–30, 349.

51. Ernst Curtius, *European Literature and the Latin Middle Ages*, trans. Williard R. Trask (1953; rpt. New York: Harper and Row, 1963), pp. 138–44.

52. See Robert of Brunne, *Handlyng Synne*, ed. F. J. Furnivall, EETS, o.s. 119 (London, 1901), p. 155. However, Davis connects William's condemnations with the Feast of Fools, not with religious plays ("The Playing of Miracles," p. 46).

53. John Bromyard, *Summa predicantium* (Venice, 1586), fol. 152^{v}, as quoted in translation by Clopper, "*Miracula* and *The Tretise of Miraclis Pleyinge*," p. 881.

54. Robert Mannyng of Brunne, *Handlyng Synne*, ed. Idelle Sullens (Binghamton: Center for Medieval and Early Renaissance Studies, 1983), pp. 117–18. See also the attack against "Karolles, wrastlinges, or somour games" in the "cherche other in cherch yerd" (ibid., p. 225). The term 'summer game' is ambiguous, but see Siegfried Wenzel, "*Somer Game* and Sermon References to a Corpus Christi Play," *Modern Philology*, 86 (1989),

274–82. For another adaptation of the *Manuel des Péchés*, see Davis, "The Playing of Miracles," pp. 42–45, and, for a discussion of summer games (as well as winter games), Sandra Billington, *Mock Kings in Medieval Society and Renaissance Drama* (Oxford: Clarendon Press, 1991), pp. 1–113.

55. Axton, *European Drama of the Early Middle Ages*, p. 162; Young, *The Drama of the Medieval Church*, II, 539.

56. Such an origin was first suggested in 1892 by Charles Davidson, *Studies in the English Mystery Plays* (1892; rpt. New York: Haskell House, 1965), pp. 83–94. For pageant wagons at Coventry, see especially R. Ingram, "The Coventry Pageant Waggon," *Medieval English Theatre*, 2 (1980), 3–14. The Northampton wagons were stored at St. George's Hall, but unfortunately nothing further is currently known about their use for pageantry or plays. It should be noted, however, that the Abraham and Isaac play which has been associated with Northampton seems to demand place and scaffold staging and hence would not be easily presented from a pageant wagon.

57. For an important study of devotional patterns and medieval drama, see Gail McMurray Gibson, *The Theater of Devotion: East Anglian Drama and Society in the Late Middle Ages* (Chicago: Univ. of Chicago Press, 1989).

58. Briscoe, "Some Clerical Notions," pp. 4–6.

59. See also John C. Coldewey, "Plays and 'Play' in Early English Drama," *Research Opportunities in Renaissance Drama*, 28 (1985), 181–88.

60. Briscoe, "Some Clerical Notions," pp. 5–6.

61. *Destructorium Viciorum* 23, as quoted in translation by Briscoe, "Some Clerical Notions," p. 5.

62. *Coventry*, ed. Ingram, p. 3; see also Lancashire, *Dramatic Texts and Records of Britain*, No. 554.

63. See above, p. 13.

64. *York*, ed. Johnston and Rogerson, II, 728; for the Latin text, see ibid., I, 43.

65. British Library MS. Add. 35,290; for a modern edition, see *The York Plays*, ed. Richard Beadle (London: Edward Arnold, 1982). A facsimile is also available: *The York Play*, introd. Richard Beadle and Peter Meredith, Medieval Drama Facsimiles, 7 (Leeds: Univ. of Leeds School of English, 1983).

66. See Alexandra F. Johnston, "The Guild of Corpus Christi and the Procession of Corpus Christi in York," *Mediaeval Studies*, 38 (1976), 372–84. On the spirituality which informed the plays, see Clifford Davidson, "Northern Spirituality and the Late Medieval Drama of York," in *The Spirituality of Western Christendom*, ed. E. Rozanne Elder (Kalamazoo: Cistercian Publications, 1976), pp. 125–51; Gibson, *The Theater of Devotion*; and Theresa Coletti, "Spirituality and Devotional Images: the Staging of the Hegge Cycle," unpublished Ph.D. diss. (Univ. of Rochester, 1975). Support for seeing civic drama as devotional is given in such statements as the passage in the *York Memorandum Book A/Y* for the year 1422 which specifically identifies devotion and the suppression of vice as purposes of the plays; see *York*, ed. Johnston and Rogerson, p. 37. But even direct statements concerning the educational or mnemonic value of the plays, as in the case of the York Creed Play, cannot be understood in any positivist way, since the purpose of the scenes was hardly the mere transmission of information about the facts or mechanics of this world.

67. *Chester*, ed. Lawrence M. Clopper, Records of Early English Drama (Toronto: Univ. of Toronto Press, 1979), p. 28; see also Chambers, *The Mediaeval Stage*, II, 351, and F. M. Salter, *Mediaeval Drama in Chester* (Toronto: Univ. of Toronto Press, 1955), pp. 33–34.

68. See Davidson, "Northern Spirituality," pp. 125–51.

69. *The Booke of Margery Kempe*, ed. Sanford Brown Meech, EETS, o.s. 212 (London, 1940), p. 148. The Franciscan William Melton was critical of Margery Kempe's hysterical weeping, and insisted that she control herself or stay away from a series of sermons he was giving at Lynn; see Emden, *A Biographical Register of the University of Oxford*, II,

1258. For a sympathetic discussion of Margery Kempe, see Gibson, *The Theater of Devotion*, pp. 47–65.

70. Reproductions in Erwin Panofsky, *Early Netherlandish Painting* (Cambridge: Harvard Univ. Press, 1953), II, figs. 322–23; see also the commentary in ibid., I, 267. The space which separates the donors from the Passion scene may be said to function very much like that which sets apart dramatic action from audience.

71. Davis, "Another View of the *Tretise of Miraclis Pleyinge*," p. 52.

72. J. W. Robinson, *Studies in Fifteenth-Century Stagecraft*, Early Drama, Art, and Music, Monograph Ser., 14 (Kalamazoo: Medieval Institute Publications, 1991), p. 57.

73. The pioneer theological study is by Gustav Aulén, *Christus Victor*, trans. A. G. Herbert (New York: Macmillan, 1960); the effect on drama is discussed by Sandro Sticca, "Drama and Spirituality in the Middle Ages," *Medievalia et Humanistica*, n.s. 4 (1973), 69–87.

74. See especially the study by F. P. Pickering, *Literature and Art in the Middle Ages* (Coral Gables, Florida: Univ. of Miami Press, 1970), pp. 223–307.

75. Walter Hilton, *The Scale of Perfection*, ed. Evelyn Underhill (London: John M. Watkins, 1948), pp. 80–81. See also Joy M. Russell-Smith, "Walter Hilton and a Tract in Defense of the Veneration of Images," *Dominican Studies*, 7 (1954), 194. For a modern appreciation of the role of vision in devotion, see Margaret R. Miles, *Image as Insight: Visual Understanding in Western Christianity and Secular Culture* (Boston: Beacon Press, 1985).

76. Quoted in translation by Wenzel, "*Somer Game* and Sermon References to a Corpus Christi Play," pp. 279–80.

77. Ibid., p. 280.

78. On Lollard antagonism to the Franciscans, see Hudson, *The Premature Reformation, passim.*

79. *Summa Theologica* II, ii, Q. 168, Art. 2; quotations are from the translation by the Fathers of the Church Dominican Province (New York: Benziger, 1947).

80. Ibid., I, ii, Q. 34, Art. 1, Reply Obj. 3.

81. Ibid., II, ii, Q. 168, Art. 3.

82. See especially Glending Olson, *Literature as Recreation in the Later Middle Ages* (Ithaca: Cornell Univ. Press, 1982), pp. 39–127.

83. Quoted by Margaret Deanesly, *The Lollard Bible* (Cambridge: Cambridge Univ. Press, 1920), p. 274; corrected reading supplied by Davis, "Another View of the *Tretise of Miraclis Pleyinge*," p. 55. Davis questions Purvey's authorship; with regard to authorship, see also Anne Hudson, *Lollards and Their Books* (London: Hambledon Press, 1985), pp. 85–110.

84. Hudson, ed., *Selections from English Wycliffite Writings*, pp. 187–88. It is likely that some if not most Lollards approved of religious drama as a means of educating the public about the content of the Bible; thus approval would be directed at the mnemonic and didactic purpose of the plays but opposed to any devotional function, though it seems inevitable that Lollards would disappove of the great expense to which the producers of the plays would go. In later years, a civic leader at Coventry known to have been sympathetic to Lollardy was William Pysford, who in his will of 1518 left both money to those guilds involved in playing and also clothing of scarlet and crimson to be used as costumes (*Coventry*, ed. Ingram, pp. 112–13).

85. Davis suggests that the writer of these verses might have been the same person as the author of the *Tretise* ("The *Tretise of Miraclis Pleyinge*: On Milieu and Authorship," p. 147). This suggestion must be rejected.

86. This poem has been edited previously a number of times, first by J. S. Brewer, *Monumenta Franciscana*, Rolls Ser. (London, 1858), I,

606–08, and most recently by Rossell Hope Robbins, ed., *Historical Poems of the XIVth and XVth Centuries* (New York: Columbia Univ. Press, 1959), pp. 163–64. Robbins, however, seems mistaken in his notes to the poem when he suggests that it "would seem more appropriate for wall paintings, such as appeared in the large churches the Franciscans built especially for their preaching," than for drama and pageantry (p. 335) as Wright had suggested in his commentary on his transcription of the poem in *Political Poems and Songs* (London, 1859), pp. 268–70. The most complete discussion of the poem is by Lawrence G. Craddock, "Franciscan Influences on Early English Drama," *Franciscan Studies*, 10 (1950), 399–415. Craddock argues that the dramatic presentations of the friars that are here being attacked were based on the account of the life of St. Francis in the *Legenda Maior* of St. Bonaventure. In line 18 of the poem, "Armachan" is Richard FitzRalph, Archbishop of Armagh in Ireland, who was a fourteenth-century enemy of the Franciscans; he died in 1360, but was remembered by Lollards and Wycliffites as a patron who from his heavenly seat might intercede against the friars (Craddock, pp. 409–10). See also the commentary by Beverly Brian, "Franciscan Scenes in a Fourteenth-Century Satire," *Medium Aevum*, 41 (1972), 27–31; Davis, "The Playing of Miracles," pp. 124–31; and (for FitzRalph) Penn R. Szittya, *The Antifraternal Tradition in Medieval Literature* (Princeton: Princeton Univ. Press, 1986), pp. 123–51. I have read the word usually transcribed as 'iape' in the final line of the poem as 'rape,' and I am also convinced by internal evidence that this is the correct reading: "Murdre" and "horedom" (l. 40) signify the Oedipal pattern.

87. Craddock, "Franciscan Influences," pp. 408–15.

88. See David L. Jeffrey, "Franciscan Spirituality and the Rise of Early English Drama," *Mosaic*, 8, No. 4 (1975), 36–40.

89. John Wyclif, *The English Works*, ed. F. D. Matthew, EETS, o.s. 74 (London, 1880), pp. 429–30. The York Pater Noster play is discussed by Alexandra F. Johnston, "The Plays of the Religious Guilds of York: The Creed Play and the Pater Noster Play," *Speculum*, 50 (1975), 70–80.

90. Davis, "The *Tretise of Miraclis Pleyinge*: On Milieu and Authorship," pp. 132–42.

91. See, for example, R. W. Hanning, "'You have begun a parlous pleye': The Nature and Limits of Dramatic Mimesis as a Theme in Four Middle English 'Fall of Lucifer' Cycle Plays," *Comparative Drama*, 7 (1973), 22–50.

92. Woolf, *The English Mystery Plays*, pp. 86–95.

93. See Margaret Aston, *England's Iconoclasts* (Oxford: Clarendon Press, 1988), I, 115–16.

94. See Ann Eljenholm Nichols, "Books-for-Laymen: The Demise of a Commonplace," *Church History*, 56 (1987), 457–73; for Gregory the Great's pronouncements with regard to images, see especially Celia M. Chazelle, "Pictures, Books, and the Illiterate: Pope Gregory I's Letters to Serenus of Marseilles," *Word and Image*, 6 (1990), 138–53.

95. E. J. M. Spargo, *The Category of the Aesthetic in the Philosophy of St. Bonaventure* (St. Bonaventure, N.Y.: Franciscan Institute, 1953), p. 15.

96. Religious images (in preference to abstract symbols, such as the Agnus Dei) were approved by the Council of 692 (Canon 82, quoted in translation by Paul J. Alexander, *The Patriarch Nicephorus of Constantinople* [Oxford: Clarendon Press, n.d.], p. 45), and Eastern theology developed a thoroughgoing defense of their use, particularly in response to iconoclasm. "The honor rendered to the images passes to the prototype," St. Basil had said (quoted by Gerhart Ladner, "The Concept of the Image in the Greek Fathers and the Byzantine Iconoclastic Controversy," *Dumbarton Oaks Papers*, 7 [1953], 3). The Western Church never adopted Eastern image theology officially, and indeed there was considerable resistance to it; see Anthony Ugolnik, "The *Libri Carolini*: Antecedents of Reformation Iconoclasm," in *Iconoclasm vs. Art and Drama*, ed. Davidson and Nichols, pp. 1–32. On the implications of the devotional image for medieval drama, see especially Coletti, "Spirituality and Devotional Images," pp. 31–100. For a general study of the role of images in the Christian West, see Miles, *Image as Insight*, *passim*.

97. See Clifford Davidson, *From Creation to Doom: The York Cycle of Mystery Plays* (New York: AMS Press, 1984), pp. 117–34.

98. Panofsky, *Early Netherlandish Painting*, II, fig. 152; see commentary, ibid., I, 133f.

99. Ibid., I, 35.

100. Meyrick H. Carré, *Realists and Nominalists* (Oxford, 1946), p. 145. The matter of the impact of nominalism and related currents of thought is, of course, complex and subject to different interpretations; see Gordon Leff, *The Dissolution of the Medieval Outlook* (New York: Harper and Row, 1976).

101. Davis, "The English Mystery Plays and 'Ciceronian' Mnemonics," pp. 78–82.

102. See Davis, "The Playing of Miracles in England," p. 152n. For criticism which points up the difficulty of seeing plays merely in terms of pictorial tradition when practical matters of production are involved, see Peter Meredith, "The Iconography of Hell in the English Cycles: A Practical Perspective," in *The Iconography of Hell*, ed. Clifford Davidson and Thomas Seiler, Early Drama, Art, and Music, Monograph Ser., 17 (Kalamazoo: Medieval Institute Publications, 1992), pp. 158–86, and Meg Twycross, "Beyond the Picture Theory: Image and Activity in Medieval Drama," *Word and Image*, 4 (1988), 589–617.

103. Gervase Mathew, *Byzantine Aesthetics* (New York: Viking Press, 1964), p. 31.

104. See John Wyclif, *Tractatus de Ecclesia*, ed. Johann Loserth (London: Trübner, 1886), p. 459; cited by John Phillips, *The Reformation of Images* (Berkeley and Los Angeles: Univ. of California Press, 1973), p. 31. This passage, to be sure, comments on images and not on drama.

105. See Davis, "The Playing of Miracles," p. 105.

106. See the surveys of Wycliffite and Lollard attitudes toward images provided by Hudson, *The Premature Reformation*, pp. 301–07, and especially Margaret Aston, *England's Iconoclasts* (Oxford: Clarendon Press, 1988), I, 96–159. In addition to such texts, there is evidence from heresy trials that widespread objection to devotional images was present among the Lollards (ibid., I, 301–02).

107. Phillips, *The Reformation of Images*, pp. 31–33; Kolve, *The Play Called Corpus Christi*, pp. 21–22; and Aston, *England's Iconoclasts*, I, 96-159. For the Byzantine background, see Ernst Kitzinger, "The Cult of Images before Iconoclasm," *Dumbarton Oaks Papers*, 8 (1954), 104, and Ladner, "The Concept of the Image," *passim*.

108. Davis, "The Playing of Miracles," p. 100.

109. Gordon Leff, *Heresy in the Later Middle Ages* (New York: Barnes and Noble, 1967), II, 501.

110. Ibid., II, 511; see also Aston, *England's Iconoclasts*, I, 100–02.

111. See Aston, *England's Iconoclasts*, I, 99–100.

112. *Selections from English Wycliffite Writings*, ed. Hudson, p. 83.

113. Ibid., p. 87.

114. Phillips, *The Reformation of Images*, p. 31; Aston, *England's Iconoclasts*, pp. 124–32; J. A. F. Thomson, *The Later Lollards* (Oxford: Oxford Univ. Press, 1965); see also G. R. Owst, *Literature and Pulpit in Medieval England*, 2nd ed. (Oxford: Blackwell, 1961), pp. 143–44.

115. It is also called Hot Cockles, and is described in an account in Bodleian MS. 649, fol. 82, of c.1420; the description quoted by Owst, *Literature and Pulpit*, p. 510, is included below in the critical notes to this edition.

116. Kolve, *The Play Called Corpus Christi*, p. 22; for an opposing

aesthetic position, see especially David L. Jeffrey, *The Early English Lyric and Franciscan Spirituality* (Lincoln: Univ. of Nebraska Press, 1975), pp. 91ff. It should be noted that aesthetic bias against the essential deceptiveness of the theater has a history as old a Plato; see the useful survey in Edward Jayne, *Negative Poetics* (Iowa City: Univ. of Iowa Press, 1992), pp. 21–58.

117. *Shakespeare's Jest Book: C. Mery Tales*, ed. H. Oesterley (London, 1866), p. 100.

118. *Dives and Pauper*, ed. Priscilla Barnum, EETS, o.s. 275 (London: Oxford Univ. Press, 1976–80), I, 293. See also Kolve, *The Play Called Corpus Christi*, pp. 132–33, who reprints Pynson's text.

119. Kolve, *The Play Called Corpus Christi*, p. 131.

120. *MED*, s.v. 'defenden' (7).

121. *Dives and Pauper*, ed. Barnum, I, 293.

122. Ibid., I, 294.

123. Ibid., I, 294–95. Recreation of certain types—e.g., dancing—was of course forbidden during time of services. For frequent infractions in the West Country, see *Herefordshire, Worcestershire*, ed. David N. Klausner, Records of Early English Drama (Toronto: Univ. of Toronto Press, 1990), *passim.*

124. Hudson, *Lollards and Their Books*, pp. 169-70. For non-Lollard uses of the word 'maumetry,' see *MED*.

125. Aston, *England's Iconoclasts*, I, 105.

126. Clifford Davidson, "The Anti-Visual Prejudice," in *Iconoclasm vs. Art and Drama*, ed. Davidson and Nichols, pp. 33–46.

127. See the important article by Richard C. Trexler, "Florentine

Religious Experience: The Sacred Image," *Studies in the Renaissance*, 19 (1972), 7–41.

128. *Rationale de divinis offiis* (Naples, 1859), as cited by Woolf, *The English Mystery Plays*, pp. 90, 367.

129. On *play* and *drama*, see especially Kolve, *The Play Called Corpus Christi*, pp. 8–32, and Coldewey, "Plays and 'Play' in Early English Drama," pp. 181–88; cf. Curtius, *European Literature and the Latin Middle Ages*, pp. 417ff. Needless to say, Kolve's understanding of the concept of *game* is somewhat misleading since his analysis does not always distinguish between medieval conceptions and controversial modern theories. Coldewey's article is a useful corrective. However, Kolve's study remains seminal since many earlier writers on the medieval drama demonstrated no understanding of the connection between *play* and *game* whatsoever; see, for example, Coffman, "The Miracle Play in England," pp. 456–61. On derisive audience response, seen as inappropriate, see the example of the play of *Fergus* at York (*York*, ed. Johnston and Rogerson, I, 47–48, and Mark R. Sullivan, "The Missing York *Funeral of the Virgin*," *EDAM Newsletter*, 1 [1979], 5–7).

130. Curtius, *European Literature and the Latin Middle Ages*, p. 420; Kolve (*The Play Called Corpus Christi*, p. 126) additionally cites the *Cursor Mundi*: "that thris he wep we find i-nogh,/ Bot we fine never quar he logh."

131. H.-G. Gadamer, *Truth and Method* (New York: Seabury Press, 1975), pp. 99–119; Martin Heidegger, "The Origin of a Work of Art," in *Poetry, Language, Thought*, trans. Albert Hofstader (New York: Harper and Row, 1971), pp. 17–87.

132. *York*, ed. Johnston and Rogerson, II, 713.

133. *Catalogue of Additions to the Manuscripts in the British Museum*, II (1877), 22. The first item in the manuscript is an attack on "the bischopes othe that he sweris to the pope" (fols. 1^{r}–13^{v}), followed by *A Tretise of Miraclis Pleyinge* (fols. 14^{r}–21^{r}). The items which follow in the

manuscript are: a treatise against dicing (fols. 21r–24r), against the showing of relics for profit (fol. 24r–24v), an epistle to a lady on knowledge of the soul (fols. 25r–26r), *A Tretise of Imagys* (fols. 26r–28v), *A Tretise of Pristis* (fols. 28v), *Of Weddid Men and ther Wivis and Ther Childere* (fols. 29r–34r), a treatise on tithes and offerings (fols. 34r–35v), *The Seven Sacramentis* by John Gaytrigg (fols. 35v–36r), *The Seven Vertues* by Gaytrigg (fol. 36v, incomplete), and a treatise against religious orders (fols. 37r–60v). For brief descriptions of the contents of these tracts, see *A Manual of the Writings in Middle English, 1050–1500*, gen. ed. J. Burke Severs (Connecticut Academy of Arts and Sciences, 1970), II, 372–73. The manuscript, from the library of Archbishop Tenison and formerly at St. Martin-in-the-Fields, London, was purchased by the British Museum in 1861.

134. Davis, "The Playing of Miracles," p. 83.

135. See *Two Coventry Corpus Christi Plays*, ed. Craig, and *Coventry*, ed. Ingram, *passim*.

136. The Northampton Abraham and Isaac play and sixteenth-century records revealing the storing of pageant wagons have been noted above. Records of pre-Reformation drama elsewhere in Northamptonshire and in the neighboring county of Huntingdonshire are sparse. Ian Lancashire notes only the presence of copies of Terence in the libraries of Ramsay Abbey and Peterborough Abbey, records containing three rather cryptic references to acting and costumes at Peterborough from c.1300, and evidence of entertainments at Culworth (a hobby horse and "pleyers") and at Kingsthorpe (a May game with a king and queen which may have predated the Reformation); see Lancashire, *Dramatic Texts and Records*, pp. 121, 234, 249–50, 252.

137. No candidates have presented themselves for the authorship of the *Tretise*. Nicholas Hereford is an even less attractive candidate when it is remembered that he did not begin his residence in the Midlands until 1417 when he joined the Charterhouse in Coventry as a member of the Carthusian Order; see Emden, *A Biographical Register*, II, 914.

The Dialect of *A Tretise of Miraclis Pleyinge*

Paul A. Johnston, Jr.

Until recently, it was not easy to locate precisely where a given Middle English text came from. Texts often exist in several copies, each a little different from the other, as scribes from other areas than the original writer (or scribe) copied the text and, either by accident or by design, partially translated the spelling system used in that original text into one more familiar to them.[1] Other scribes from yet other dialect areas copied the copies, and so forth, resulting in dialect "layers" that only could be exposed with close analysis.[2] Since such mixed texts are the rule rather than the exception, there are few "pure" manuscripts that could serve as reference points to locate the layers. While nineteenth-century and early twentieth-century scholars used external and modern dialect evidence to localize a few manuscripts, often successfully[3] (up to a point, in any case, with only the unsystematic Ellis[4] and Wright[5] modern English surveys to work with), there were a few "howlers" long accepted by traditional scholarship. For example, the language of Wycliffite writings, including both earlier and later versions of the Bible[6] and the sermons of Wyclif's followers, were taken as representing "Oxford dialect" since we know that Wyclif lived there[7] even though it is largely devoid of the Southwestern and Southwest Midland forms that mark real Oxford writing.[8] Nevertheless, a list of linguistic criteria for dialect membership was eventually abstracted out and plotted on a series of maps by Moore, Meech, and Whitehall;[9] while this survey combines manuscripts from a number of periods and so compares apples and oranges in some respects,[10] it was definitely a step in the right direction.

More recently, the localization process has been carried much further, making the task of discovering the location of an "unknown" manuscript—or the scribal layers within it, if the language is mixed—that much easier. For the 1290–1350 period, Gillis Kristensson at the University of Lund has published two volumes of a projected four-volume *Survey of Middle English Dialects*,[11] using early fourteenth-century Lay Subsidy Rolls and similar documents containing place- and personal-name information, and the thirteenth century will soon be covered by a *Linguistic Atlas of Early Middle English*[12] being prepared by researchers based at the University of Glasgow. The same team of researchers, together with others based at the University of Edinburgh, have already developed an atlas for the 1350–1450 period, the *Linguistic Atlas of Late Middle English (LALME)*,[13] which was published in 1986. The Glasgow-Edinburgh approach is to start with as many externally placeable texts (literary and non-literary) as possible and to use measures of linguistic similarity to place other manuscripts, which, once localized, can serve as "anchor texts"[14]—reference points—to localize still more material, and so on. This cumulative process results in a grid of localities finer than that found in most modern dialect surveys, and therefore is sometimes capable of quite precise localizations.

Since the two parts of the *Tretise of Miraclis Pleyinge* belong to the early fifteenth century, the most obvious way to localize them would be to compare the forms in them to reference points in *LALME*. This has actually been done for two other sections of the same manuscript which appear as sample profiles in the survey. Language 3, which begins immediately following the *Tretise* in British Library Add. MS. 24,202 and continues to fol. 36^{v}, was assigned to an area around Chesterfield, Derbyshire,[15] and Language 4, the dialect of the remaining sections of the manuscript, was placed in eastern Northamptonshire, around the villages of Thrapston and Raunds.[16] The language of the *Tretise* was itself treated as a unit and called Language 2, with a (tentative) assignment to Northamptonshire in the *LALME* index,[17] though no precise placement was made and no profile appears.

Following my description of the dialect of the *Tretise*, I will attempt below to make a more precise localization for this text by using a cumulative, multi-stage, highly-detailed analysis to compare the spellings found in it with *LALME* material in different ways until a placement to a specific area of about thirty-six square miles is achieved.[18] As a by-product of this process, it will be shown that the two parts of the *Tretise* come from separate areas within the same subdialect group and therefore that they were composed by different men although copied by the same person during the compilation of the present manuscript. It will also be shown that *LALME*'s assignment of the *Tretise* to Northamptonshire is more reasonable in the case of Part II than of Part I.

Features of the language. The first step in the performance of the analysis necessarily involves the construction of a linguistic profile parallel to those used in the *LALME* survey. These profiles examine the spellings and forms used for 289 diagnostic graphological, phonological, morphological, and lexical linguistic features—e.g., whether Old English *ā*, as in words of the *stone* class, is spelled <a(a)> or <o(o)>; whether *hi/he* forms or *they* types are used for the third-person plural pronoun; or whether present participles take *-ynge* or *-ande/-ende/-inde* as a suffix. Of the surveyed features, 189 appear in the *Tretise*. All the spellings of these items are listed below in Table 1 and incorporate the *LALME* conventions indicating the forms' frequency. Majority forms (the most frequent) and those appearing down to half as often as the majority forms appear without parentheses; those appearing between a half and a quarter as often are listed within single parentheses; and rarer forms, with less than a quarter frequency, are enclosed within double parentheses. In this way, the variability within a manuscript can be accounted for quite easily and can be incorporated into any comparison with other material.

Since the two parts of the *Tretise* are not precisely identical, an **A** before a form means that it is found only in Part I, and a **B** identifies it as appearing only in Part II. Otherwise, we may assume that the form is found in both parts.

TABLE 1
LINGUISTIC PROFILE
OF *A TRETISE OF MIRACLIS PLEYINGE*

THE:	þe	TO: +sb.	to
THESE:*	þes, **A** þese, **A** ((þise))	+inf.	to
THOSE:*	þo	FROM:*	fro
SHE:*	**A** sche (she)	AFTER:*	after ((**A** aftire, **B** aftir))
HER:	hir	THEN:*	þanne, **B** (þan)
IT:	it	THAN:*	þan
THEY:*	þei, **A** ((þey))	THOUGH:*	**A** þouȝ, **B** þof
THEM:*	hem	IF:*	ȝif (yif), **B** if
THEIR:*	þer, **A** (þeire), **A** ((þeir, þeyre, her))	AS:	as
		AS . . . AS:	as . . . as
		AGAINST:*	aȝenus, agenus, **B** (aȝen), **B** ((aȝens))
SUCH:*	siche ((suche))		
WHICH:*	whiche, **A** ((whyche))	SINCE:*	syþen ((**A** siþen, **A** siþ, **B** siþþe))
EACH:*	eche		
MANY:*	many	YET:*	**A** ȝit
MAN:*	man	WHILE:*	**A** while (whil)
ANY:*	ony	WH-:*	wh-
MUCH:*	myche, **B** ((miche))	NOT:*	not
		NOR:	ne, **B** (nor)
ARE:*	ben	A, O:	o ((oo))
WERE:	were, weren	WORLD:*	world, **B** (worlde)
IS:	is		
WAS:	was	THERE:	þer ((þere))
SHALL:*	schal ((shal, **B** schalle))	WHERE:*	wher, **A** where
		MIGHT:	**A** myȝt-, **B** miȝte
SHOULD:*	shulde, **B** ((schulde))		
		WHEN:*	whanne (whan)
WILL:	wil	THROUGH:*	**A** þoru
pl.	wolen	-s:*	-is (-es) ((-ys, -us))
WOULD:*	wolde		

Table 1: Linguistic Profile—*A Tretise of Miraclis Pleyinge* (cont.)

pres part:*	-ynge, -yng (-inge, -ing), ((**A** -ande, **B** -ende))
vb. n.:*	-ynge, -yng (-inge, -ing)
3 p. sing.*	-iþ (-yþ, -eþ), **A** ((-is))
vb. pl.*	-en, -yn ((-in, -un))
pret.*	-ide (-yde, -ede)
p. pt.*	-id (-yd, -ed) ((-ud))
strg. vb.*	-en, -yn (-un, -in)
ABOUT:	aboute
AFTERWARDS:	afterward
ALL:	alle (al), **A** ((all))
AMONG:	**B** among
ANSWER:	**A** answer-, **B** answere
ASK:*	**A** ax- (aske)
AWAY:*	awey, **A** ((aweye))
BEEN:	ben, **A** been, **B** ((bien))
BEFORE:*	**A** byforn, bifore, **B** beforn (byfore), **B** ((bifore, before))
BETWEEN:*	**B** bitwene, betwene
BOTH:*	boþe, **A** ((boþ))
BROTHER:	**B** broþer
BURN:*	**A** brinn-
BUSY:*	bisi-, **A** bysi-
BUT:	but
BY:	by, **B** (bi)
CALL:	clep-
CAME:	cam
CAST:	**A** cast
CHOOSE:	**B** chosyn
CHURCH:*	**A** chirche
DAUGHTER:*	douȝter
DAY:*	day/dayes, **B** (dayees), **A** ((daies))
DEATH:*	deþ, **A** deþe
DIE:	**B** dye-
DO:*	doþ (doiþ)
pret.*	dyde, **A** dude, **B** dide
pret. pl.	**A** dyden, **B** diden
DREAD:*	drede
EARTH:*	erþe
EITHER:*	eyþer, **A** eiþer
EITHER-OR:*	ouþer
EVIL:*	yuel, **A** yuele, **B** vuel ((**A** vuil, **B** yuil))
EYE:*	**A** eyen, **B** eȝen (eyȝen)
FAR:*	fer
FATHER:*	**B** fadir ((fader))
FELLOW:	felaw-
FILL:	fulfill-, **A** fulfyll-
FIRST:*	first, **A** Ffirste, **B** ((firste))
FIVE ord:	**A** fifte
FLESH:*	fleysh, **A** fleyssh (flesche, **A** fleyss, **B** fleys-)
FOLLOW:	**A** folowe
FOUR:	**B** four-

Table 1: Linguistic Profile—*A Tretise of Miraclis Pleyinge* (cont.)

FOWL:	**B** fowl-
FRIEND:	frend **B** ((frynde, frynd, fren-))
GIVE: pt.	**A** ȝaf
p. pt.*	ȝyuen (**A** ȝiuen, **B** ȝifen)
GO: 3 ps.	**A** goþ
GOOD:*	good, gode
HAVE:*	han (**A** haue)
3 ps.	haþ
pret.	hadde
HEAD:*	**A** heued, heuyd, **B** hede
HEAR:*	her-
HEAVEN:*	heuene
HELL:	**A** helle
HENCE:*	**A** hennys
HIGH:	**A** heie
HILL:*	**B** hil
HIM:	hym ((him))
HOW:*	how ((hou, houȝ))
HUNDRED:	hundrid, hundid
I:	**A** y, **B** J (I)
KIND:*	kynde, mynde, **B** (kinde)
KNOW:	knowe
LAUGH:	**A** lawþ-, **B** lawȝ-
pret. pl.	**A** lowen
LAW:*	**B** lawe
LESS:	lasse (lesse)
LIE:*	**A** ly- (li-, lyy-)
LIFE:	lif (lyf)
LITTLE:*	litil
LORD:*	lord
LOVE:	loue, **B** ((looue))
LOW:	**B** low-
MAY:	may
pl.	mowen
MON:	**A** moten, **B** moot
MOTHER:	**B** modir
MY:	my/min
NAME:	name, **B** ((naame))
NEITHER:*	neyþer, **B** nouþer
NEVER:*	neuer, **A** neuere
NEW:	newe
NIGH:	A neye-, **B** neȝ, neiȝ- (**A** ney-, neie-, **B** neȝe-, neȝþe)
NOW:	now ((nowe))
OLD:	olde
ONE:*	oon
OR:	or, **A** ((ore))
OTHER:	oþere ((oþer))
OUR:	oure
OUT:	oute, out
OWN:*	owne, **A** ((oune))
PEOPLE:*	puple
PRAY:	prey-, **B** preye
PRIDE:	pride
SAY:*	sey, **B** seye, **B** (seie)
3 p. sing.	seiþ
pret./ppt.	**B** seide/seid
SEE:*	**A** se, **B** see
ppt.	seen
SEEK:	**A** sech-
SELF:*	silf ((silfe, **B** self))

Table 1: Linguistic Profile—*A Tretise of Miraclis Pleyinge* (cont.)

SIN:*	synne, **B** ((sinne))	WORSE:*	**A** worse, **B** werse
SIX:	**B** sixti	WORSHIP:*	worschip-, **A** worschipe, **A** ((worschyp, worship-))
SLAIN:*	**B** sleyn		
SOME:	**A** sum, summe		
SON:*	sone		
SORROW:*	**A** sorw-, **B** sorowe	YE:	yee, **B** ȝee, **A** ((yhe))
SOUL:	soule	YOU:	**A** you, **B** ȝou
SPAKE:	**B** spac	YOUR:	**A** youre, **B** ȝoure
THEE:*	þe, **B** þee		
THOU:	þou, **B** (þu)	YEAR:	**B** ȝeer
THY:	þi, **B** þyn	YIELD:	**A** yilding
THOUSAND:*	**B** thousend	YOUNG:*	**A** ȝonge
THREE:	þre; þridde	-ALD:	-old
TOGETHER:*	togidere	-AND:	-ond ((-and))
TRUE:*	trew-, treu-, trwe, **B** (trow-, trw-)	-ANG:	**B** -ong
		-ANK:	**B** -ank
		-DOM:	-dam, **A** ((-dum))
TWENTY:	**B** twenty		
TWO:	two	-ER:*	-ere, -er- ((-er, -our))
UPON:	upon		
WAY:	weye, **B** weies	-FUL:	-ful
WELL:*	wel	-HOOD:	**A** -hod, **B** -hed, -hode
WHAT:	what, **A** ((watte))	-LY:*	-ly, **B** ((-liche))
WHO:	**A** who	-NESS:	-nesse, **A** ((-nes))
WHOM:	**A** whom		
WHY:	why, whi	-SHIP:	**A** -schip-, **B** -schip, ((**A** -chipe,-schyp, -ship-, **B** -schipe, -chip))
WITEN: inf.	witen		
pres. pl.	witen		
pret. sg.	**A** woost 2p		
WITHOUT:	**A** wiþoute		

Given the forms in this profile, it is fairly easy to show that the language of both parts belongs to the East Central Midlands—an area roughly contained within a quadrilateral with corners at Wisbech, Burton-on-Trent, Bicester, and Cambridge—by a process of elimination. The North can be easily excluded by the fact that OE *ā* as in *lord, who, two* yields <o>, not <a>;[19] that OE *ō* as in *good* shows <o> spellings, implying a back vowel, rather than <u> = [ø:];[20] and additionally that there are no present indicative verb plurals in *-is/-es*.[21]

The Kentish-speaking Southeast and the Southwest can likewise be excluded. In fact, one feature alone—the development of OE *y, ȳ* to <i, y>= [ι i:] in words like *church, hill, busy, mind, kind*—will rule out both areas, since Kentish would have <e> and Southwestern, <u> = [y(:)][22] in this class of words. Furthermore, Kentish would not show <þ, th> instead of <d> for initial /θ/,[23] <ou> instead of <au> in *daughter, though*,[24] or <e> as the usual outcome of OE *ēo* in *seen, been* instead of <ye, ie>.[25] Southwestern Middle English would have a prefix <y-, i-> before past participles, which would end in schwa or zero, not *-n*,[26] without prefix, as here. Southern dialects would also have <segge, ligge> for *say* and *lie*[27] and quite possibly <u, v> and <z> for initial /f/ and /s/ respectively.[28] The *Tretise* therefore must be written in a Midland dialect of some sort—and not a transitional one like East Anglian, Thames Valley, or Southwest Midland English, since at least some of the Southern features enumerated above are characteristic of these areas also.[29]

Within the remaining area, the West Midlands can be instantly excluded, since no rounded vowels from OE *an* appear except in *ony*, which is very generally distributed throughout the Midlands.[30] Also, <u> forms for OE /y(:)/ and <vche> for *each* would be the rule in Western documents.[31] The two rounded vowel spellings for *did, evil*[32] may provide evidence that the East Midland/West Midland dialect boundary is not far away, though the prevalence of forms implying /i(:)/ suggests a point on the eastern side of the line.

The North Midland/South Midland line might be close also since North Midland forms are found sporadically; examples include third person singular present tense <-is>,[33] *less* = <lesse>,[34] *against* = <agenus>[35] in addition to the regular Central/South Midland *-iþ,* <lasse>, <aȝen(u)s>. However, these forms are rare (and mostly confined to Part I), and there is no trace of North Midlandisms such as <m(e/i)kyll, whilk, ilk> for *much, which, each*;[36] or <callen> in the sense of *be called* = "be named" instead of <clepen>,[37] and the like.

The language can therefore be localized to the above-mentioned quadrilateral, which contains cities such as Leicester, Northampton, Cambridge, Peterborough, Coventry, and Bedford and their hinterlands. This dialect region is a sort of "transition zone to everywhere," the linguistic/geographical center of England,[38] full of features shared with adjacent dialect areas and with few exclusive to itself.

There is one problem: this transitional nature, which would have made this dialect easily understood in most regions of England, combined with the social prestige it would have had as coming from one of the most "tony" areas of the country,[39] led to the development of a *lingua franca* based on the East Central Midland dialect, which was especially employed not only by proselytizing preachers, both orthodox and Wycliffite, as a vehicle for their writings[40] but also by some authors of secular literature.[41] While the variety, called Type I Standard or Central Midlands Standard (CMS) by Samuels,[42] is not employed in the North for the most part, there are many early fifteenth-century documents from all parts of the Midlands or the first row of counties south of the Thames (Gloucestershire, Somerset, Wiltshire, Berkshire, Surrey, Kent) that have a majority of CMS features, and one would expect that religious treatises like this one would be especially prone to possess them. East Midland features are therefore no guarantee of East Midland provenance.

Now, if CMS were a Standard in the same sense as modern Standard English, fully codified and virtually invariable (at least ideally), the *Tretise*, if proven to be in CMS, could not be localized at all. Indeed, Anne Hudson, who mentions the contemporary comment that Wycliffite preachers all sounded alike,[43] suggests as much. However, this judgment probably referred to the vocabulary choice and rhetorical style being uniform—a feature to be observed in any tightly-knit in-group's language, from that of Marxists to that of "born-again" evangelicals—and thus may not have anything to do with grammatical forms *per se*; after all, CMS was only a written Standard, not a spoken one,[44] and vocabulary choice would be more salient than grammatical structures to an audience of non-linguists in any case; most of the lay commentators on usage today concentrate primarily on definition and use of words and secondarily on syntax to the exclusion of other factors.[45] The preachers may have been influenced by the dialect of their own writing somewhat, but probably this influence was not enough to call their speech an invariable Standard.

Even in writing, there is considerable variation in CMS. While there are certainly typical CMS spellings for some words—Samuels mentions <myche> for *much*, <silf> for *self*, <siȝe> for *saw*, <ȝouun> for *given*, and so on[46]—there does seem to be a distinction between "Native" CMS, written in the East Midlands, presumably by locals to whom East Central Midland English was their own dialect, and "Outlying" CMS, invariably with some telltale forms indicating the manuscript's true origins, written in other areas by native speakers of other dialects. The latter is indeed localizable; a close analysis of a given manuscript will reveal clusters of items that do not belong to the East Central Midlands, and if they point towards a single area the manuscript can be assumed to have been written there. If there are no such clusters of any significant size, even if there are a few isolated non-East Midland forms, the document must in fact be an East Midland one. To illustrate, Language 3, which appears in British Library Add. MS. 24,202 (the manuscript to which the *Tretise* also belongs) and assigned by *LALME* to the heart of the North Midlands, even has East Midland characteristics as a common feature throughout the whole manuscript (see below). However, Language 3 exhibits a number of consistent telltale Derbyshire forms:[47] the third person singular ending is always in *-s;* forms of *give* start with <g->; *church* = <kirk>;[48]

worse = *warr*, from Old Norse *verra*, not Old English (Anglian) *wersa*;[49] forms of *nine* have <e>,[50] showing the Northern development of Old English /i-γ/, and so on. Note that these forms are not sporadic North Midlandisms, which might simply show dialect borrowing into the Standard, but are majority forms within the section of the manuscript in which they appear. It is their presence that makes this language "Outlying" CMS and determines the impossibility that it might have come from, say, Northamptonshire.

Therefore, the next step in the analysis must involve teasing apart the different dialect layers within the *Tretise* to establish whether any such non-East Central Midland stratum of forms exists. In this way it can be determined whether or not it is a true East Central Midland manuscript or merely an example of "Outlying" CMS. Such a form-by-form study is set forth in the next section.

The vertical analysis: the geographical distribution of forms. The type of form-by-form analysis needed to determine the provenance of the *Tretise* is a multistage process. The first step is a simple comparison of the features in the above profile with the equivalent form in each *LALME* manuscript in turn, and devising some quantitative measure of the extent of similarity, preferably in some way that takes frequency within a manuscript into account. Then one must determine which of these forms are shared by the majority of manuscripts in each county. From there, the majority forms for each dialect group that are also present in the *Tretise* can be identified. Finally, the variants can be sorted into clusters having similar geographical distribution across dialect groups—'layers,' to use Carver's terminology[51]—and it then can be determined whether or not the *Tretise* qualifies as "Outlying" CMS, "Native" CMS, or non-Standard East Midland dialect of some kind.

In the first stage of analysis, the decision was made to take a random sample of one hundred of the 189 features in the profile in order to facilitate later computation; this type of sampling should not affect the representativeness of the variables chosen. The features sampled are marked with asterisks in the profile above. Their reflexes in the *Tretise* were then compared with those in every *LALME* profile containing them. This involved using a quadrille pad to list the number of the feature assigned by *LALME*[52] on the vertical lines and the *LALME* profile numbers on the horizontal ones, marking correspondences to show frequency as follows. A match between majority forms of a *LALME* manuscript and in the *Tretise* was indicated by a solid dot at the relevant intersection on the paper. Where the majority form of the *LALME* manuscript matched a frequent minority form (shown in single parentheses) in the *Tretise*, or vice versa, a circle was drawn, and any other sort of a match was shown by a double circle. Complete mismatches were indicated by a blank space, and if the form being analyzed did not appear in the *LALME* manuscript in question, an X was drawn through the appropriate quadrille square. The analysis was continued to completion with each county or administrative unit having its own quadrille sheet(s) to facilitate the next stage of the process.

The results were then quantified by turning the patterns of dots and circles into a number called a Similarity Index Score, calculated separately for each form in each county. This was derived by awarding one point for each dot, a half point for each single circle, and a quarter point for each double circle—then summing the point totals down each column for each individual county, and dividing the sum by the number of manuscripts in that county minus the number of X's. The resulting figure, which ranges between zero and one, is a sort of percentage, weighted for frequency, measuring how common the form being studied is within the county corpus. Scores above .5 indicate that it is a majority form.

The scores were then transferred to a second piece of quadrille paper with the same form numbers on the vertical axis but with the county name, sorted roughly by dialect group according to the breakdown listed in Table 2,[53] on the horizontal one. Once again dots were inserted if the index score was .5 or over; if it was less than this, but the majority of manuscripts had single or double circles, whatever symbol was most frequent was written. Otherwise, the square was left blank (or given an X if there were no responses).

TABLE 2
BREAKDOWN OF DIALECT GROUPS BY COUNTY

DIALECT GROUP	COUNTIES
Scots	All Scotland
Northern English:	
Far Northeast	Northumberland; Durham
Northwest	Cumberland; Westmorland
Near Northeast	Yorkshire, North and East Ridings; City of York
Midland English:	
Northeast Midlands	Yorkshire, West Riding; Lincolnshire; Nottinghamshire
Northwest Midlands	Lancashire; Cheshire; Derbyshire; Isle of Man
West Central Midlands	Shropshire; Staffordshire; Warwickshire; North Welsh counties
Mid Central Midlands	Leicestershire; Rutland; Northamptonshire
East Central Midlands	Huntingdonshire; Bedfordshire; Buckinghamshire; Peterborough
East Anglia	Norfolk; Suffolk; Cambridgeshire; Ely
Southwest Midlands	Worcestershire; Gloucestershire; Herefordshire; Oxfordshire; South Welsh counties
Southeast Midlands	Hertfordshire; Essex; London; Middlesex
Southern English:	
Far Southeast	Surrey; Sussex; Kent
Near Southwest	Berkshire; Hampshire; Wiltshire; Somerset; Dorset
Far Southwest	Devon; Cornwall

Finally, the same procedure of dotting and circling was carried up to the dialect group level by indicating the forms for which the majority of counties within a group had symbols. Having become visible, the forms with similar patterns of dots by county and dialect group were gathered into layers with each one given an appropriate label—e.g., "Britain," "Midlands," "Midlands and South without the Northeast Midlands," and so on[54]—according to what area was covered. Forms having a discontinuous distribution were assigned to whatever layer most nearly matched the part of the distribution in or nearest to the Midlands so that a word appearing in Scotland and the Southwest Midlands would be assigned to the latter layer and its Scottish distribution ignored.

Now, any Standard, because of its *lingua franca* function, should be rich in words or forms belonging to layers extending over a wide area, and poor in localized forms. We might expect, therefore, that a CMS manuscript would not have many words belonging to the East Central Midlands alone but would have quite a few belonging to the Midlands, South Midlands, and East Midlands layers—and even layers of wider distribution, such as the British layer (covering all counties), the English layer, and composite layers such as the Midlands and North or the Midlands and South, which all extend over more than one dialect group. Once these wide-distribution layers are accounted for, any residue should indicate the specific dialect area to which the manuscript belongs. If this is the Mid or East Central Midlands, the *Tretise* must be a "Native" CMS work, if it is Standardized at all.

Table 3 shows the final results, with "modified" layers counted with the appropriate "unmodified" layer in the totals. The results show that the *Tretise* ought to be tentatively counted as a CMS manuscript. Of the 100 features, forty-three—nearly half—are found as majority or frequent minority forms in layers that include at least every Midland county. Another forty are found in more than one dialect group within the Midlands; these include forms shared throughout the Mid and East Central Midlands (tied for the "thickest layer," with sixteen forms) alone or with the addition of East Anglia

TABLE 3
SPELLINGS IN THE *TRETISE* BY DIALECT LAYER

LAYER	**NO. OF WORDS** **PLAIN**	**MODIFIED**	**TOTAL**
BRITAIN	7	---	7
ENGLAND	6	2	8
MIDLANDS & NORTH	2	2	4
MIDLANDS & SOUTH	6	10	16
MIDLANDS	3	1	4
NORTH MIDLANDS	1	---	1
SOUTH MIDLANDS	5	3	8
WEST MIDLANDS	5	---	5
EAST MIDLANDS	9	1	10
CENTRAL MIDLANDS	16	---	16
S.E. MIDLANDS	2	---	2
S.W. MIDLANDS	2	---	2
EAST ANGLIA	2	---	2
E.C. MIDLANDS	8	---	8
N.E. MIDLANDS	1	---	1
Other	6	---	6

and the Southeast Midlands (the East Midland layer, with ten forms, the third thickest layer). Comparison with Samuels' article on CMS[55] shows that the most distinctive CMS features not shared with Chancery or other English Standards-in-embryo belong to either the Central or East Midland layers, particularly the former. In all, eighty-three forms qualify as widely distributed.

Furthermore, among the remaining seventeen spellings belonging to one and only one dialect group, there is only one cluster that stands out: the East Central Midland layer, with eight forms. When considered along with the thickness of the East Midland, South Midland, and Central Midland layers, this result probably indicates an origin from within this group or near to it even after all the CMS forms have been accounted for. Therefore, the language of the *Tretise* is not an "Outlying" form of CMS but a "Native" form of that dialect.[56]

One can obtain a rough idea of the most likely counties from which this dialect comes by returning to the county-level analysis and applying the same scoring system as before, but summing them across a row, by county, instead of adding the points down a column (by form). Using this procedure, Huntingdonshire scores highest with an index score of 78, the Soke of Peterborough is next with 75, and then Bedfordshire (73), Cambridgeshire (66), and Northamptonshire (60). This reinforces the conclusion reached above since these are all East Central Midland counties or in areas abutting this part of the Midlands. A clue is also given as to where within the dialect area to look for a more specific placement.

It must be emphasized, however, that this procedure does not really give such a placement because the score also depends on how uniform the language is across the county. In this case, Huntingdonshire is quite uniform, but Bedfordshire and Northamptonshire are criss-crossed by isoglosses separating the Southeast Midlands and the Mid Central Midlands from the East Central Midlands respectively; Oundle in northeast Northamptonshire, for example, would group linguistically with Huntingdon, but Northampton or Daventry are more similar to Coventry. The Northamptonshire score then represents an "average" between the two parts of the county, and should not be relied upon too heavily. If a more precise placement is desired, another type of analysis not depending on county boundaries must be tried.

The horizontal analysis: the similarity of other manuscripts. The easiest way to perform such an analysis is to sum similarity points for all forms as was done at the county level in the last section, but this time at the manuscript level, returning to the first stage of analysis above and using the same sort of system of dots and circles and the same method of computing Similarity Index Scores. The *LALME* placings of the manuscripts scoring the highest should be correspondingly close to the actual point of origin; at the very least, the set of manuscripts most similar to the *Tretise* should bunch up geographically in a way that should indicate the rough area in which this point lies. Since no groupings by county are involved, isoglosses within a county should not distort the results, but, if anything, the placement of these dialect boundaries should be highlighted. To this extent, one should arrive at a more precise localization than the previous analysis could provide, perhaps to the subdialect group level.

TABLE 4
SIMILARITY INDICES
OF *LALME* MANUSCRIPTS WITH *A TRETISE OF MIRACLIS PLEYINGE*, PARTS I AND II

PART I:

COUNTY	**PROFILE**	**MS. NUMBER**	**SCORE**
HUNTS	541	New College (Oxford) MS. 95, Hand A, Lang. 1	81.95
DERBS	577	Brit. Lib., Add. MS. 24,202, Lang. 3	80.65
NTHNTS	562	Brit. Lib., Add. MS. 24,202, Lang. 4	80.51
NTHNTS	742	Brit. Lib., Royal 18B. ix., Hand A	78.05
HUNTS	427	Lambeth Palace MS. 369	77.62
NTHNTS	4707	Trinity College (Dublin) MS. 75, Hand D	77.48
HUNTS	755	Brit. Lib., Add. MS. 40,672	77.16
HUNTS	51	Bodleian Lib., Douce 321	76.90
HUNTS	518	Brit. Lib., Royal 17B. ix.	76.04
HUNTS	709	Rylands Lib. Eng. MS. 86	75.76
WARWS	4675	Huntington Lib. MS. HM 502	75.66
CAMBS	698	Oxford University College 45, Hand A	75.16

Table 4: Similarity Indices (cont.)

PART II:

COUNTY	**PROFILE**	**MS. NUMBER**	**SCORE**
NTHNTS	562	Brit. Lib., Add. MS. 24,202, Lang. 4	85.80
DERBS	577	Brit. Lib., Add. MS. 24,202, Lang. 3	81.92
HUNTS	541	New College (Oxford) MS. 95, Hand A, Lang. 1	78.13
NTHNTS	742	Brit. Lib., Royal 18B. ix., Hand A	77.52
HUNTS	51	Bodleian Lib., Douce 321	77.37
HUNTS	755	Brit. Lib., Add. MS. 40,672, Hand C	77.16
HUNTS	427	Lambeth Palace MS. 369	77.12
HUNTS	518	Brit. Lib., Royal 17B. ix.	76.97
HUNTS	745	Oxford Lincoln College Lat. MS. 119	76.88
HUNTS	709	Rylands Lib. Eng. MS. 86	76.72
BEDS	4708	Brit. Lib., Sloane 73	76.55
NTHNTS	4707	Trinity College (Dublin) MS. 75, Hand D	76.49
HUNTS	761	Brit. Lib., Harley 2396, Main Hand	76.42
NTHNTS	762	Bodleian Lib., Bodley 959, Hand D/E	75.96
LINCS	905	Lincs. Archives, Maddison Deposit 2/11	75.55
ELY	60	Bodleian Lib., Bodley 60	75.44
HUNTS	461	Cambridge Univ. Lib. MS. Ii. V. 41, Hand B	75.31
HUNTS	561	Bodleian Lib., Bodley 771	75.15

However, since greater precision is wanted, two modifications to this method were felt to be essential. First, since no information should be omitted, it was decided to analyze the other eighty-nine variables not included in the vertical analysis. Second, since there are in fact some systematic differences (mentioned above) between the spelling systems of Parts I and II of the *Tretise*, separate comparisons of each part with the *LALME* manuscripts were perceived to be necessary to test whether these differences are merely accidental or whether they in fact reflect separate geographical origins. The analysis therefore had to be redone completely.

The results for manuscripts with a Similarity Index Score of 75 or more are shown in Table 4, above. It will be noticed first of all that both parts of the *Tretise* are "most similar" to many of the same manuscripts, an indication that they probably both at least come from the same subdialect area. Almost all Huntingdonshire documents are on both lists, but there are quite a few Northamptonshire profiles on each one as well as a few outliers from Ely, South Lincolnshire, and Bedfordshire nearby—and Warwickshire and Derbyshire farther afield.

Close inspection of the outliers reveals that the great similarity involves features of the East and Central Midland layers, or layers even more widely distributed than this—in other words, features of CMS. The Derbyshire manuscript has already been mentioned, and the other outliers also show signs of their real origin. Maddison Deposit MS. 2/11, for instance, contains typical North Midland majority forms like <swilk, whilk(e), ilk(one), mykil> for *such, which, each, much*, and <kirke> for *church*,[57] while Huntington Library MS. HM 502 contains West Midlandisms such as frequent <u> forms in *bury, first, church*; <ligg-> for *lie*; and <amoung> for *among*.[58] Since neither part of the *Tretise* contains such features more than sporadically, any outlying origin like this can be ruled out.

Maps 1 and 2 plot all manuscripts on the lists above geographically, for Part I and Part II, using the grid position given in *LALME*. Those scoring between 75 and 80 are indicated by small dots, and over 80 by larger ones. It can be seen that, except for the outliers, dots concentrate in an area starting in northeastern Northamptonshire, circling around to take in northern Huntingdonshire, and coming back into Northamptonshire. There are also smaller enclaves around St. Neots-Sandy, where Huntingdonshire and

MAP 1
THE PLACEMENT OF THE MOST SIMILAR MANUSCRIPTS TO *A TRETISE OF MYRACLIS PLEYINGE*, PART I

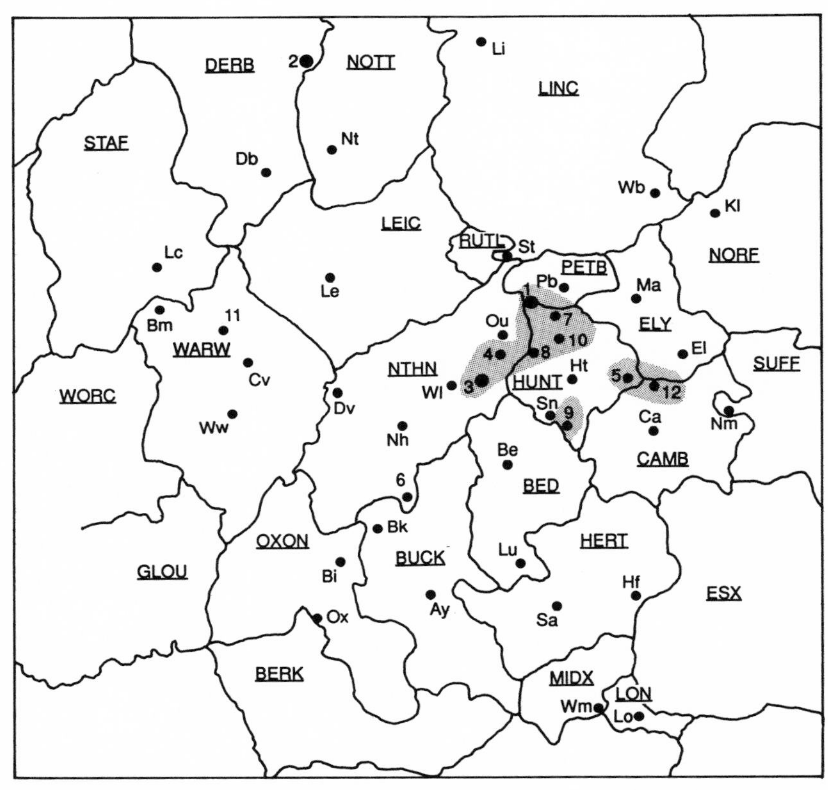

MAP 2
THE PLACEMENT OF THE MOST SIMILAR MANUSCRIPTS TO *A TRETISE OF MYRACLIS PLEYINGE*, PART II

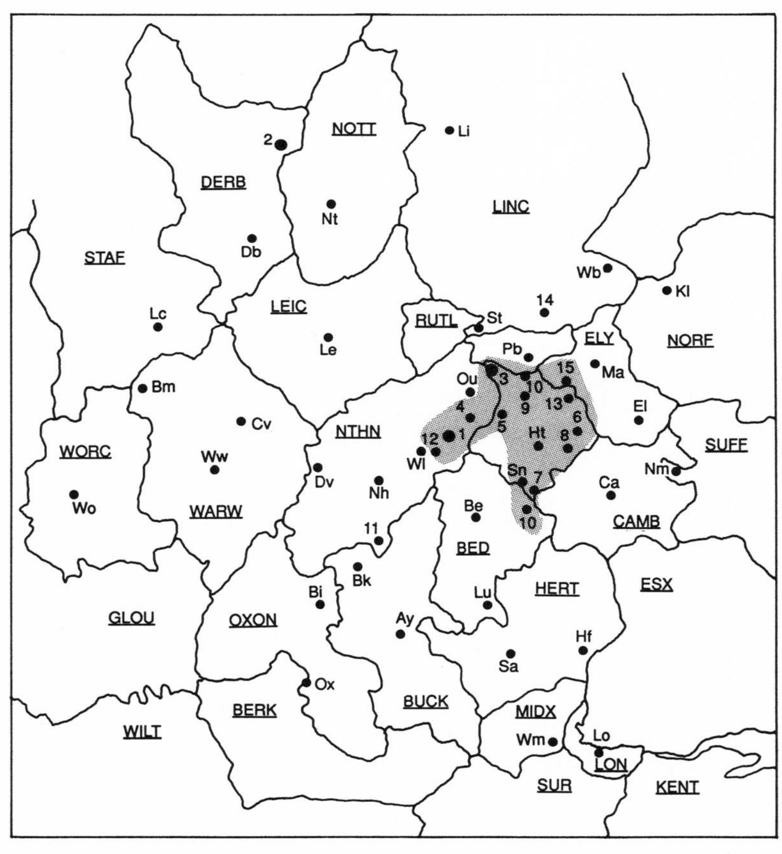

MAP 3
GEOGRAPHICAL PLACEMENT
OF *A TRETISE OF MIRACLIS PLEYINGE*,
PARTS I AND II

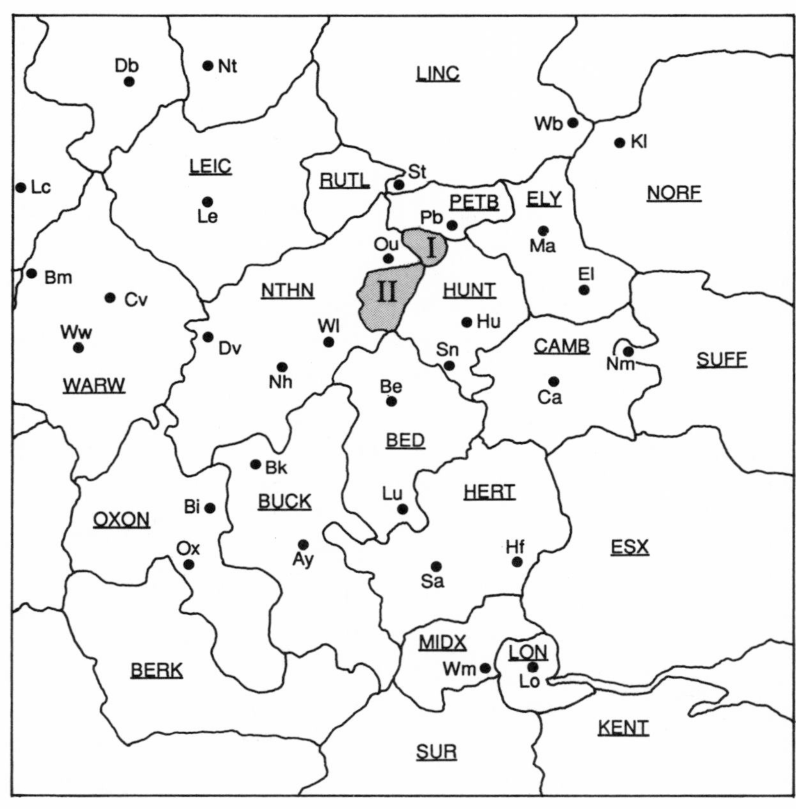

Bedfordshire meet, and St. Ives-Fenstanton on the Huntingdonshire-Cambridgeshire border; these are joined to the main area in the case of Part II. These districts comprise the most likely subdialect area for both parts of the *Tretise*, with the region around Northampton, the Peterborough area, North Buckinghamshire, and most of Bedfordshire excluded.

Even though both parts of the *Tretise* probably belong to the outlined region, whether or not they come from the same identical town or were written by the same person is, however, a different matter. The data suggest that they do not. The dialect of Part II, as shown by the score breakdown, is very much like Language 4, as it appears in the same manuscript with the *Tretise* (from Thrapston or Raunds, Northamptonshire); there is, in fact a four-point jump in score between Language 4 and any other *LALME* profile. Part I, on the other hand, is slightly closer to the collection of Wycliffite material collected in New College (Oxford) MS. 95, Hand A, a North Huntingdonshire work, than to any other profile including Languages 3 and 4. It seems, therefore, that the two parts of the *Tretise* have different origins, but our methodology thus far is too crude to prove or disprove it; this hypothesis will be explored in the next and final section.

The "Benskin Fit": an attempt at maximal localization. In order further to refine the placement of both parts of the *Tretise* and to resolve the problem of whether or not they came from the same town—and thus whether or not it is possible to assert common authorship—it was decided to use a modification of the technique the *LALME* editors themselves used to place manuscripts. This methodology has been described by Michael Benskin, one of the editors of *LALME*, in his article "The 'Fit-Technique' Explained."[59] Like the methods pursued here, this procedure involves a comparison of forms in a document of unknown provenance with their equivalents in already placed manuscripts but uses maps instead of lists and is qualitative rather than quantitative in approach. First, a tracing of a map of Britain is placed over a series of dialect maps of each form in turn. Areas where the form(s) found in the unknown does/do not occur are then shaded in until a small, contiguous area—its size depends on the density of surveyed localities—is left unshaded. The manuscript is then placed there. In the East Central Midlands, the fineness of the grid is such that a placement within a forty-square-mile region, an area about the size of the city of Northampton, can be easily achieved.

Benskin envisioned this "fitting" process as a multi-stage procedure,[60] with the first pass using the small-scale dot maps of Volume I of *LALME* yielding the dialect group, and subsequent passes refining the placement further. However, since the subdialect group has already been determined, it was decided to proceed to the second stage of "fitting," using the detailed, large-scale maps of Volume II. A separate tracing was made for each part of the *Tretise*, and the forms were examined one by one; the areas within the East Midlands were shaded in wherever the particular reflexes used in that part did not occur until the small contiguous area of unshaded space appeared. Twelve comparisons were required for this to happen for Part II, and eighteen for Part I. Any part of this space not in the region outlined in the previous section was also shaded in.[61] The result represents the most specific placement of the manuscript that can be made on linguistic grounds; it is shown in Map 3, with the region of origin for each part of the manuscript labelled "I" and "II" respectively.

The map reveals that the two parts of the *Tretise* in fact do appear as coming from different towns, lying about fifteen to twenty miles apart as the crow flies. Part II is located on the map in about the same locality as Language 4—i.e., Thrapston or Raunds, Northamptonshire, or nearby, between Wellingborough and Huntingdon. This agrees with the results of the horizontal analysis, which shows a special affinity with Language 4 and with the *LALME*'s own tentative placing. Further investigation of the tone and style needs to be done before one can prove common authorship with the Language 4 material, but at least the dialect can be proved to be the same—or sufficiently close that differences are minimal.

The area of origin of Part I, on the other hand, is further northeast; in fact, the "Benskin fit" yields an area taking in the whole of the Soke of Peterborough, the Whittlesey area to the east, and part of North Huntingdonshire. However, given the results of the horizontal analysis and an inspection of Peterborough-North Ely material in *LALME*[62] which on the whole contains much more frequent North Midlandisms, only a North Huntingdonshire placement is possible, specifically around Yaxley or, better yet, Stilton, close to the place of origin of the New College manuscript. Stilton would be close to the absolute southwestern limit for North Midlandisms and East Anglianisms to appear, and this would explain why they are so sporadic; this location would be more or less on the line where <ȝ> in words like *eyes* is written in invariably—one of the main differences between Part I and II—and is too far north and west for <iȝen> to appear for *eyes* or <ȝouun> exclusively for *given*, both of which characterize most of Huntingdonshire.[63]

Conclusion. The analysis of the spellings and forms in the *Tretise* leads to the following conclusions:

1. The *Tretise* is written in somewhat Standardized East Central Midland English, fairly similar to that found in the Wycliffite Bible and other Wycliffite works coming from this part of England. There are a few sporadic North Midland, West Midland, and East Anglian forms, but the biggest stratum of closely localizable spellings points to an area between Northampton, Peterborough, and Huntingdon. There exist no *systematic* differences from East Central Midland dialect, which is not the case even for the language of the item that immediately follows the *Tretise* in the manuscript which is an incompletely rendered Central Midland Standard on a Derbyshire base. The language of the *Tretise*, especially that of Part II, however, is quite similar to that of the material beginning on fol. 37^{v} (Language 4) of British Library Add. MS. 24,202 which stems from the vicinity of Thrapston or Raunds, Northamptonshire, and that part of the *Tretise* was most probably composed in the same area.

2. Part I, however, shows more North Midlandisms, differences in incidence of final <e> and in word-internal <ȝ> after /ei/, which probably place it a little further northeast, around Stilton or Yaxley, Huntingdonshire, between Peterborough and Huntingdon. The language is closest to that of the Wycliffite sermons collected in New College (Oxford) MS. 95, Hand A. The difference in language between the two parts of the *Tretise* in my view precludes common authorship, although the writers may have been active in the same Wycliffite community since the two places of origin are only fifteen miles apart. The effect of scribal "regularizing" is minimal; we note that the scribe did not edit out such features as *-is* as a third person singular present-tense verbal ending in the Derbyshire material that follows the *Tretise*. He apparently copied the manuscript *literatim* when compiling, joining the Huntingdonshire material to an "in-house" sermon on the same subject.

3. While no miracle play activity has yet been documented either for Peterborough, the nearest cathedral city to either area, or for Huntingdon, the nearest county town, there are records of plays, represented by the extant text of a play of *Abraham*,[64] and sixteenth-century notices of pageant wagons in Northampton.[65] Undoubtedly the *Tretise* authors, living but short distance away, were familiar with plays like the Northampton *Abraham*, and they were likely also very much aware of the famous Coventry Corpus Christi cycle fifty to fifty-five miles away. The localities proposed for the manuscript's origin place it in a region where a direct familiarity with miracle plays seems extremely likely.

4. The methodology used here, if a little involved, provides an exercise in using the *LALME* profiles to localize "unknown" texts and to determine the amount of Standardization and of dialect mixture. Each type of analysis provides an output easily "recycled" to become the input of the next pass, resulting in very precise localizations, down to an area the size of a modern large town or small city, probably as good a fit as anyone might need. The method is capable of testing whether dialects, even varieties of Central Midland Standard, are identical to each other or not—a technique

which may help in deciding authorship questions. It therefore could easily be useful in matters of non-specialized textual analysis as well as in the further study of types of Middle English *qua* dialect. The methodology may also be recommended as being of further use for the analysis of the extant plays in the late medieval vernacular drama of England in those instances in which local provenance has not been established with certainty.

NOTES

1. Michael L. Samuels, "Scribes and Manuscript Traditions," in *Regionalism in Late Mediaeval Manuscripts and Texts*, ed. Felicity Riddy (Woodbridge, Suffolk: Boydell and Brewer, 1991), p. 1.

2. Ibid., p. 1.

3. For a largely successfully-localized list of manuscripts, see, for example, Karl W. Luick, *Historische Grammatik der Englischen Sprache* (Leipzig: Tauchniz, 1914–40), I, 41–48.

4. Alexander J. Ellis, *Early English Pronunciation* (1869–89; rpt. New York: Haskell House, 1969), vol. V.

5. Joseph Wright, *English Dialect Grammar* (London: Frowde, 1905).

6. For a linguistic profile of Wycliffite biblical English, see Angus McIntosh, Michael L. Samuels, and Michael Benskin, *A Linguistic Atlas of Later Middle English* (Aberdeen: Aberdeen Univ. Press, 1989), III, 2–3, 12–13, 16, 28, 183–84, 186, 190–91, 375–76. The bulk of biblical material is assigned to Northamptonshire by the *Atlas*, but portions have been located in surrounding counties.

7. Michael L. Samuels, "Some Applications of Middle English Dialectology," in Angus McIntosh, Michael L. Samuels, and Margaret Laing, *Middle English Dialectology* (Aberdeen: Aberdeen Univ. Press, 1989), p. 67.

8. For an interpretation of this dialect as London-based (probably equally wrong, for similar reasons), see Karl Brunner, *Die Englische Sprache* (Halle: Niemayer, 1950), I, 95.

9. Samuel Moore, S. G. Meech, and W. Whitehall, *Middle English Dialect Characteristics and Dialect Boundaries*, Essays and Studies in English and Comparative Literature: University of Michigan Publications in Language and Literature, 13 (Ann Arbor: Univ. of Michigan Press, 1935).

10. Angus McIntosh, "A New Approach to Middle English Dialectology," in McIntosh, Samuels, and Laing, *Middle English Dialectology*, p. 25.

11. Gillis Kristensson, *A Survey of Middle English Dialects, 1290–1350: The Six Northern Counties and Lincolnshire* (Lund: Gleerup, 1967), and Gillis Kristensson, *A Survey of Middle English Dialects, 1290–1350: The West Midland Counties* (Lund: Gleerup, 1988).

12. Margaret Laing, "Anchor Texts and Literary Manuscripts in Early Middle English," in *Regionalism in Late Mediaeval Manuscripts and Texts*, ed. Riddy, p. 27.

13. See n. 6, above.

14. Laing, "Anchor Texts," p. 28.

15. Linguistic Profile 577; McIntosh, Samuels, and Benskin, *Linguistic Atlas*, III, 78–79.

16. Linguistic Profile 562; Ibid., III, 366–67.

17. Ibid., I, 100.

18. The precision of location possible with these methods varies greatly over England, depending on the number of manuscripts surveyed for a county. We are fortunate here to be dealing with one of the most densely covered regions, making "town-level" placements possible. This would not

be so for, say, a Scottish or a Cornish manuscript—or even for a manuscript from Kent.

19. Richard Jordan, *Handbook of Middle English Grammar: Phonology*, trans. Eugene C. Crook (The Hague: Mouton, 1974), pp. 72–73.

20. Ibid., p. 86.

21. Angus McIntosh, "The Present Indicative Plural in the Later Middle English of the North Midlands," in McIntosh, Samuels, and Laing, *Middle English Dialectology*, p. 117.

22. Jordan, *Handbook*, pp. 67–68.

23. McIntosh, Samuels, and Benskin, *Linguistic Atlas*, I, 549; III, 194–200.

24. Jordan, *Handbook*, p. 124.

25. Ibid., pp. 110–13.

26. McIntosh, Samuels, and Benskin, *Linguistic Atlas*, I, 520, 525, 531.

27. Ibid., I, 525, 531, 535–36.

28. Luick, *Historische Grammatik*, II, 930–38.

29. Jordan, *Handbook*, pp. 68, 110, 124; McIntosh, Samuels, and Benskin, *Linguistic Atlas*, I, 431, 533–34, 549; II, 321–26.

30. Jordan, *Handbook*, pp. 50–55; McIntosh, Samuels, and Benskin, *Linguistic Atlas*, II, 69–74.

31. Jordan, *Handbook*, pp. 67–68; Samuels, "Applications," p. 67.

32. <Vuel> for *evil* represents /ʏvəl/ or the like, as <v> is usually used for both high rounded vowels and /v/ word-initially, and <u> word-internally.

33. McIntosh, "Present Indicative Plural," p. 117.

34. Jordan, *Handbook*, pp. 77–78.

35. McIntosh, Samuels, and Benskin, *Linguistic Atlas*, II, 153–58.

36. Ibid., II, 39–56, 75–80.

37. Ibid., I, 399.

38. Gloria Cigman, *Lollard Sermons* (London: Oxford Univ. Press, 1989), p. xli.

39. Henry C. Darby, *Historical Geography of England before 1800* (Cambridge: Cambridge Univ. Press, 1964), p. 232.

40. Samuels, "Applications," pp. 67–70.

41. There is a version of *Piers Plowman*, for instance, listed in the Table 4 below in this variety from Cambridgeshire; see McIntosh, Samuels, and Benskin, *Linguistic Atlas*, III, 26–27.

42. Samuels, "Applications," pp. 67–72.

43. Anne Hudson, *The Premature Reformation: Wycliffite Texts and Lollard History* (Oxford: Clarendon Press, 1988), pp. 9–10, 19.

44. Samuels, "Applications," p. 67.

45. See James Milroy and Lesley Milroy, *Authority in Language* (London: Routledge and Kegan Paul, 1985), pp. 36–47; most of their examples concern vocabulary and syntax.

46. Samuels, "Applications," p. 67.

47. See n. 15, above.

48. McIntosh, Samuels, and Benskin, *Linguistic Atlas*, II, 249–54.

49. Ibid., I, 454.

50. Jordan, *Handbook,* p. 122.

51. Craig M. Carver, *American Regional Dialects* (Ann Arbor: Univ. of Michigan Press, 1987), pp. 16–19.

52. McIntosh, Samuels, and Benskin, *Linguistic Atlas,* III, xviii–xix.

53. For the basis of the breakdown, see Paul A. Johnston, Jr., "English Vowel Shifting: One Great Vowel Shift or Two Small Vowel Shifts," *Diachronica*, 9, No. 2 (1992), 209–10.

54. Forms of the type of the last example are called "modified" layers; they are viewed as a subtype of the "Midlands and South" layer. See Table 3.

55. Michael L. Samuels, "Spelling and Dialect in the Late and Post-Middle English Periods," in *So meny people longages and tonges: Philological Essays on Scots and Mediaeval English Presented to Angus McIntosh*, ed. Michael Benskin and Michael L. Samuels (Edinburgh: Michael Benskin and Michael L. Samuels, 1981), pp. 43–54.

56. The "other" group consists of spellings with exceedingly narrow distributions, often over only part of a dialect group. Two, <aȝenus> and <biforn>, are only the majority form in Huntingdonshire. <Sleyn> pops up in that county also, but also in Staffordshire and Warwickshire. <Bitwene> straddles the East and Mid Central counties, but not over the whole of either area. <Eyþer> is present in most of Gloucestershire and Sussex manuscripts, though it does appear in the East Central Midlands as a minority form alongside a more frequent <eiþer>; <syþen> is rarer than <siþen> in the East Midlands generally, but is common in Staffordshire, Oxfordshire, and the East Riding of Yorkshire. At least four of these words probably really belong to the East Central or Central Midland layer. See McIntosh, Samuels, and Benskin, *Atlas*, III, *passim.*

57. Ibid., II, 249–54.

58. Ibid., III, 519–20.

59. Michael Benskin, "The 'Fit-Technique' Explained," in *Regionalism in Late Mediaeval Manuscripts and Texts*, ed. Riddy, pp. 9–25.

60. Ibid., pp. 17–25.

61. This step was superfluous in the case of Part II, where the whole area was within the subdialect area arrived at by the horizontal analysis.

62. McIntosh, Samuels, and Benskin, *Linguistic Atlas*, pp. 98–113, 438–41.

63. Ibid. I, 410–11; II, 262–66.

64. Ibid., III, 377. For the extant Northampton play of *Abraham*, see *Non-Cycle Plays and Fragments*, ed. Norman Davis, EETS, s.s. 1 (London: Oxford Univ. Press, 1970), pp. 32–42.

65. Ian Lancashire, *Dramatic Texts and Records of Britain: A Chronological Topography to 1558* (Toronto: Univ. of Toronto Press, 1984), p. 234.

Selected Bibliography

Manuscript:

Catalogue of Additions to Manuscripts in the British Museum, II. London: British Museum, 1877.

Davis, Nicholas M. "The Playing of Miracles, c.1350 to the Reformation." Unpubl. diss., Cambridge Univ., 1978.

__________. "The *Tretise of Miraclis Pleyinge*: On Milieu and Authorship," *Medieval English Theatre*, 12 (1990), 124–51.

Hudson, Anne, ed. *English Wycliffite Writings.* Cambridge: Cambridge Univ. Press, 1978.

Talbert, Ernest W., and S. Harrison Thomson. "Wyclyf and His Followers." In *A Manual of the Writings in Middle English, 1050–1500*, gen. ed. J. Burke Severs (Connecticut Academy of Arts and Sciences, 1970).

Editions—The Complete Text:

Halliwell, James Orchard, and Thomas Wright, eds. *Reliquiae Antiquae.* 1843; rpt. New York: AMS Press, 1966. Vol. II.

Hazlitt, W. C., ed. *The English Drama and Stage Under the Tudor and Stuart Princes, 1543–1644.* 1869; rpt. New York: Burt Franklin, n.d. (Reprints Halliwell's text.)

Eduard Mätzner, ed. *Altenglische Sprachproben.* Berlin: Wiedmann, 1969. Vol. I, Pt. 2.

Davis, Nicholas M. "The Playing of Miracles, c.1350 to the Reformation." Unpubl. Ph.D. diss., Cambridge Univ., 1978.

Editions—Selections:

Coulton, G. G., ed. *A Medieval Garner* (London: 1910). (Translation of selection.)

Cook, Albert Stanburrough, ed. *A Literary Middle English Reader*. Boston: Ginn, 1915.

Benham, Allen Rogers. *English Literature from Widsith to the Death of Chaucer: A Source Book* (1968; rpt. New York: Phaeton Press, 1968). (Translation of selection.)

Loomis, Roger Sherman, and Rudolph Willard. *Medieval English Verse and Prose in Modernized Versions*. New York: Appleton-Century-Crofts, 1948. (Translation of selection.)

Matthews, William, ed. *Later Medieval Prose*. New York: Appleton-Century-Crofts, 1963. (Translation of selection.)

Hudson, Anne, ed. *Selections from English Wycliffite Writings*. Cambridge: Cambridge Univ. Press, 1978. (Part I, abridged.)

Happé, Peter, ed. *Medieval English Drama: A Casebook*. London: Macmillan, 1984.

Critical Studies:

Aston, Margaret. *England's Iconoclasts*. Oxford: Clarendon Press, 1988. Vol. I.

Selected Bibliography

Barish, Jonas. *The Antitheatrical Prejudice*. Berkeley and Los Angeles: Univ. of California Press, 1981.

Briscoe, Marianne. "Some Clerical Notions of Dramatic Decorum in Late Medieval England," *Comparative Drama*, 19 (1985), 1–13.

Chambers, E. K. *The Mediaeval Stage*. London: Oxford Univ. Press, 1903. 2 vols.

Clopper, Lawrence M. "*Miracula* and *The Tretise Against Miraclis Pleyinge*," *Speculum*, 65 (1990), 878–905.

Coffman, George R. "The Miracle Play in England—Nomenclature," *PMLA*, 31 (1916), 448–65.

Coletti, Theresa. "Spirituality and Devotional Images: The Staging of the Hegge Cycle." Unpubl. Ph.D. diss., Univ. of Rochester, 1975.

Craddock, Lawrence G. "Franciscan Influences on Early English Drama," *Franciscan Studies*, 10 (1950), 399–415.

Davidson, Clifford. *Drama and Art: An Introduction to the Use of Evidence from the Visual Arts for the Study of Early Drama*. Early Drama, Art, and Music, Monograph Ser., 1. Kalamazoo: Medieval Institute, 1977.

__________. *From Creation to Doom: The York Cycle of Mystery Plays*. New York: AMS Press, 1984.

__________ and Ann Eljenholm Nichols, eds. *Iconoclasm vs. Art and Drama*. Early Drama, Art, and Music, Monograph Ser., 11. Kalamazoo: Medieval Institute Publications, 1989.

Davis, Nicholas M. "The Playing of Miracles, c.1350 to the Reformation." Unpubl. Ph.D. diss., Cambridge Univ., 1978.

__________. "The Art of Memory and Medieval Dramatic Theory," *EDAM Newsletter*, 6, No. 1 (Fall 1983), 1–3.

__________. "The English Mystery Plays and 'Ciceronian' Mnemonics." In *Atti del IV Colloquio della Société Internationale pour l'Etude du Théâtre Médiéval*, ed. M. Chiabò, F. Doglio, and M. Maymone. Viterbo: Centro Studi sul Teatro Medioevale e Rinascimentale, 1983. Pp. 75–84.

__________. "Another View of the *Tretise of Miraclis Pleyinge*," *Medieval English Theatre*, 4 (1982), 48–55.

__________. "The *Tretise of Miraclis Pleyinge*: On Milieu and Authorship," *Medieval English Theatre*, 12 (1990), 124–51.

Davis, Norman, ed. *Non-Cycle Plays and Fragments*, EETS, s.s. 1. London: Oxford Univ. Press, 1970.

Fraser, Russell. *The War Against Poetry*. Princeton: Princeton Univ. Press, 1970.

Gardiner, Harold C. *Mysteries' End*. 1946; rpt. Hamden, Conn.: Archon Books, 1967.

Gibson, Gail McMurray. *The Theater of Devotion: East Anglian Drama and Society in the Late Middle Ages*. Chicago: Univ. of Chicago Press, 1989.

Hudson, Anne. *Lollards and Their Books*. London: Hambledon Press, 1985.

__________. *The Premature Reformation: Wycliffite Texts and Lollard History*. Oxford: Clarendon Press, 1988.

Jeffrey, David L. "Franciscan Spirituality and the Rise of Early English Drama," *Mosaic*, 8, No. 4 (1975), 17–46.

Kendall, Ritchie D. *The Drama of Dissent: The Radical Poetics of Nonconformity, 1380–1590*. Chapel Hill: Univ. of North Carolina Press, 1986.

Kolve, V. A. *The Play Called Corpus Christi*. Stanford: Stanford Univ. Press, 1966.

Lancashire, Ian. *Dramatic Texts and Records of Britain: A Chronological Topography to 1558*. Toronto: Univ. of Toronto Press, 1984.

Leff, Gordon. *Heresy in the Later Middle Ages*. Manchester: Manchester Univ. Press, 1967. 2 vols.

Mills, David. "Medieval and Modern Views of Drama." In *Medieval Drama*, gen. ed. Lois Potter. Revels History of Drama in English, 1. London: Methuen, 1983. Pp. 79–91.

Owst, G. R. *Literature and Pulpit in Medieval England*, 2nd ed. Oxford: Blackwell, 1961.

Olson, Glending. *Literature as Recreation in the Later Middle Ages*. Ithaca: Cornell Univ. Press, 1982.

Robinson, J. W. *Studies in Fifteenth-Century Stagecraft*. Early Drama, Art, and Music, Monograph Ser., 14. Kalamazoo: Medieval Institute Publications, 1991.

Woolf, Rosemary. *The English Mystery Plays*. Berkeley and Los Angeles: Univ. of California Press, 1972.

Dialect:

Benskin, Michael, and Michael L. Samuels, eds. *So meny people longages and tonges: Philological Essays on Scots and Mediaeval English Presented to Angus McIntosh*. Edinburgh: Michael Benskin and Michael L. Samuels, 1981.

Brunner, Karl. *Die Englische Sprache*. Halle: Niemayer, 1950.

Selected Bibliography

Cigman, Gloria, ed. *Lollard Sermons*, EETS, o.s. 294. London: Oxford Univ. Press, 1989.

Darby, Henry C. *Historical Geography of England before 1800.* Cambridge: Cambridge Univ. Press, 1964.

Davis, Norman, ed. *Non-Cycle Plays and Fragments*, EETS, s.s. 1. London: Oxford Univ. Press, 1970.

Ellis, Alexander J. *Early English Pronunciation.* 1869–89; rpt. New York: Haskell House, 1969. Vol. V.

Hudson, Anne. *The Premature Reformation: Wycliffite Texts and Lollard History*. Oxford: Clarendon Press, 1988.

Johnston, Paul A. "English Vowel Shifting: One Great Vowel Shift or Two Small Vowel Shifts?" *Diachronica*, 9 (1992), 199–228.

Jordan, Richard. *Handbook of Middle English Grammar: Phonology*, trans. Eugene C. Crook. The Hague: Mouton, 1974.

Kristensson, Gillis. *Survey of Middle English Dialects, 1290–1350: The Six Northern Counties and Lincolnshire*. Lund: Gleerup, 1967.

__________. *Survey of Middle English Dialects, 1290–1350: The West Midland Counties*. Lund: Gleerup, 1988.

Lancashire, Ian. *Dramatic Texts and Records of Britain: A Chronological Topography to 1558*. Toronto: Univ. of Toronto Press, 1984.

Luick, Karl W. *Historische Grammatik der Englischen Sprache*. Leipzig: Tauchniz, 1914–40.

McIntosh, Angus, Michael L. Samuels, and Michael Benskin. *Linguistic Atlas of Later Middle English.* Aberdeen: Aberdeen Univ. Press, 1986. 4 vols.

McIntosh, Angus, Michael L. Samuels, and Margaret Laing. *Middle English Dialectology*. Aberdeen: Aberdeen Univ. Press, 1989.

Milroy, James, and Lesley Milroy. *Authority in Language*. London: Routledge and Kegan Paul, 1985.

Moore, Samuel, S. G. Meech, and W. Whitehall. *Middle English Dialect Characteristics and Dialect Boundaries*. Ann Arbor: Univ. of Michigan Press. 1935.

Riddy, Felicity, ed. *Regionalism in Late Mediaeval Manuscripts and Texts.* Woodbridge: Boydell and Brewer, 1991.

Wright, Joseph. *English Dialect Grammar*. London: Frowde, 1905.

Bibliography:

Talbert, Ernest W., and S. Harrison Thomson. "Wyclyf and His Followers." In *A Manual of the Writings in Middle English, 1050–1500,* gen. ed. J. Burke Severs. Connecticut Academy of Arts and Sciences, 1970.

A Tretise of Miraclis Pleyinge

Here beginnis a tretise of miraclis pleyinge. f. 14r

PART I

Knowe yee, cristen men, that as Crist, God and man, is bothe weye, trewth, and lif, as seith the gospel of Jon—weye to the erringe, trewthe to the unknowing and douting, lif to the styinge to hevene and weryinge—so Crist dude no thinge to us but efectuely in weye of mercy, in treuthe of ritwesnes, and in lif of yilding everlastinge joye for oure contunuely morning and sorwinge in this valey of teeres. Miraclis, therfore, that Crist dude heere in erthe outher in himsilf outher in hise seintis weren so efectuel and in ernest done that to sinful men that erren they broughten forgivenesse of sinne, settinge hem in the weye of right bileve; to doutouse men not stedefast they broughten in kunning to betere plesen God, and verry hope in God to been stedefast in him; and to the wery of the weye of God, for the grette penaunce and suffraunce of the tribulacion that men moten have therinne, they broughten in love of brynninge charite to the whiche alle thing is light, yhe to suffere dethe, the whiche men most dreden, for the everlastinge lif and joye that men most loven and disiren of the whiche thing verry hope puttith awey all werinesse heere in the weye of God.

Thanne, sithen miraclis of Crist and of hise seintis weren thus efectuel, as by oure bileve we ben in certein, no man shulde usen in bourde and pleye the miraclis and werkis that Crist so ernystfully wroughte to oure helthe. For whoevere so doth, he errith in the byleve, reversith Crist, and scornyth God. He errith in the bileve, for in that he takith the most precious werkis of God in pley and bourde, and so takith his name in idil and so misusith oure byleve. A, Lord, sithen an erthely servaunt dar not takun in pley and in bourde that that his erthely lord takith in ernest, myche more we shulden not maken oure pleye and bourde of tho miraclis and werkis that God so ernestfully wrought to us. For sothely whan we so doun, drede to sinne is takun awey, as a servaunt, whan he bourdith with his maister, leesith his drede to offendyn him, namely whanne he bourdith with his maister in that that his maister takith in ernest. And right as a nail smiten in holdith two thingis togidere, so drede smiten to Godward holdith and susteineth oure bileve to him.

Therfore right as pleyinge and bourdinge of the most ernestful werkis of God takith aweye the drede of God that men shulden han in the same, so it takith awey oure bileve and so oure most helpe of oure savacion. And sith taking awey of oure bileve is more venjaunce taking than sodeyn taking awey of oure bodily lif, and whanne we takun in bourde and pley the most ernestful werkis of God as ben hise miraclis, God takith awey fro us his grace of mekenesse, drede, reverence and of oure bileve; thanne, whanne we pleyin his miraclis as men don nowe on dayes, God takith more venjaunce on us than a lord that sodaynly sleeth his servaunt for he pleyide to homely with him. And right as that lord thanne in dede seith to his servaunt, | [f. 14v] “Pley not with me but pley with thy pere,” so whanne we takun in pley and in bourde the miraclis of God, he, fro us takinge his grace, seith more ernestfully to us than the forseid lord, “Pley not with me but pley with thy pere.”

Therfore siche miraclis pleyinge reversith Crist. Firste in taking to pley that that he toke into most ernest. The secound in taking to miraclis of oure fleyss, of oure lustis, and of oure five wittis that that God tooc to the bringing in of his bitter deth and to teching of penaunse doinge, and to fleyinge of feding of oure wittis and to mortifying of hem.

And therfore it is that seintis myche noten that of Cristis lawghing we reden never in holy writt, but of his myche penaunse, teris, and scheding of blod, doying us to witen therby that alle oure doing heere shulde ben in penaunce, in disciplining of oure fleyssh, and in penaunce of adversite. And therfore alle the werkis that we don that ben out of alle thes thre utturly reversen Cristis werkis. And therfore seith Seint Poul that "Yif yee been out of discipline of the whiche alle gode men ben maad perceneris, thanne avoutreris yee ben and not sones of God." And sith miraclis pleynge reversen penaunce doying as they in greet liking ben don and to grete liking ben cast biforn, there as penaunce is in gret mourning of hert and to greet mourning is ordeinyd biforne.

It also reversith dissipline, for in verry discipline the verry vois of oure maister Crist is herd as a scoler herith the vois of his maister, and the yerd of God in the hond of Crist is seyn, in the whiche sight alle oure othere thre wittis for drede tremblyn and quaken as a childe tremblith seing the yerde of his maister. And the thridde in verry dissipline is verry turning awey and forgeting of alle tho thingis that Crist hatith and turnyde himsilf awey heere as a childe undir dissipline of his maister turnith him awey fro alle thingis that his maister hath forbedun him, and forgetith hem for the greet minde that he hath to doun his maistris wille.

And for thes thre writith Seint Petur, seyinge, "*Be yee mekid undur the mighty hond of God that he henhaunce you in the time of visiting, all youre bisinesse throwinge in him.*" That is, "*be yee mekid*," that is, to Crist, heringe his voice by verry obeschaunce to his hestis; and "*undur the mighty hond of God*," seeing evere more his yird to chastisen us in his hond yif we waxen wantown or idil, bethenking us, seith Seint Petre, that "*hidous and ferful it is to fallen into the hondis of God on live*." For right as most joye it is to steyen up into the hond of the mercy of God, so it is most hidous and ferful to fallen into the hondis of the wrathe of God. Therfore mekely drede we him heere evere more seing and thenkinge his yerde overe oure hevyd, and thanne he shal *enhauncyn* | us elliswhere in time of his graceous *visiting*. So f. 15[r] that *alle oure bisinesse* we *throwyn in him*, that is, that alle othere erthely werkis we don not but to don his gostly werkis, more frely and spedely and more plesauntly to him tristing, that *to him is cure over us*, that is, yif we don to him that that is in oure power he schal merveIousely don to us that that is in his power, bothe in dylivering us fro alle perilis and in giving us graciously al that us nedith or willen axen of him.

And sithen no man may serven two lordis togydere, as seith Crist in his gospel, no man may heren at onys efectuely the voice of oure maister Crist and of his owne lustis. And sithen miraclis pleyinge is of the lustis of the fleyssh and mirthe of the body, no man may efectuely heeren hem and the voice of Crist at onys, as the voice of Crist and the voice of the fleysh ben of two contrarious lordis. And so miraclis pleying reversith discipline, for as seith Seint Poul, "*Eche forsothe discipline in the time that is now is not a joye but a mourninge*." Also sithen it makith to se veine sightis of degyse, aray of men and wymmen by yvil continaunse, either stiring othere to leccherie and debatis as aftir most bodily mirthe comen moste debatis, as siche mirthe more undisposith a man to paciencie and ablith to glotonye and to othere vicis, wherfore it suffrith not a man to beholden enterly the yerde of God over his heved, but makith to thenken on alle siche thingis that Crist by the dedis of his passion badde us to forgeten. Wherfore siche miraclis pleyinge, bothe in penaunce doying in verry discipline and in pacience reversyn Cristis hestis and his dedis.

Also, siche miraclis pleying is scorning of God, for right as ernestful leving of that that God biddith is dispising of God, as dide Pharao, so bourdfully taking Goddis biddingis or wordis or werkis is scorning of him, as diden the Jewis that bobbiden Crist, thanne, sithen thes miraclis pleyeris taken in bourde the ernestful werkis of God, no doute that ne they scornen God as diden the Jewis that bobbiden Crist, for they lowen at his passioun as these lowyn and japen of the miraclis of God. Therfore as they scorneden Crist, so theese scorne God. And right as Pharao, wrooth to do that that God bad him, dispiside God, so these miraclis pleyeris and maintenours, leevinge plesingly to do that God biddith hem, scornen God. He forsothe had beden us alle to halowyn his name, giving drede and reverence in alle minde of his werkis withoute ony pleying or japinge, as al holinesse is in ful ernest. Men thanne pleyinge the name of Goddis miraclis as plesingly, they leeve to do that God biddith hem so they scornen his name and so scornyn him.

But here agenus they seyen that they pleyen these miraclis in the worschip of God and so diden not thes Jewis that bobbiden Crist.

Also ofte sithis by siche miraclis pleyinge ben men commited to gode livinge, as men and wymmen seing in miraclis pleyinge that the devul by ther aray, by the whiche they moven eche on other to leccherie and to pride, makith hem his servauntis to bringen | hemsilf and many othere to f. 15^{v} helle, and to han fer more vilenye herafter by ther proude aray heere than they han worschipe heere, and seeinge ferthermore that al this worldly being heere is but vanite for a while, as is miraclis pleying, wherthoru they leeven ther pride and taken to hem afterward the meke conversacion of Crist and of hise seintis. And so miraclis pleying turneth men to the bileve and not pervertith.

Also ofte sithis by siche miraclis pleyinge men and wymmen, seinge the passioun of Crist and of his seintis, ben movyd to compassion and devocion, wepinge bitere teris, thanne they ben not scorninge of God but worschiping.

Also prophitable to men and to the worschipe of God it is to fulfillun and sechen alle the menes by the whiche men mowen leeve sinne and drawen hem to vertues; and sithen as ther ben men that only by ernestful doinge wilen be convertid to God, so ther been othere men that wilen not be convertid to God but by gamen and pley. And now on dayes men ben not convertid by the ernestful doing of God ne of men, thanne now it is time and skilful to assayen to convertyn the puple by pley and gamen as by miraclis pleyinge and other maner mirthes.

Also summe recreacion men moten han, and bettere it is (or lesse yvele) that they han theire recreacion by pleyinge of miraclis than by pleyinge of other japis.

Also sithen it is leveful to han the miraclis of God peintid, why is not as wel leveful to han the miraclis of God pleyed, sithen men mowen bettere reden the wille of God and his mervelous werkis in the pleyinge of hem than in the peintinge? And betere they ben holden in mennes minde and oftere rehersid by the pleyinge of hem than by the peintinge, for this is a deed bok, the tother a quick.

[1.] To the first reson we answeryn seying that siche miraclis pleyinge is not to the worschipe of God, for they ben don more to ben seen of the worlde and to plesyn to the world thanne to ben seen of God or to plesyn to him, as Crist never ensaumplide hem but onely hethene men that evere more dishonouren God, seyinge that to the worschipe of God, that is to the most veleinye of him. Therfore as the wickidnesse of the misbileve of hethene men lyith to themsilf, whanne they seyn that the worshiping of theire maumetrie is to the worschipe of God, so mennus lecherye now on dayes to han ther owne lustus lieth to hemself whanne they seyn that suche miracles pleying is to the worschip of God. For Crist seith that folc of avoutrie sechen siche singnys as a lecchour sechith signes of verrey love but no dedis of verrey love. So sithen thise miraclis pleyinge ben onely singnis, love withoute dedis, they ben not onely contrarious to the worschipe of God—that is, bothe in signe and in dede—but also they ben ginnys of the devvel to cacchen men to byleve of Anticrist, as wordis of love withoute verrey dede ben ginnys of the lecchour to cacchen felawchipe to fulfillinge of his leccherie. Bothe for these miraclis pleyinge been verrey leesing as they ben signis withoute dede and for they been verrey idilnesse, as they taken the miraclis of God in idil after theire owne lust. And certis idilnesse and leesing been the most ginnys of the dyvul to drawen men to the byleve of Anticrist. And therfore to pristis it is uttirly forbedyn not onely to | been miracle pleyere, but also to heren or to seen f. 16r miraclis pleyinge lest he that shulde been the ginne of God to cacchen men and to holden men in the bileve of Crist, they ben maad agenward by ypocrisie, the gin of the devel to cacchen men to the bileve of Anticrist. Therfore right as a man sweringe in idil by the names of God and seyinge that in that he worschipith God and dispisith the devil, verrily lyinge doth the reverse; so miraclis pleyers, as they ben doers of idilnesse, seyinge that they don it to the worschip of God, verreyly liyn. For, as seith the gospel, “Not he that seith ‘Lord, Lord’ schal come to blisse of hevene, but he that doth the wille of the fadir of hevene schal come to his kindam.” So myche more not he that pleyith the wille of God worschipith him, but onely he that doith his wille in deede worschipith him. Right therfore as men by feinyd tokenes bygilen and in dede dispisen ther neighboris, so by siche feinyd miraclis men bygilen hemsilf and dispisen God, as the tormentours that bobbiden Crist.

[2.] And as anentis the secound reson, we seyen that right as a vertuous deede is othere while occasioun of yvel, as was the passioun of Crist to the Jewis, but not occasioun given but taken of hem, so yvele dedis ben occasioun of gode dedis othere while, as was the sinne of Adam occasioun of the coming of Crist, but not occasion given of the sinne but occasion takun of the grete mercy of God. The same wise miraclis pleyinge, albeit that it be sinne, is othere while occasion of converting of men, but as it is sinne it is fer more occasion of perverting of men, not onely of oon singuler persone but of al an hool comynte, as it makith al a puple to ben ocupied in vein agenus this heeste of the Psauter book that seith to alle men and namely to pristis that eche day reden it in ther servise: "*Turne awey min eyen that they se not vanitees,*" and efte, "*Lord, thou hatidest alle waitinge vanitees.*" How thanne may a prist pleyn in entirlodies or give himsilf to the sight of hem sithen it is forbeden him so expresse by the forseide heste of God, namely sithen he cursith eche day in his service alle tho that bowen awey fro the hestis of God. But, alas, more harme is, pristis now on dayes most shrewyn hemsilf and al day as a jay that al day crieth, "Watte shrewe!" shrewinge himsilf. Therfore miraclis pleyinge, sithen it is agenus the heest of God that biddith that thou shalt not take Goddis name in idil, it is agenus oure bileve and so it may not given occacioun of turninge men to the bileve but of perverting. And therfore many men wenen that ther is no helle of everelastinge peine, but that God doth but thretith us, not to do it in dede, as ben pleyinge of miraclis in signe and not in dede. Therfore siche miraclis pleying not onely pervertith oure bileve but oure verry hope in God, by the whiche seintis hopiden that that the more they absteneden hem fro siche pleyes, the more mede they shulden have of God, and therfore the holy Sara, the doughter of Raguel, hopinge heie mede of God, seith, | [f. 16v] "*Lord, thou woost that nevere I coveytide man, and clene I have kept my soule fro all lustis, nevere with pleyeris I mingid me mysilfe persin*," and by this trwe confessioun to God, as she hopide, so sche hadde hir preyeris herd and grete mede of God. And sithen a yonge womman of the Olde Testament for keping of hir bodily vertue of chastite and for to worthily take the sacrament of matrimonye whanne hir time shulde come, abstenyde hir fro al maner idil pleying and fro al cumpany of idil pleyeris, myche more a prist of the Newe Testament, that is passid the time of childehod and that not onely shulde kepe chastite but alle othere vertues, ne onely ministren the sacrament of matrimonye but alle othere sacramentis and namely sithen him owith to ministre to alle the puple the precious body of Crist, awghte to abstene him fro al idil pleying bothe of miraclis and ellis. For certis, sithen the quen of Saba, as seith Crist in the gospel, schal dampne the Jewis that wolden not reseive the wisdom of Crist, myche more this holy womman Sara at the day of dom schal dampnen the pristis of the Newe Testament that givis heem to pleyes, reversen hir holy maners aprovyd by God and al holiy chirche; therfore sore aughten pristis to be aschamyd that reversen this gode holy womman and the precious body of Crist that they treytyn in ther hondis, the whiche body never gaf him to pley but to alle siche thing as is most contrarious to pley, as is penaunce and suffring of persecution.

And so thes miraclis pleyinge not onely reversith feith and hope but verry charite by the whiche a man shulde weilen for his owne sinne and for his neieburs, and namely pristis, for it withdrawith not onely oon persone but alle the puple fro dedis of charite and of penaunce into dedis of lustis and likingis and of feding of houre wittis. So thanne thes men that seyen, "Pley we a pley of Anticrist and of the Day

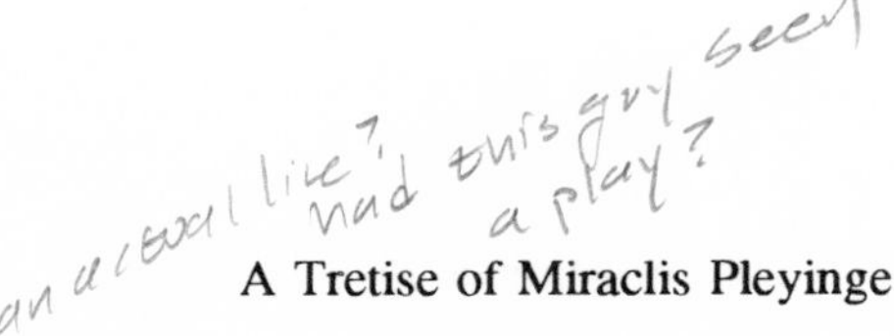

of Dome that sum man may be convertid therby," fallen into the herisie of hem that, reversing the aposteyl, seiden, "Do we yvel thingis, that ther comyn gode thingis," of whom, as seith the aposteyl, "dampning is rightwise."

[3.] By this we answeren to the thridde resoun seyinge that siche miraclis pleyinge giveth noon occasioun of werrey wepinge and medeful, but the weping that fallith to men and wymmen by the sighte of siche miraclis pleyinge, as they ben not principaly for theire oune sinnes ne of theire gode feith withinneforthe, but more of theire sight withouteforth is not alowable byfore God but more reprowable. For sithen Crist himsilf reprovyde the wymmen that wepten upon him in his passioun, myche more they ben reprovable that wepen for the pley of Cristis passioun, leevinge to wepen for the sinnes of hemsilf and of theire children, as Crist bad the wymmen that wepten on him.

[4.] And by this we answeren to the furthe resoun, seyinge that no | man may be convertid to God but onely by f. 17r
the ernestful doyinge of God and by noon vein pleying, for that that the word of God worchith not ne his sacramentis, how shulde pleyinge worchen that is of no vertue but ful of defaute? Therfore right as the weping that men wepen ofte in siche pley comunely is fals wittnessenge that they lovyn more the liking of theire body and of prosperite of the world than likinge in God and prosperite of vertu in the soule, and, therfore, having more compassion of peine than of sinne, they falsly wepyn for lakkinge of bodily prosperite more than for lakking of gostly, as don dampnyd men in helle. Right so, ofte sithis the convertinge that men semen to ben convertid by siche pleyinge is but feinyd holinesse, worse than is othere sinne biforehande. For yif he were werrily convertid, he shulde haten to seen alle siche vanite, as biddith the hestis of God, albeit that of siche pley he take occasion by the

grace of God to fle sinne and to folowe vertu. And yif men seyn heere that yif this pleyinge of miraclis were sinne, why wile God converten men by the occasion of siche pleyinge, heereto we seyen that God doith so for to comenden his mersy to us, that we thenken enterly hou good God is to us, that whil we ben thenkinge agenus him, doinge idilnesse and withseyinge him, he thenkith upon us good, and sendinge us his grace to fleen alle siche vanite. And for ther shulde no thinge be more swete to us than siche maner mercy of God, the Psauter book clepith that mercy "blessinge of swetnesse" where he seith, "*Thou cam bifore him in blessinges of swetnesse*"—the whiche swetnesse, albeit that it be likinge to the spirit, it is while we ben here ful travelous to the body, whan it is verry as the flesche and the spirit ben contrarious; therfore this swetnesse in God wil not been verely had while a man is ocuped in seinge of pleyis. Therfore the pristis that seyn hemsilf holy and bysien hem aboute siche pleyis ben verry ypocritis and lieris.

[5.] And herby we answeren to the fifte resoun seyinge that verry recreacion is leeveful, ocupyinge in lasse werkis, to more ardently worschen grettere werkis. And therfore siche miraclis pleyinge ne the sighte of hem is no verrey recreasion but fals and worldly, as provyn the dedis of the fautours of siche pleyis that yit nevere tastiden verely swetnesse in God, traveilinge so myche therinne that their body wolde not sofisen to beren siche a traveile of the spirite, but as man goith fro vertue into vertue, so they gon fro lust into lust that they more stedefastly dwellen in hem. And therfore as this feinyd recreacioun of pleyinge of miraclis is fals equite, so it is double shrewidnesse, worse than though they pleyiden pure vaniteis. For now the puple giveth credence to many mengid leesingis for othere mengid trewthis and maken wenen to been gode that is ful yvel, and so ofte sithis lasse yvele it were to pleyin | rebaudye than to f. 17v pleyin siche miriclis. And yif men axen what recreacion men shulden have on the haliday after theire holy contemplacion in the chirche, we seyen to hem two thingis—oon, that yif he hadde verily ocupiede him in contemplacion byforn, neither he wolde aske that question ne han wille to se vanite; another we seyn, that his recreacioun shulde ben in the werkis of mercy to his neiebore and in diliting him in alle good comunicacion with his neibore, as biforn he dilitid him in God, and in alle othere nedeful werkis that reson and kinde axen.

[6.] And to the laste reson we seyn that peinture, yif it be verry withoute menging of lesingis and not to curious, to myche fedinge mennis wittis, and not occasion of maumetrie to the puple, they ben but as nakyd lettris to a clerk to riden the treuthe. But so ben not miraclis pleyinge that ben made more to deliten men bodily than to ben bokis to lewid men. And therfore yif they ben quike bookis, they ben quike bookis to shrewidenesse more than to godenesse. Gode men therfore seinge ther time to schort to ocupien hem in gode ernest werkis, and seinge the day of ther rekeninge neighen faste, and unknowing whan they schal go hennys, fleen alle siche idilnessis, hyinge that they weren with her spouse Crist in the blisse of hevene.

✠

PART II

An half frynde tarriere to soule helthe, redy to excusen the yvil and hard of bileve, with Thomas of Inde, seith that he wil not leevyn the forseid sentense of miraclis pleyinge but and men schewen it him by holy writt opynly and by oure bileve. Wherfore that his half frenschip may be turnyd to the hoole, we preyen him to beholden first in the seconde maundement of God that seith, “Thou schalt not take

Goddis name in idil," and sithen the mervelous werkis of God ben his name, as the gode werkis of a craftisman been his name, than in this hest of God is forbeden to takun the mervelouse werkis of God in idil. And how mowen they be more takyn in idil than whanne they ben maad menis japinge stikke, as whan they ben playid of japeris? And sithen ernestly God dide hem to us, so take we hem of him; ellis forsothe we taken hem in vein. Loke thanne, frend, yif thy byleve tellith that God dide his miraclis to us for we shulden pleyn hem—and yn trowe it seith to the, "Nay, but for thou schuldist more dredyn him and lovyn him." And certis greet drede and gret effectuel loove suffrith no pleyinge nor japing with him. Thanne sithen miraclis pleyinge reversith the wille of God and the ende for the whiche he wrought miraclis to us, no doute but that miraclis pleyinge is verre taking of Goddis name in idil.

And yif this suffisith not to thee, albeit that it shulde suffisen to an hethene man that therfore wil not pleyin the werkis of his mawmete, I preye thee rede enterly in the book of lif that is Crist Jhesus and if thou mayst finden in him that he | evere exsaumplide that men shulden pleye miraclis, but alwey the revers and oure byleve cursith that hadden or f. 18r
lassen over that Crist exsaumplide us to don. Hou thanne darst thou holden with miraclis pleyinge sithen alle the werkis of Crist reversiden hem, and in none of his werkis they ben groundyd?—namely, sithen thou seyst thyselven that thou wolt nothing leven but that may be schewid of oure bileve, and sithen in thing that is acording with the fleyssh and to the liking of it, as is miraclis pleyinge, thou wilt nothing don agenus it, but yif it be schewid of oure bileve; myche more in thing that is with the spirit, and alwey exsawmplid in the lif of Crist and so fully writen in the booke of lif, as is leving of miraclis pleyinge and of alle japing, thou shuldest not holden agenys it but if it mighte ben

schewid agens the bileve, sithen in al thing that is dowtous men schulden holden with the partye that is more favowrable to the spirit and more exsawmpplid in the lif of Crist. And so as eche sinne distruyith himsilf and eche falshed, so thy answere distruyith himsilfe and therby thou mayst wel witen that it is not trewe, but verre unkindenesse; for if thou haddist hadde a fadir that hadde suffred a dispitouse deth to geten thee thin heritage, and thou therafter woldest so lightly hern it to make therof a pley to the and to alle the puple, no dowte but that alle gode men wolden denien the unkinde, miche more God and alle his seintes denien alle tho cristen men unkinde that pleyen or favouren the pley of the deth or of the miracles of ther most kinde fadir Crist that diede and wroughte miraclis to bringen men to the everelastande heretage of hevene.

But peraventure heere thou seist that of pleyinge of miraclis be sinne, never the latere it is but litil sinne. But herfore, dere frend, knowe yee that eche sinne, be it never so litil, if it be maintenyd and prechid as gode and profitable, is deadely sinne; and therfore seith the prophite, "*Wo to hem that seyen gode, yvel, and yvel, good.*" And therfore the wise man dampneth hem that gladen whan they don yvel; and therfore alle seintis seyen that mannische it is to fallen, but develiche it is to abiden stille therinne. Therfore, sithen thes miraclis pleyinge is sinne, as thou knowlechist, and is stedefastly meintenyd, and also men deliten hem therinne, no dowte but that it is deadly sinne—dampnable, develiche, not mannisch. Lord, sithen Adam and Eve and al mankinde weren dampnyd out of paradise not onely for eting of the appul, but more for the excusing therof, myche more pleyinge of miraclis not onely excusid but stedefastly meintenyd is dampnable and deadly, namely sithen it not onely pervertith oon man but al a puple that they seyen good, yvel, and yvel, gode.

And if this wil not suffise thee, albeit that it shulde suffisen to eche cristen man (that nothing schulde donn oute of the teching that Crist taughte), tac hide to the dedis that God hath donn, of whiche we reden that at the bidding of God, for Ismael pleyide with his brother Isaac, bothe Ismael and his modir weren throwen out of the hous of Abraham, of the whiche the cause was for by siche pleyinge Ismael, that was the sone of the servant, mighte han begilid Isaac of his | heretage, that was the sone of the fre wif of Abraham. f. 18v Another cause was sithen Ismael was born after the fleysh, and Isaac after the spirit, as seith the apostele, to exsaumplen that pley of the fleysh is not covenable ne helpely to the spirit but to the bynimming of the spiritus heretage.

And the thridde cause was to figuren that the Olde Testament, that is testament of the fleysh, may not ben holdun with the Newe Testament, that is testament of the spririt; and yif it be hooly kept with the testament of the spirit, it doith awey verre fredom and bynimmeth the heretage of hevene. Thanne sithen the pley of Ismael was not leveful with Isaac, myche more fleysly pley is not leveful with the gostly werkis of Crist and of his seintis, as ben hise miraclis to converten men to the bileve, bothe for fer more distaunce of contrarite is bitwene fleyshly pley and the ernestful dedis of Crist than bitwene the pley of Ismael and Isaac, and also for the pley betwene Ismael and Isaac was figure of the pley bitwene the fleysh and the spirit. Therfore, as two thingis most contrarious mowen not pleyn togidere withouten hurting of either, as experiens techith, and most that party schal hurtyn that is most meintenyd, and that partie schal be most hurt that is lest meintenyd; than pleyinge that is fleschely with the werkis of the spirit is to harming of ever either, and most schal the fleysh hurtyn the spirit, as in suche pleyinge the fleysh is most meintenyd and the spirite lasse. And as in good thingis the figuride is evermore bettere than that that is figure; so in yvel thingis that that is figurid is fer werse than the figure; than sithen the pleyinge of Ismael with Isaac is figure of the pleyinge of the fleysh with the spirit, and the ton is yvel, thanne fer werse is the tother. Than pleyinge with the miraclis of God disservith more venjaunce and more sinne is than disservyde the pleyinge of Ismael with Isaac, and lasse yvel was; and as felawchip of a thral with his lord makith his lord dispisid, so myche more pleyinge with the miraclis of God makith hem dispisid sithen pleyinge to comparisoun of the mervelouse werkis of God is fer more cherl than ony man may ben cherl of a lord; and therfore the pleyinge of Ismael, that was the sone of the servant, with Isaac, that was the sone of the fre womman, was justly reprovyd, and bothe the damme and the sone put out of his cumpanye; myche more mennus pley with the mervelouse werkis of God is reprovable and worthy to ben put out of ther cumpanye.

And therfore, as seith the apostel, as ther is no gode comuning betwene the devel and God, so ther is no gode comuning betwene the develis instrument to perverten men, as pleying of the fleysh, and Goddis instrewment to converten men, as be his mervelous werkis; therfore, as this is a verre lesinge to seyen that for the love of God he wil ben a good felowe with the devul, so it is a werry lesing to seyen that for the love of God he wil pleyen his miraclis, for in neither is the love of God schewid but his hestis tobrokun.
And sithen | the serymonies of the olde lawe, albeit that they f. 19r
weren given by God, for they weren fleyshly, they shulden not be holde with the Newe Testament, for it is gostly. Myche more pleyinge, for it is fleysly, never bedyn of God, shulde not ben don with the mervelouse werkis of God, for they ben gostly. For as the pleyinge of Ismael with Isaac shulde han bynomyn Isaac his heretage, so in the keping of the seremonies of the olde lawe in the Newe Testament

shulde han bynomen men ther bileve in Crist, and han made men to gon bacward, that is to seye, fro the gostly living of the Newe Testament to the fleyshly living of the Olde Testament.

Myche more pleyinge of miraclis benemeth men ther bileve in Crist and is verre goinge bacward fro dedis of the spirit to onely signes don after lustis of the fleysh that ben agenus alle the deedis of Crist, and so miraclis pleyinge is verre apostasye fro Crist. And therfore we schal nevere findyn that miraclis pleying was usid among Cristene men but sithen religious onely in tokenes shewiden ther religioun and not in dedis, and sithen pristis onely in signes and for money schewiden ther pristhode and not in dedis. And therfore the apostasye of these drawith myche of the puple after hem, as the apostasie of Lucifer the first aungel droowgh myche of hevene after him.

If this, frend, wil not suffisen to thee that the eyghen of the blind wite takun sighte, take hede how the pleyinge of two contrary partis togidere, as of the pleyinge of the childre of Abner and of the childre of Joab weren thre hundrid men and sixty sleyn and mo, out of doute myche more harm doth pleyinge of gostly werkis after lustus of the fleysh as they ben more enemies. For it is of miraclis pleyinge as it is of thes apostatas that prechen for bodily avauntage. For right as thes han bodily avauntage at more pris than the word of God, as they maken the word of God but a mene to ther avauntage, so these miracle playeris and the fautours of hem as they maken the miraclis of God onely a mene to ther pley, and the pley the ende of the miraclis of God, han at more pris ther pley than the miraclis of God. And so thes miraclis pleyeris and the fawtours of hem ben verre apostatas, bothe for they puttun God bihinde and ther owne lustis biforn, as they han minde of God onely for sake of ther pley and also for they deliten hem more in the pley than in the miraclis silf, as an apostata more delitith him in his bodily winning than in the trowthe of God and more preisith seemely thingis withouteforth than ony fairnesse withinneforth to Godward. And herfore it is that siche miraclis pleyinge thretith myche venjaunse of God. For right as a jelous man seeinge his wif to japun with his kindnessis, and to lovyn by hem another man more than him, abidith not longe to don venjaunse to chastisinge of hyr, so sithe God is more jelous over his puple as he more lovyth it than ony man is jelous upon his wif, he seeinge the kindnessis of his miraclis put | byhinde and (f. 19v) mennus lustis beforn, and so menis wil to ben more lovyd than his owne wille, no wondir thof he sende sone venjaunse therafter, as he moot nede, for his grete rightwessnesse and mersy. And therfore it is that the wise man seith, "*The ende of mirthis is sorowe,* and efte *youre lawghing shal be medelid with sorowe.*" And therfore, as experience proveth, ever sithen regnyde siche maner apostasie in the puple, seside never the venjaunce of God upon us, outher of pestilence, outher of debate, outher of flodis, other of derthe, and of many othere, and comunely whan men be most unsckilfuly merye sone after fallith sorowe.

Therfore siche miraclis pleyinge now on dayes witnessith thre thingis. First is grete sinne biforne. The second, it witnessith grete foly in the doinge. And the thridde, greet venjaunse aftir. For right as the children of Israel, whan Moyses was in the hil bisily preying for hem, they mistristing to him, honouriden a calf of gold and afterward eetyn and drinken and risen to pleyn, and afterward weren sleyn of hem thre and twenty thousend of men. So thanne as this pleyinge wittnesside the sinne of ther maumetrie beforn and her mistryst to Moyses whanne they shulde most han tristenede to him, and after ther foly in ther pleyinge, and the thridde, the venjaunce that cam after. So

this miraclis pleyinge is verre wittnesse of mennus averice and coveytise byfore—that is, maumetrie, as seith the apostele—for that that they shulden spendyn upon the nedis of ther negheboris, they spenden upon the pleyis; and to peyen ther rente and ther dette they wolen grucche, and to spenden two so myche upon ther pley they wolen nothinge grucchen. Also to gideren men togidere to bien the derre there vetailis, and to stiren men to glotonye and to pride and boost, they pleyn these miraclis, and also to han wherof to spenden on thes miraclis and to holden felawschipe of glotenye and lecherie in siche dayes of miraclis pleyinge, they bisien hem beforn to more gredily bygilen ther neghbors in byinge and in selling. And so this pleyinge of miraclis now on dayes is werre witnesse of hideous coveytise—that is, maumetrie. And right as Moyses was that time in the hil most travelinge aboute the puple, so now is Crist in hevene with his fader most bisily preinge for the puple; and never the latere as the children of Israel diden that time that in hem was, in ther pleyinge of ther maumetrie, most folily to distroyen the grete travele of Moyses, so men now on dayees, aftere ther hidouse maumetree of coveytise in ther pleying of miraclis they don that in hem is to distroye the ententive preyere of Crist in hevene for hem, and so ther miraclis pleyinge witnessith ther most folye in ther doinge. And therfore as unkindely seiden to Aaron the children of Israel, Moyses beinge in the hil, "We witen never hough it is of Moyses, make us therfore goddis that gon biforn us," so unkindely seyen | men nowe on dayes, "Crist doth now no f. 20r
miraclis for us, pleye we therfore his olde," adding many lesingis therto so colowrably that the puple gife as myche credense to hem as to the trwthe.

And so they forgeten to ben percener of the preyere of Crist, for the maumetrye that men don to siche miraclis pleyinge—maumetrye, I seye, for siche pleyinge men as myche honoryn (or more than) the word of God whanne it is prechid, and therfore blasfemely they seyen that siche pleyinge doith more good than the word of God whanne it is prechid to the puple. A, Lord, what more blasfeme is agenis thee than to seyen to don thy bidding as is to prechen the word of God, doth fer lasse good than to don that that is bodyn onely by man and not by God, as is miraclis pleyinge? Rit forsothe as the licnesse of miraclis we clepen miraclis, right so the golden calfe the children of Israel clepiden it God, not for it was in itsilf, but for they maden it to licnesse of God, in the whiche they hadden minde of the olde miraclis of God beforn and for that licnesse they worschipiden and preiseden, as they worschipiden and preisiden God in the dede of his miraclis to hem. And therfore they diden expresse maumetrye. So sithen now on dayes myche of the puple worschipith and preisith onely the lickenesse of the miraclis of God as myche as the word of God in the prechours mowth by the whiche alle miraclis be don. No dowte that ne the puple doth more maumetre now in siche miraclis pleyinge than dide the puple of Israel that time in heringe of the calf in as myche as the lesingis and lustus of miraclis pleyinge that men worschipen in hem is more contrarious to God and more acordinge with the devul than was that golden calf that the puple worschipid. And therfore the maumetrye that time was but figure and lickenesse of mennus maumetrye nowe, and therfore, seith the apostel, "Alle thes thingis in figure fellen to hem," and therfore in siche miraclis pleyinge the devel is most plesid, as the dyvel is best payid to disceive men in the licnesse of that thing in whiche by God men weren convertid biforhond and in whiche the devel was tenyd byfornhond. Therfore oute of doute siche miraclis pleying thretith myche more venjaunce than dide the pleyinge of the children of Israel after the heryinge of the calf, as this pleyinge settith but japis grettere and mo benfets of God.

A, Lord, sithen childres pleyinge witnessith ther fadirs sinnes before hem and ther owne original sinnes beforn and ther owne defaute of wisdum whanne they pleyen, and ther chastising afterward schal more greve hem, so myche more this miraclis pleyinge witnessith mennys hidous sinnes befornhond and the forgeting of ther maister Crist, and ther owne folye and the folye of malice passinge the folye of childre, and that ther is grete venjaunce to comyn to hem | f. 20v
more than they shul mowen paciently boren, for the grete liking that they han in ther pley.

But, frend, peraventur yee seyen that no man schal make you to byleven but that it is good to pleyen the passion of Crist and othere dedis of him. But here agenus herith how whanne Helise steyede up into Bethel, childre pleyingly coming agenus him seiden, "Steye up, ballard! steye up, ballard!" And therfore he cursid hem, and two bores of the wyilde wode al totoren of hem, two and fourty childre. And, as alle seintis seyen, the balledness of Helisee betokeneth the passion of Crist, thanne sithen by this storye is opynly schewid that men schulden not bourden with the figure of the passion of Crist ne with an holy prophete of Crist, myche more in the Newe Testament. And whanne men shulden be more wis, ferthere fro alle maner pleyinge and ernestful dedis more comaundid now than that time, and the passion of Crist more schuld ben in drede than that time schulde han ben Helisee. Men schulden not pleyn the passion of Crist upon peine myche grettere than was the venjaunce of the childre that scornyden Helisee.

For siker pleyinge of the passion of Crist is but verre scorning of Crist, as it is seid beforn; therfore, dere frend, beholdith how kinde tellith that the more eldere a man waxith the more it is agen kinde him for to pleyn, and therfore seith the booc, "Cursid be the childe of han hundrid yeer." And certis the world, as seith the apostil, is now at his ending, as in his laste age; therfore for the grete neghing of the day of dome alle creaturis of God nowe weryen and wrathen of mennus pleyinge, namely of miraclis pleyinge, that most schuln ben schewid in ernest and into venjaunce at the day of dome; therfore agen kinde of alle creaturis it is now miraclis pleyinge, and therfore God now on dayes sendith souner wisdam to children than herbyforn, for they schulden now on dayees leven pleyinge and given hem more to ernestful werkis, plesaunt to God.

Also, frend, take hede what Crist seith in the gospelle that, "right as it was in the dayes of Noye agenus the greet flood, men weren etinge and drinkinge and ther likingis taking, and feerely cam the venjaunce of God of the grete flode upon hem; so it schalle ben of the coming of Crist to the day of dom," that whanne men gifen hem most to ther pleyinge and mirthis, ferely schal come the day of dome upon hem with greet venjaunce beforn. Therfore oute of dowte, frynd, this miracle pleyinge that is now usid is but trewe threting of sodeyn venjaunce upon us.

And therfore, dere frend, spende we nouther oure wittis ne oure money aboute miraclis pleying, but in doinge hem in dede, in grette drede and penaunce, for sikir the weping and the fleyshly devocion in hem ben but as strokis of han hamer on either side to drive out the nail of oure drede in God and of the day of dome, and to maken the weye of Crist slidir and hevy to us, as rein on erthe and cley weies. Than, frend, yif we | wilen algate pleyen, pleyne we f. 21r
as Davith pleyide bifore the harke of God, and as he spac byfor Michol his wif, dispising his pleyinge, wherfore to hir he seide in this wise: "The Lord liveth, for I shal pleyn bifore the Lord that hath chosen me rather than thy fadur, and al the hous of him, and he comaundide to me that I were

duke upon the puple of the Lord of Israel, and I schal pleyn, and I schal be maad fowlere more than I am maad, and I schal ben meke in min eyen, and with the handwymmen of the whiche thou speeke I schal more glorious aperen."

So this pleyinge hath thre parcelis. The firste is that we beholden in how many thingis God hath given us his grace passinge oure neghyeboris, and in so myche more thanke we him, fulfilling his wil and more tristing in him agen alle maner reproving of oure enmys. The secound parcel stant in continuel beinge devowt to God almighty and fowl and reprovable to the world, as Crist and his apostelis schewiden hemself and as Davith seide. The thridde parcel stant in beinge as lowly in oure owne eyen or more than we schewen us withouteforthe, settinge lest by in us silf as we knowen mo sinnes of us silf than of ony other, and thanne beforn alle the seintis of hevene and biforn Crist at the day of dome and in the blisse of hevene we schul ben more glorious in as myche as we pleyn betere the thre forseid perselis heer, the whiche thre perselis wel to pleyn heere and after to comyn to hevene, graunt the holy Trinite. Amen.

Textual Notes

Emendations in the text of the *Tretise* presented above are indicated in the textual notes; the manuscript readings and, in only a few instances, the readings presented by other editors are noted here. No attempt has been made to present all the variant readings of nineteenth-century editors, nor are their inadvertent omissions of passages from the text indicated.

The following abbreviations appear in the textual notes:

MS. : British Library MS. Add. 24,202

Davis : Nicholas Davis, "The Playing of Miracles in England between c.1350 and the Reformation" (1977).

Hudson : Anne Hudson, *Selections from English Wycliffite Writings* (1978).

Mätzner : Eduard Mätzner, *Altenglische Sprachproben* (1869), II, Pt. 1.

---

8. contunuely] contunuiely *MS.*
9. Miraclis] In miraclis *MS.*
23. efectuel] eflectuel *MS.;* ef[f]ectuel *Hudson*
31. his] her *MS.*
68. that ben] and ben *MS.*
70. that] ȝat *MS.;* [þ]at *Hudson*
104. *cure*] *curer MS.*
120. and debatis] and of debatis *MS.*
153. other] othe *MS.*
174. pleyinge] ?pleynge *MS.*
185. quick] quck *MS.*

186. answeryn] answeryng *MS.*
215. they ben] *MS.;* be *Hudson*
218. verrily] verrrily *MS.*
244. hatidest] hatistde *MS.*
250. hemsilf and al] *MS.;* hemsilf al *Hudson*
275. matrimonye] matmonye *MS.*
294. houre] *MS.;* hore *Hudson*
331. wile] while *MS.;* wile *Hudson*
335. good, and sendinge] good, sendynge *Hudson*
370. communicacion] comunicaciou *MS.*
373–74. yif it] yif it it *MS.*
414. hadden] *MS.;* adden *Mätzner*
462. donn] doun *MS.*
493. meintenyd] meytenyd *MS.*
496. than sithen] thau sithen *MS.*
521. serymonies] sermonyes *MS.*
534. and is verre] *Mätzner;* and verre *MS.*
546. wite] pite *MS.;* wite *Mätzner*
555. miracle] ?miraclo *MS.*; miracl(is) *Davis.*
559. apostatas] apostaas *MS.*
562. they] ther *MS.*
563. apostata] postata *MS.*
612. preinge] *MS;* preyinge *Mätzner*
613. children] chlyndren *MS.;* chyldren *Mätzner*
621. hough] *MS.;* how *Mätzner*
630. honouryn] houoryn *MS.*
674. peraventur] perauntur *MS.*
686. ferthere] fethere *MS.*
710. taking] takyng takyng *MS.*
721. either] eiiþer *MS.*
743. settinge] ?sittinge

Critical Notes

Abbreviations

Aston	Aston, Margaret. *England's Iconoclasts*. Oxford: Clarendon Press, 1988.
Barish	Barish, Jonas. *The Antitheatrical Prejudice*. Berkeley and Los Angeles: Univ. of California Press, 1981.
Chambers	Chambers, E. K. *The Mediaeval Stage*. London: Oxford Univ. Press, 1903. 2 vols.
Clopper	Clopper, Lawrence M. "*Miracula* and *The Tretise of Miraclis Pleyinge*," *Speculum*, 65 (1990), 878–905.
Coventry	*Coventry*, ed. R. W. Ingram. Records of Early English Drama. Toronto: Univ. of Toronto Press, 1981.
"Milieu"	Davis, Nicholas. "The *Tretise of Miraclis Pleyinge*: On Milieu and Authorship," *Medieval English Theatre*, 12 (1990), 124–51.
Fraser	Fraser, Russell. *The War Against Poetry*. Princeton: Princeton Univ. Press, 1970.
Gardiner	Gardiner, Harold. *Mysteries' End*. 1946; rpt. Hamden, Conn.: Archon Books, 1967.
Hazlitt	*The English Drama and Stage under the Tudor and Stuart Princes 1543–1664*, ed. W. C. Hazlitt. 1869; rpt. New York: Burt Franklin, 1978.
Kolve	Kolve, V. A. *The Play Called Corpus Christi*. Stanford: Stanford Univ. Press, 1966.

Leff — Leff, Gordon. *Heresy in the Later Middle Ages.* Manchester: Manchester Univ. Press, 1967. 2 vols.

Mätzner — *Altenglische Sprachproben*, ed. Eduard Mätzner. Berlin: Wiedmann, 1869. Vol. I, Pt. 2.

Selections — *Selections from English Wycliffite Writings*, ed. Anne Hudson. Cambridge: Cambridge Univ. Press, 1978.

Vulgate — *Biblia Sacra iuxta vulgatam versionem*, ed. Robert Weber *et al.* 1969; rpt. Stuttgart: Deutsche Bibelgesellschaft, 1983.

WB — *The Holy Bible, Containing the Old and New Testaments, with the Apocryphal Books, in the Earliest English Versions Made from the Latin Vulgate, by John Wycliffe and His Followers*, ed. Josiah Forshall and Frederic Madden. Oxford: Oxford Univ. Press, 1850. 4 vols.

Woolf — Woolf, Rosemary. *The English Mystery Plays.* Berkeley and Los Angeles: Univ. of California Press, 1972.

1 **miraclis:** The term 'miraclis' as used in the *Tretise of Miraclis Pleyinge* appears in this work to cover a very wide range of vernacular drama of a religious nature, especially plays on the Passion and on the lives and martyrdoms of the saints but also including non-sacred plays and summer games presented on religious festivals and Sundays; see Introduction, above, pp. 1–3. The polemical nature of the *Tretise*, however, must be kept in mind throughout both parts of the document; the reader is intended to see the contrast between the real miracles of Christ and the false spectacle of the drama in which such effects are done in play. Compare the curious form 'steraclis' as used in *Dives and Pauper*—a term which

combines the terms 'miracles' and 'spectacles'; see *OED*, s.v. 'steracle.' On this term cf. Clopper, pp. 891–93.

2 **Knawe yee, cristen men:** Davis ("Milieu," p. 143) calls attention to a joint statement by Nicholas Hereford and Philip Repton which also begins as an address to "cristen men"; for the text of the Hereford-Repton declaration, see Margaret Aston, "Wyclif and the Vernacular," in *From Ockham to Wyclif*, ed. Anne Hudson and Michael Wilks, Studies in Church History, Subsidia, 5 (Oxford: Basil Blackwell, 1987), p. 328. For commentary on the dialect of the *Tretise* which establishes it from a different dialect area, see above, pp. 53–84.

3–4 **gospel of Jon:** *John* 14.6: "Jhesu seith to [Thomas], 'I am weye, treuthe, and lif . . ." (*WB*).

9 **Miraclis:** For the MS. reading "In miraclis," see textual notes. Davis ("Milieu," p. 138) defends the reading of the manuscript as an effort by the author to apply the insights of the Oxford Calculators "to differentiate the intrinsic force of Christ's redemptive action from its observable effects, dynamics from kinetics." The sentence, when unemended, is ungrammatical.

18 **yhe to suffere dethe:** This reference to the threat of martyrdom suggests the persecution of Wycliffites, Lollards, and their sympathizers; while Davis' attribution of the *Tretise* to Nicholas Hereford leads him to date this text in the 1380's when Hereford was undergoing persecution for his beliefs (see A. B. Emden, *A Biographical Register of the University of Oxford to A.D. 1500* [Oxford: Clarendon Press, 1958], II, 914), very severe persecution of Lollards only intensified in the early fifteenth century with the first execution (of William Sawtrey) oc-

curring in 1401 by order of King Henry IV.

23 **efectuel:** In his unpublished Cambridge University dissertation, Nicholas Davis suggests that 'efectuel' ('effectual') is a word associated with Oxford thinking and notes that it is a derivation from *effectus* ("The Playing of Miracles, c.1350 to the Reformation" [1978], p. 85).

oure bileve: A common synonym for the Creed, but when appearing in a treatise by a Lollard or Lollard sympathizer this terminology might have a more specific connotation implying either (1) a more sincere belief in the Creed and Scripture, or (2) a different interpretation of scripture and tradition.

24 **bourde and pleye:** The first of these terms is synonymous with 'jest,' 'joke' (*OED*, s.v. 'bourd') and is also to be associated with 'game,' a word understood as indicating play, including in the sense of theatrical presentation. "Playing" among young children is below in the *Tretise* even seen as unavoidable but inappropriate behavior indicative of the lapsarian condition. See the extended discussion of the ambiguity of the term 'play' by John Coldewey, "Plays and 'Play' in Early English Drama," *Research Opportunities in Renaissance Drama*, 28 (1985), 181–88, and also the comments of Kolve, pp. 8–32. The idea of *playing* in sacred scenes in religious drama would also eventually cause objections in officialdom after the Protestant Reformation; see Gardiner, *passim*, and also, for a useful example, the condemnation of the Chester pageants in Archdeacon Rogers' *Breviary*, copied and brought up to date with additions by David Rogers in the early seventeenth century. The *Breviary*, after providing commentary on the plays as well as their alleged history (a late set of banns is also included),

complained about the plays as "beinge nothinge profitable to anye use excepte it be to showe the Ignorance of our forefathers" (*Chester*, ed. Lawrence M. Clopper, Records of Early English Drama [Toronto: Univ. of Toronto Press, 1979], p. 248). Queen Elizabeth's proclamation "Prohibiting Unlicensed Interludes and Plays," issued on 16 May 1559, focused on vernacular drama played during the summer and fall months—drama which included "some that have been of late . . . not convenient in any good ordered Christian commonwealth to be suffered" (*Tudor Royal Proclamations*, ed. Paul L. Hughes and James F. Larkin, I [New Haven: Yale Univ. Press, 1969], 115). The Queen's officers are ordered to "permit none to be played wherein either matters of religion or of the governance of the estate of the commonweal shall be handled or treated, being no meet matters to be written or treated upon but by men of authority, learning, and wisdom, nor to be handled before any audience but of grace and discreet persons" (ibid.). This proclamation did not affect the civic drama directly at this time, however. The Coventry Corpus Christi plays were not suppressed until 1580; see R. W. Ingram, "Fifteen Seventy-Nine and the Decline of Civic Religious Drama in Coventry," in *The Elizabethan Theatre VIII*, ed. G. R. Hibbard (Port Credit, Ontario: P. D. Meany, 1982), pp. 114–28. The feast of Corpus Christi, which had long been the occasion for the Coventry plays, would be abolished in the sixteenth century. But Corpus Christi and other festivals had come under attack by the more ascetically minded, especially Lollards, long before Protestantism raised objections to a celebration and veneration of the Eucharist. See *Selections*, p. 25, for Lollard denunciation of Corpus Christi, the liturgy for which is described as "untrewe and peintid ful of false miraclis" (*Twelve Conclusions of Lollards*, IV).

26 **reversith:** For the Lollard understanding of the contemporary Church as *reversing* the values for which Christ stood and his law, see Anne Hudson, *Lollards and Their Books* (London: Hambledon Press, 1985), pp. 171, 179. Davis observes that the *Tretise* used drama as a means to a larger end: "the absolute discrediting of a contemporary Church establishment which, in practice, tolerates or extends its sanctions to certain kinds of theatrical *ludus*" ("Milieu," p. 125).

29 **in idil:** i.e., in vain. Such use of language is prohibited by the Ten Commandments; see *Exodus* 20.7.

33–39 The political stance is highly conservative. The social order envisioned by Lollardy indeed depended upon aristocratic control, which it was expected should expel the power of the pope from the land and establish conditions favorable to "true" religion. See the selection from the *Tractatus de Regibus* in *Selections*, pp. 127–31. As Gordon Leff notes, for Wyclif "the principle of kingship was inherent in all forms of human association; it applied in the church before the fall and the coming of endowment, when with a minimum of civil law it had been subject to the king's guidance. . . . Wyclif, although frequently reiterating the king's obligation to act in conformity with God's decrees, which was his *raison d'être*, attributed to him virtually limitless powers over his kingdom" (Leff, II, 543–44). In this kind of society, no *playing* of roles either above or below one's status would appear to be appropriate. For a post-Reformation condemnation of role playing (1625), see Hazlitt, p. 244.

34 **drede to sinne:** As a reform movement, Lollardy was motivated by a fear of divine punishment for infractions against divine law; such dread meant that *Matthew* 25,

including its account of the Last Judgment and the parable of the Wise and Foolish Virgins, would be taken extremely seriously. Though this parable is not mentioned in the *Tretise*, it assists in an important way to explicate the meaning of the text: to play thus means being lax and failing to address the demand that one always should be vigilant. Lollards and Wycliffites returned to the Augustinian understanding of sin as qualitative rather than quantitative; hence they rejected penitential practices that implied a hierarchy of sins which might be greater and more dangerous or smaller and less threatening to the soul. Any sin, if not terminated and forgiven, was to be seen as a mortal threat to the soul. See Christina von Nolken, *The Middle English Translation of the Rosarium Theologie* (Heidelberg: Carl Winter, 1979), pp. 105–06.

57–60 **Firste . . . wittis:** The argument is from the *jest and earnest* commonplace; see the discussion in the Introduction, above, and Kolve, pp. 125ff. For Wyclif, there had been no "mingling of divine and human traditions" (Leff, II, 539); hence his followers were unable to understand how jest could legitimately be utilized for the advancement of a serious purpose. The association of playing with the flesh, desire, and the senses links together those aspects of human life which the Lollards and Wycliffites, like more orthodox ascetics, distrusted most. Because playing of plays is a source of pleasurable experience for men, it is therefore of the "fleyss" as is church music (ibid., II, 576), which likewise appeals to sense and emotionally stimulates people. The distrust of man's "five wittis" stands, of course, in contrast to the emphasis on them as gateways to the soul in Franciscan and other thought of the period. See also Fraser, p. 41, and compare Stephen Gosson's assertion in *Playes Confuted* *in five Actions* (London, 1582), sig. F1^{v}, that playwrights "studie to make our affections overflow, whereby they draw the bridle from that parte of the mind, that should ever be curbed, from runninge on heade: which is manifest treason to our soules. . . ."

63–64 **of Cristis lawghing:** See Introduction, above, for the Patristic source of the idea that Christ never laughed. Hudson (*Selections*, p. 188) cites Wyclif's statement "we rede not of Cristis laughtir, but of his weping we reden diverse times." For the *Tretise* this is a central point: jest, game, and play are symptoms of the Fall and hence are to be set apart from the sacred and from divinity. Christ, as perfect man, could thus have had no sense of humor but must have been perfectly "ernest."

70–72 **"Yif . . . God":** *Hebrews* 12.8: cf. *WB*: "That if ye ben out of disciplin, of which alle ben maad parceners, therfore ye ben avowtreris, and not sones." Wycliffite versions of the Bible themselves differ; quotations from the Wycliffite Bible in these notes are from the earlier Wycliffite version printed in *WB* unless otherwise noted. The author of the *Tretise* also does not necessarily follow any extant Wycliffite version of the Bible exactly; such freedom in presenting the English translation was, however, usual with Lollard and Wycliffite writers, who sometimes quoted passages quite freely translated from the Vulgate.

78 **yerd of God:** The rod of God, seen as an emblem of his punishment of those who violate the presciptions of his law. See, for example, *Job* 9.34 and Psalm 2.9; the Vulgate uses the same term—'virga'—at *Proverbs* 13.24 where the rod or "yerde" is the instrument used for disciplining a child. Further, this term is used three times

as a symbol of God's power and wrath in the *Apocalypse* (2.27, 12.5, 19.15), where it is identified, as in Psalm 2, as a rod of iron (*WB*: "an irene yerde"). Below, at 124 in the *Tretise*, the "yerde of God" is poised "over his heved"—a statement typical of ascetic writers who maintained that bodily delights should be entirely given up by those who have surrendered themselves totally to spiritual thoughts and actions. See, for example, the parable of the man who fell into the abyss in the section devoted to SS. Barlaam and Josaphat in the *Golden Legend*: though the bush (i.e., human life) to which he clings is being gnawed away at its roots by mice (temporality), he becomes enraptured by some honey dripping from above and forgets about all danger. The honey is, of course, the pleasurable experience available in this world that leads people to forget the ever-present reality of one's precarious state as a mortal human being. At the Last Day of history, the unrighteous who have failed to be spiritually vigilant in their earthly lives will feel the wrath of God's rod or "yerde," for they may expect to be condemned to the everlasting bonfire of hell.

87–90 ***"Be yee . . . him"*****:** *1 Peter* 5.6–7.

94–95 **"hidous and ferful . . . live":** Not St. Peter's words but a passage from *Hebrews* 10.31: "It is feerful for to falle into hondis of God livinge" (*WB*).

100 **time of his graceous *visiting:*** The Last Judgment.

109–10 **And sithen . . . gospel:** *Matthew* 6.24: "No man may serve to two lordis, forsothe ethir he shal haat the toon, and love the tother; other he shal susteine the toon, and dispise the tothir" (*WB*); see also *Luke* 16.13. As the Protestant antitheatrical writer Stephen Gosson later indicated, there should be no idea of a truce between God and the devil (*Plays Confuted*, sig. B4).

117–18 ***"Eche . . . mourninge"*:** *Hebrews* 12.11.

118–19 **veine sightis of degyse, aray:** Here the controversial subject of costume, which is essential to dramatic presentation, is introduced. Distrust of disguise within a play would even make Shakespeare uneasy, for in his *Macbeth*, for example, he established his guilty hero's villainy through the imagery of stolen and ill-fitting clothing; the Scottish tyrant in the end of the play becomes a mere actor exhibiting outward show and inward emptiness. Through costume, actors appear to be something that they are not. The spectacles in which such costumed actors take part are, according to the author of the *Tretise*, "veine sightis" since they allegedly lack the substance of reality.

The later sixteenth- and seventeenth-century enemies of the stage would agree with the *Tretise*'s view of disguise and costume, as had many earlier writers, including Herrad of Landsberg (see Introduction, above). In William Prynne's opinion, any attempt to appear to be something other than what one is—e.g., through "the common *accursed hellish art of face-painting*"—involves sinful falsification; God "enjoines all men at all times, to *be such in shew, as they are in truth: to seeme that outwardly which they are inwardly;* to act themselves, not others . . ." (*Histriomastix* [London, 1633], p. 159). See also Barish, pp. 90–106. A further objection, articulated in the later anti-theatrical writings, involves the contoversial matter of cross-dressing; see Meg Twycross, "Transvestism in the Mystery Plays," *Medieval English Theatre*, 5 (1983), 123–80.

Medieval dramatic records collected by Records of Early English Drama and the Malone Society accumulate considerable evidence concerning costumes used in medieval plays. Even Adam and Eve in the Garden of Eden were presented in leather garments to simulate nudity and hence would have been regarded as not what they seem; as fallen human beings they could only *pretend* to be unfallen creatures by wearing such garments. For costumes in the Coventry plays, see *Coventry*, *passim*; the disguises included masks, beards, wigs, costumes for God, devil costumes, armor, vestments, coats, cloaks, gowns, caps, jackets, kirtles, crowns, hats, head-dresses, helmets, mitres, hoods, shoes, and wings for angels as well as other items (see the index in ibid., pp. 657–58).

120 **stiring othere to leccherie:** Playing, since it is the source of pleasure through experiences entering by way of the senses, is associated with the body and the flesh; the flesh, along with the world and the devil, is understood in terms of the concept of the Three Enemies of Man. Associated with the flesh is the sin of gluttony, which is mentioned later in the sentence along with "othere vicis" that likewise function to draw the mind away from the urgency of spiritual realities. While this concern is a paramount one in anti-theatrical writings, including such earlier documents as Tertullian's *De Spectaculis*, it seems that contemporary temptations at local sites were in the writer's mind; the Corpus Christi fair at Coventry, held annually at the time when the Coventry Corpus Christi plays were performed, would most likely hold sufficient temptations to be offensive to some Lollards, who probably considered the play a prelude to vice. See also Introduction, above.

121 **debatis:** See Herrad of Landsberg's insistence that at

plays the conclusion of the entertainment is often rowdiness: "Rarely does such a gathering break up without quarrelling" (Chambers, II, 98n). As noted in the Introduction, some less than pious behavior also characterized the gatherings at the York plays at the feast of Corpus Christi when unruly persons engaged in actions that seemed at variance with the devotional intent of the pageants or the wish of the city corporation that they should be presented to the honor of the city. That such indecorous behavior did not cancel the serious intent of the plays can be verified by the York records, while at Coventry William Pysford, a former mayor and also a citizen sympathetic to Lollardy, felt that the Corpus Christi plays continued "the laudable custumes of the Citie"; hence in his will, probated in 1518, Pysford contributed financially to the plays and also in his will left garments to be used as costumes (*Coventry*, pp. 112, 576).

131 **Pharao:** See *Exodus* 7–12.

133 **Jewis that bobbiden Crist:** Hot cockles, or "*the bobbid* game," is described by the writer in MS. Bodley 649 (as quoted by G. R. Owst, *Literature and Pulpit in Medieval England*, 2nd ed. [Oxford: Blackwell, 1961], p. 510) as "a common game in use nowadays . . . which the soldiers played with Christ at his Passion. . . ." The writer continues:

> In this game, one of the company will be *blindfold* and set in a prone position; then those standing by will hit him on the head and say—
>
> "*A bobbid, a bobbid, a biliried:*
> *Smite not her, bot thu smite a gode!*"
>
> And as often as the former may fail to guess correctly

> *and rede amis*, he has to play a fresh game. And so, until he *rede him that smote him*, he will be *blindfold stille and hold in* for the post of player.

The game is identified as "popse" in the York plays (*The York Plays*, ed. Richard Beadle [London: Edward Arnold, 1982], p. 252) and "Whele and pylle" in the N-town *Trial before Annas and Cayphas* (*The N-town Play*, ed. Stephen Spector, EETS, s.s. 11 [1991], I, 303); both cycles, along with the plays in the Towneley manuscript, utilize this game for the presentation of the Passion. See the discussion of this game in relation to the vernacular plays in Kolve, pp. 185–86. For a list of available illustrations of hot cockles, see Lilian M. C. Randall, *Images in the Margins of Gothic Manuscripts* (Berkeley and Los Angeles: Univ. of California Press, 1966), p. 111. On the anti-Semitism implicit in these passages in the plays and in the plays generally, see Stephen Spector, "Anti-Semitism and the English Mystery Plays," *Comparative Drama*, 13 (1979), 3–16. See also the comments of Davis, "Milieu," p. 128.

141–42 **to halowyn his name:** The command implicit in the invocation at the beginning of the Lord's Prayer.

153 **pride:** Chief of the Seven Deadly Sins but also the sin that is regarded as containing within it the essence of all the others.

157–58 **al this . . . pleying:** A commonplace; see Ernst Robert Curtius, *European Literature and the Latin Middle Ages*, trans. Willard R. Trask (1953; rpt. New York: Harper and Row, 1963), pp. 139–44. Life is transitory, like the playing of a role in a theatrical scene. Cf. Macbeth's speech in V.v.24–26: "Life's but a walking shadow, a poor player/ That struts and frets his hour upon the stage,/ And then is heard no more."

163–64 **seinge . . . bitere teris:** The nature of the devotional response to certain religious plays is here established as consistent with the affective spirituality prevalent in Northern Europe in the late Middle Ages; see Introduction, above.

The display of emotion, particularly upon viewing an image, was hardly a new response in the late Middle Ages; in Patristic literature there is the instance of Gregory of Nyssa who was brought to tears each time he saw a certain image illustrating the Sacrifice of Isaac, which typologically represents the Crucifixion of Christ on the cross (Gerhart B. Ladner, "The Concept of the Image in the Greek Fathers and the Byzantine Iconoclastic Controversy," *Dumbarton Oaks Papers*, 7 [1953], 4). In the late Middle Ages, however, art and drama shared a common aim in their attempt to present the Passion of Christ *feelingly*, even to the point of "bitere teris." Michelangelo is reported to have sneered at such expressions of Northern piety in response to Flemish painting; such works, he is believed to have said, might well bring tears to the eyes of the pious, though on the whole those who responded were "women, young girls, clerics, nuns, and gentlefolk without much understanding for the true harmony of art" (quoted by Erwin Panofsky, *Early Netherlandish Painting* [Cambridge: Harvard Univ. Press, 1953], I, 2).

Affective piety of this sort, though in raising the level of lay religious consciousness it helped to create a basis among the people for reform that eventually expressed itself in Protestantism, was nevertheless offensive to many early Protestants—a response which is reflected in the description of Corpus Christi day with its processions and plays in Barnabe Googe's *The Popish Kingdome* (London, 1570), fols. 53^{v}–54^{r}. (This work is a translation of Thomas Kirchmayer's *Regnum Papisticum.*) Googe's text complains that "Christes passion here derided is, with sundrie maskes and playes," including pageants "playde in worship of this bred [of the Eucharist],/ That please the foolish people well." The streets are strewn with rushes and decked out for the occasion, and people fall upon their knees in devotion. Father Gardiner, who mentions this text (p. 15n), also calls attention to another example of such piety (pp. 18–19, citing Marcel Dieulafoy, *Le Théâtre édifiant* [Paris: Librairie Bloud, 1907], p. 6), though it is from the post-Reformation period in a Catholic territory; in this instance Mme. d'Aulnoy is reported to have said in a letter in 1679 "that she saw the audience fall on their knees and strike their breasts when the character of St. Anthony said his *confiteor* on the stage."

176–78 **summe recreacion . . . japis:** The recreational argument in favor of drama; see the Introduction, above, and Glending Olson's chapter "The Recreational Justification," in his *Literature as Recreation in the Later Middle Ages* (Ithaca: Cornell Univ. Press, 1982), pp. 90–127.

179–85 **Also . . . quick:** This statement has been interpreted to indicate that the writer actually approved of certain images—a stance indicative of the more moderate Lollard or Wycliffite position, which nevertheless tended to encourage iconomachy and, eventually, some iconoclasm (cf. *Selections*, pp. 83–88, and see Aston, I, 96–159). However, the reference to "dead" images is indicative of the Lollard rejection of the practice of the veneration of images; see Introduction, above.

These sentences are some of the most important in the *Tretise* since they verify that drama from the standpoint of its aesthetics was regarded as having a basis in common with the visual arts—a basis in the appeal to the sense of sight. According to the understanding of vision prevalent in both learned and popular circles at this time, *seeing* meant coming into direct visual contact with the object, which if it were idolatrous would contaminate the viewer; see Clifford Davidson, "The Anti-Visual Prejudice," in *Iconoclasm vs. Art and Drama*, ed. Clifford Davidson and Ann Eljenholm Nichols, Early Drama, Art, and Music, Monograph Ser., 11 (Kalamazoo: Medieval Institute Publications, 1988), pp. 23–46. The object that was seen would thus make a direct impression upon the viewer's memory. That the connection between the visual arts and drama was a commonplace one, with theatrical representation seen as having certain advantages, is also indicated in Reginald Pecock's *The Repressor of Over Much Blaming of the Clergy*, ed. Churchill Babington, Rerum britannicarum medii aevi scriptores, 19 (London, 1860), pp. 216–22. Pecock (p. 221) suggests that a crucifix of wood or stone in "the likenes of Crist hanging on a cros nakid and woundid" is normally the best means of coming to understand Christ in his "manhode"; the only more effective means is "whanne a quik man is sett in a pley to be hangid nakid on a cros and to be in seming woundid and scourgid." Unfortunately, he laments, plays showing the Passion are staged "ful seelde and in fewe placis and cuntrees."

The defense of the religious stage thus depended especially upon a belief in the efficacy of the dramatic scene—efficacy which was in turn explained in terms of mnemonic theory; the natural condition of memory was to keep in mind those images that had appeared most vividly to the senses. The fullest discussion of mnemonic theory in relation to the *Tretise* is provided by Nicholas Davis ("The English Mystery Plays and 'Ciceronian' Mnemonics," *Atti del IV Colloquio della Société Internationale pour l'Etude du Théâtre Médiéval* [Viterbo: Centro Studi sul Teatro Medioevale e Rinascimentale, 1983], pp. 75–84), who especially makes reference to the pseudo-Ciceronian *Ad Herennium.*

According to memory theory, repetition was also an important factor in assisting one to retain mental impressions in the memory, and this would be particularly so if the plays, as in Coventry at the feast of Corpus Christi, were in fact ones that were mounted each year in an annual repetition of the sacred story. The point is an important one and may be linked to the urgency with which recollection through memory of the sacred narrative of the New Testament was regarded. The *Tretise* reports belief in the usefulness of plays for re-imprinting the images illustrating salvation history upon the mind, though its authors will strongly reject such a view—a rejection that also is itself based in part on memory theory, for the impressions made on the mind by plays are felt by the authors to be produced by false images, not by the true images that could only have been witnessed visually by Christ's contemporaries.

194 **maumetrie:** Idolatry. Concern with idolatry was a widespread concern among Lollards and their sympathizers; see Introduction, above, pp. 29–30.

198 **folc of avoutrie . . . singnys:** Cf. *Matthew* 12.39: "An ivel generacioun and avoutrere [adultera] sekith a tokne,

and tokne shal nat be goven to it, no but the tokne of Jonas, the prophete" (*WB*); the later Wycliffite version printed in *WB* translates the word *adultera* of the Vulgate as "spouse brekere."

198–99 **siche singnys . . . love:** Miracles are compared with the insincere lover, who is only interested in seduction, not in commitment; see Introduction, above, and the note on line 207, below, for discussion of *signs* in late medieval thought. Barish calls attention to the demand for sincerity in Puritan aesthetics and cites (p. 96) Iago's ironic "Men should be what they seem" (*Othello* III.iii.126).

204 **Anticrist:** On the obsession with Anti-Christ among Wyclif and his followers, see Leff, II, 504, 518, 520, 528, 530–31, 535–41, 575–76, 580–81. Like many Protestants in the sixteenth century, Lollards before very long came to see the official Church as an arm of the powers of darkness. The power of the pope—a power which came to be identified with Anti-Christ— was questioned, and his right to issue decrees was denied (ibid., II, 576). Ironically, much of the argument in the *Tretise* is related to the prohibitions concerning the theater to be found in such papal decrees. The connection of Anti-Christ with the theater, however, is a logical one; according to the *Rosarium*, the initial way of demonic subversion "is deceivabel persuasion" (von Nolken, *The Middle English Translation of the Rosarium*, p. 60); thus, as an effective way of persuading through the (alleged) deception of the stage, plays are thought to be a way to entrap men and women to false belief. For an extended study of the Anti-Christ tradition, see Richard Kenneth Emmerson, *Antichrist in the Middle Ages* (Seattle: Univ. of Washington Press, 1981).

207 **signis withoute dede:** For the *Tretise* this is precisely the aesthetic problem that needs to be addressed in theatrical representation. See the Introduction, above, for some general comments on the relation of this interpretation to contemporary philosophical trends. The sign detached from reality in mimesis was, of course, a point upon which the Church Fathers had denounced dramatic representation, and in the Early Modern period the deceptiveness of such representation was again under attack. See Fraser, pp. 3–51. The charge of "idilnesse" also appears in the sixteenth century; see Stephen Gosson's *School of Abuse*, a book that labels players "the Sonnes of idlenesse" (quoted by Fraser, p. 59).

211–13 **to pristis . . . pleyinge:** Hudson notes (*Selections*, p. 188) that the Wycliffite *Floretum*, an alphabetical listing which includes an entry under *histrio*, cites canon law forbidding clergy participation in plays and similar events. Some medieval legislation against drama is noted by Gardiner, pp. 4–19. Fraser (p. 42) calls attention to Rossiter's quotation from the Dean of the Faculty of Theology at Paris in the fifteenth century who condemned "priests and clerks" who, "wearing masks and monstrous visages," run and leap through "the whole church in unblushing shameless iniquity" or drive "about the town and its theatres in carts and deplorable carriages to make an infamous spectacle for the laughter of bystanders and participants, with indecent gestures of the body and language most unchaste and scurrilous" (A. P. Rossiter, *English Drama from Early Times* [1950; rpt. New York: Barnes and Noble, 1967], pp. 64–65). See also Introduction, above, pp. 9–11. While it is more or less obvious what theatrical activity was specifically condemned in such complaints, there clearly was also considerable flexibility in the interpretation of various decrees against clergy participation in drama, though masked entertainments seem consistently to be singled out as not allowed and events such as the Feast of Fools and games in the churchyard receive frequent mention. Abuses must have been common. The *miraculum* at Carlisle which caused a disturbance in 1345 (see Introduction, above) was presented by clerks (*Cumberland, Westmorland, Gloucestershire*, ed. Audrey Douglas and Peter Greenfield, Records of Early English Drama [Toronto: Univ. of Toronto Press, 1986], p. 17; see also the interpretation of Clopper, p. 880). Alexander Carpenter, in his *Destructorium Viciorum* of c.1425, includes drama within the various categories of *games*; he lists two types of dramatic action ("acting" of illusion, and erotic dancing and interludes as well as "theatrical plays which are called plays of the theater—that is, of a public place where people are accustomed to come for playing") that are condemned and one "socially honorable" type (*ludus socialis honestatis*) that is approved as recreation (see Marianne Briscoe, "Some Clerical Notions of Dramatic Decorum in Late Medieval England," *Comparative Drama*, 19 [1985], 4–6). Carpenter, however, attempts to adopt prohibitions directed at the clergy in his sources in canon law and to extend them to the general laity (ibid., p. 9), which is in fact a tactic used in the *Tretise of Miraclis Pleyinge*.

The clergy were naturally supposed to be held to a higher standard than the laity, though even in monasteries there seems to have been much theatrical activity. Included were such lively liturgical plays as the St. Nicholas dramas in the Fleury Playbook that probably derive from a Benedictine house—and there are copious records showing that monks were treated to plays in monasteries by visiting players. Allardyce Nicoll cites the condemnation of clergy participation at the synod at Tours in 813 as an example of a Church council's action; in this case it was declared that the clergy ought to flee "the obscenity of the players and the scurrilities of debased jesting" (*Masks, Mimes, and Miracles* [London: George G. Harrap, 1931], p. 147). These prohibitions were not interpreted to include such liturgical dramas as the *Visitatio Sepulchri* (the Easter play of the three Marys) for which clergy participation is documented from the earliest records of religious drama (see Pamela Sheingorn, *The Easter Sepulchre in England*, Early Drama, Art, and Music, Reference Ser., 5 [Kalamazoo: Medieval Institute Publications, 1987], pp. 18–22).

It is it difficult to say if the average clergyman would have regarded the prohibitions as directed against vernacular drama that was in part or primarily devotional or religious in character. Woolf, p. 363, quotes a gloss on the decretals of Gregory IX (repeating the decree of Innocent III; see Introduction, above) which excludes from condemnation plays on subjects such as the Nativity, Holy Innocents, and the Magi because "such things conduce to devotion rather than to lasciviousness and delight of the senses, just as at Easter Christ's sepulchre and other things are represented in order to stimulate devotion." Clopper notes (p. 882) commentary which indicates that unacceptable plays occurred on such feasts as Holy Innocents or the feast of St. John (probably Midsummer, associated with John the Baptist); these are not allowed. At York, the author of the Creed Play was almost certainly a chantry priest named William Revetour, whose role we may assume was not untypical in the presentation of civic drama. Revetour's 1446 will, quoted in *York*, ed. Alexandra F. Johnston and Margaret Rogerson, Records of Early English Drama (Toronto: Univ. of

Toronto Press, 1979), I, 68 (trans., ibid., II, 746), also refers to stage props associated with the play which are contributed along with the book containing "le Crede Play" to the Corpus Christi guild. See also Alexandra F. Johnston, "The Plays of the Religious Guilds of York: The Creed Play and the Pater Noster Play," *Speculum*, 50 (1975), 57–59.

215 **ypocrisie:** Cf. Prynne's demand that we see 'hypocrisy' as a word that signifies "*but the acting of anothers part or person on the Stage:* or what else is an *hypocrite, in his true etimologie, but a Stage-player, or one who acts anothers part*. . . . And hence it is, that . . . not onely divers *moderne* . . . Writers, but likewise *sundry Fathers . . . stile Stage-players, hypocrites; Hypocrites, Stage-players, as being one and the same in substance* . . ." (*Histriomastix*, pp. 158–59). The Patristic evidence from "*sundry Fathers*" is supplied in Prynne's long footnote, pp. 158–59.

221–23 **"Not he that seith . . . kindam":** *Matthew* 7.21.

229 **tormentours that bobbiden Crist:** See note to 133, above.

230–36 **And as anentis the secound reson . . . God:** Hudson notes: "The distinction is between the sin itself which is evil, as was the sin of Adam or the rejection of Christ by the Jews, and the response of God to this evil action through which good results. The paradox is expressed neatly in the lyric *Adam lay ybounden* . . ." (*Selections*, p. 188). The theological term for the event in the Garden of Eden is 'fortunate Fall': because of his fall, humankind will paradoxically be given eventually a place higher than the angels—a place that would not have been made available had the Fall not occurred. However, the *Tretise* insists that the ends do not justify the means and that neither the fortunate Fall nor the Crucifixion, which also involves evil converted into great good, can be made to defend the acting of plays.

243–44 ***"Turne awey min eyen . . . vanitees":*** Psalm 118 (119).37.

244–45 ***"Lord . . . vanitees":*** Mätzner (p. 231) cites Psalm 30 (31).7: "Thou hatedist aboute waiteris vanites overveinliche." On the liturgical use in the Sarum rite of this passage and of the verse quoted in lines 243–44, above, see *Selections*, pp. 188–89.

250–51 **as a jay . . . himsilf:** Cf. Thomas Wright, *The Political Songs of England*, Camden Soc., 6 (London: Nichols, 1839), p. 328:

> For riht as me thinketh hit fareth by a prest that is
> lewed,
> As by a jay in a kage, that himself hath bishrewed.
> . . .

255–56 **many men wenen . . . peine:** The reference here has not been convincingly traced, but see *Selections*, p. 189, for Hudson's note that "some of the more extreme members of the Brethren of the Free Spirit appear to have denied the existence of hell." Perhaps the writer is merely jeering at those who do not take seriously enough the threat of hell fire. In this case, the author is using a straw man to emphasize the importance of giving attention to the end of one's life and one's condition in eternity.

263–66 ***"Lord, thou woost . . . persin":*** *Tobit* 3.14–17, following the Vulgate, "numquam cum ludentibus miscui me," which in the Wycliffite version appears as "Nevere with pleyeres I mengde me" (quoted by Mätzner, p. 231). Barish comments: "The case of Sara happens to be nearly the sole instance among the scriptural citations made by the preacher that supports his own interpretation" (p. 72); see, however, Clopper, pp. 898–99.

272–74 **myche more a prist . . . vertues:** The *Tretise*'s extended attention to priests who take part in plays, or otherwise encourage them, provides additional evidence that the clergy did indeed play a substantial role in the religious theater of the time. See note to 211–13, above.

275–77 **alle othere sacramentis . . . Crist:** There is no hint here whatever of a heterodox view of the Sacraments. Cf. *Selections*, pp. 110–15.

278–79 **quen of Saba . . . Crist:** See *Matthew* 12.42: "The queen of the south shal rise in dome with this generation, and shal condempne it; for she came fro the eendis of the erthe, for to here the wisdam of Salomon, and loo! heere is more than Salomon" (*WB*).

285–86 **the precious . . . hondis:** This statement again corroborates the orthodoxy of the writer with regard to the Sacraments; there is no suggestion that he has any reservations about the Eucharist or about transubstantiation.

295–96 **pley of Anticrist . . Dome:** Among the extant medieval English plays, Anti-Christ appears only in the Chester cycle, but there is a continental play on the subject from an earlier date reprinted in Karl Young, *The Drama of the Medieval Church* (Oxford: Clarendon Press, 1933), II, 371–87). See additionally the discussion in John

Wright, ed., *The Play of Antichrist* (Toronto: Pontifical Institute of Mediaeval Studies, 1967), which also provides a translation of the continental play. The Chester Clothworkers' and Dyers' plays of *Antichrist's Prophets* and *Antichrist* have been edited by R. M. Lumiansky and David Mills in *The Chester Cycle*, EETS, s.s. 3 (1974), I, 396–438.

The Judgment play, which in each of the Middle English civic cycles (but not in the Cornish *Origo Mundi*) concluded the cycle, dramatizes the events of Doomsday. At York, the Doomsday play was produced by the Mercers, the most affluent of the local guilds, who were able to provide a production which must have been spectacular indeed as a closing for the cycle. See Alexandra F. Johnston and Margaret Dorrell [Rogerson], "The York Mercers and Their Pageant of Doomsday, 1433–1526," *Leeds Studies in English*, n.s. 6 (1972), 10–35. At Coventry, the Doomsday play was presented by the Drapers, again an affluent guild able to finance a spectacular show, in this case involving the burning of the world with fire at three stations to represent the end of history. For the Drapers' Doomsday play, see Clifford Davidson, "The Lost Coventry Drapers' Play of Doomsday and Its Iconographic Context," *Leeds Studies in English*, n.s. 17 (1986), 141–58. The choice of the Anti-Christ and Doomsday plays as examples would seem to have been in part the result of familiarity with one or both of them. However, the criticism in the *Tretise* perhaps more importantly reflects an obsession with Anti-Christ and the end of time.

297–99 **"Do we yvel . . . rightwise":** *Romans* 3.8: "Do we yvele thingis, that goode thingis come. Whos dampnacioun is just" (*WB*).

307–08 **Crist himsilf reprovyde . . . passioun:** See *Luke* 23.27–28: "Sothly ther [on the way to the cross] suede him moche cumpanye of peple, and of wymmen that weiliden, and bymoornyden him. Sothly Jhesu turnyd to hem [and] seide, 'Doughtris of Jerusalem, nyle ye wepe on me, but wepe ye on youre silf, and on youre sones'" (*WB*). The author's argument about tears, which is resumed in 317–23 below, is crucial; see the note to 163–64, above.

315 **word of God . . . sacramentis:** Earnest and sincere preaching and the Sacraments are the way to salvation, not false plays in which things are not as they seem.

339–40 ***"Thou cam bifore him . . . swetnesse"*:** Psalm 20 (21).4.

346 **verry ypocritis and lieris:** A traditional accusation which would be repeated by critics of the stage in the late sixteenth century. On hypocrisy and actors, see the note on 215, above. Sir Philip Sidney's refutation of the claim that the poet-playwright is a liar may be found in his *Apology for Poetrie*, which explains: "Now, for the Poet, he nothing affirmes, and therefore never lieth" (*Elizabethan Critical Essays*, ed. G. Gregory Smith [London: Oxford Univ. Press, 1904], I, 184). Gosson had insisted that plays "are no Images of trueth" since "they handle such thinges as never were" or else distort reality (*Plays Confuted*, sig. D5[r]).

360–61 **for othere mengid trewthis . . . ful yvel:** Hudson glosses this passage as follows: "for others mixed truth (with lies), and make that which is really evil to be considered to be good" (*Selections*, p. 189).

363–67 **what recreacion . . . vanite:** The writer's attitude foreshadows the later Puritan condemnation of Sunday games, sports, and recreation of other kinds. See the chapter entitled "Sabbatarianism" in M. M. Knappen, *Tudor Puritanism* (Chicago: Univ. of Chicago Press, 1939), pp. 442–50. But ascetic hostility to recreation throughout the Middle Ages, especially among the clergy, has been well established. Normally, however, monastic life allowed some recreation if it was not inconsistent with decency and order (see Olson, *Literature as Recreation*, pp. 109–15).

368–69 **werkis of mercy:** The Corporal Acts of Mercy described in *Matthew* 25 and commonly depicted in art, as in the famous painted glass in the window in All Saints, North Street, York (see E. A. Gee, "The Painted Glass of All Saints Church, North Street, York," *Archaeologia*, 102 [1969], pp. 162–64, Pls. XXIV–XXVI); for other examples in painted glass, see Christopher Woodforde, *The Norwich School of Glass-Painting in the Fifteenth Century* (London: Oxford Univ. Press, 1950), pp. 193–96, Pl. XLII. The Corporal Acts were at the heart of Catholic attitudes toward charity in the late Middle Ages—attitudes that were to suffer under the Protestant condemnation of "works righteousness" in the sixteenth century. For the *Tretise*, such sincere *acts*—feeding the hungry, giving drink to the thirsty, giving shelter to the homeless, supplying clothing for the naked, visiting the sick and those in prison—are to replace the hypocritical and lying *actions* of the drama and theater. (A seventh corporal act, burying the dead, is not mentioned in *Matthew* 25.)

373–77 **peinture . . . treuthe:** 'Peinture' could include wall paintings or panel paintings on wood, but mainly would seem to indicate images such as figures of saints or crucifixes, which were always painted and never bare wood or stone. The writer is concerned about the honesty of presentation, and hence realistic art containing imaginative details such as those introduced by the Flemish painters would be excluded. Images that are "not to curious" are plain and unadorned, relatively speaking; they would not be clothed with rich clothing or adorned with jewels. *The Lanterne of Light*, a Lollard treatise written prior to 1414, complains, "The peintour makith an image forgid with diverse colours til it seme in foolis iyen as a lively creature. This is sett in the chirche in a solempne place. . . . Priestis . . . seyn that Goddis powere in worching of hise miraclis loweth doun in oo image more than anothir . . ." (ed. Lilian M. Swinburn, EETS, o.s. 151 [1917; rpt. New York: Kraus, 1971], pp. 84–85; attention is called to this passage by Aston, I, 114). The *Tretise*'s insistence that "maumetrie" be avoided is consistent with the Lollard rejection of the veneration of images and of their use as a means of encouraging gifts to the clergy in pilgrimage centers (see Aston, I, 114–15).

378–79 **bokis to lewid men:** A direct reference to the opinion, definitively set forth for the West by Pope Gregory to Bishop Serenus of Marseilles, that "a picture especially serves as a book [pro lectione] to the common people" (Woolf, pp. 87, 365).

382 **day of ther rekeninge:** Doomsday, which the writer expected in the near future.

384–85 **hyinge . . . hevene:** The eschatological hope of heaven is visualized in terms of a marriage; this emotional and even ecstatic view of the union of Christ with his Church at the Last Day is based on an allegorical reading of the

Song of Songs and the parable of the Wise and Foolish Virgins in *Matthew* 25. See also the useful though in some ways misleading account by Colleen McDannell and Bernhard Lang, *Heaven: A History* (New Haven: Yale Univ. Press, 1988), pp. 94–107.

386 **An half frynde:** Because of the shift in tone and the identification of a different audience, the second part of the *Tretise* which begins here is to be regarded as a continuation of Part I produced at a different time—and, as the dialect evidence shows, by a different writer. It is specifically directed to a "half frynde" who, while he sympathizes with Lollard or Wycliffite attitudes and doctrine, refuses to reject plays though the writer implies widespread antagonism to such drama by those who share "oure bileve." This portion of the *Tretise*, designed to convince the "frynde" of the wrongness of his opinions and actions with regard to playing and patronage of plays, is more distinctively heterodox than the first part of the work. See the dissertation by Nicholas M. Davis ("The Playing of Miracles," pp. 103–04). There is evidence that many Lollards found religious plays useful toward encouraging belief. One early Lollard, William Ramsbury, appears to have used the occasion of gatherings to see plays as opportunities for preaching; see Hudson, *Lollards and Their Books*, p. 114. Lollard sympathizers such as William Pysford at Coventry (see note to 121, above) were active supporters of plays, and among the Protestants who were the successors of the Lollards at Coventry there is the case of John Careles who was jailed for religion in the time of Queen Mary but "upon his worde he was let out to play in the Pageant about the City with his other companions" in 1556 (John Foxe, *Acts and Monuments*, as quoted in *Coventry*, pp. 207–08). Davis' speculation concerning the

identity of the "half frynde" as Sir William Neville ("Milieu," p. 145) cannot be sustained.

387 **Thomas of Inde:** The apostle, who according to medieval accounts such as the *Golden Legend* became a missionary to India. His scepticism is proverbial, for he would not believe in the risen Christ until confronted with him physically; thus the "half frynde" will not stay away from plays or otherwise refrain from supporting them until confronted with proof from holy writ and the doctrine derived from it.

392–93 **Thou schalt not . . . in idil:** The Second Commandment, which is central to the argument presented in the *Tretise* against religious plays. As Barish notes (p. 76), the *Tretise* "finds . . . impiety not in the interpolation of alien matter, not in levity of tone, but in the fact of representing sacred story at all, from which it would seem to follow that *any* attempt to depict scriptural episodes mimetically, whether out of doors and in the vernacular, or inside the church and in Latin, must be blasphemous."

397–98 **japinge stikke:** Fool stick, carried by a jester; here used figuratively.

410–11 **an hethene man . . . mawmete:** Davis ("Milieu," p. 127) calls attention to Wyclif's interest in Islam and his sympathy for this non-Christian religious tradition. The writer of the *Tretise* is referring to the Islamic prohibition against the representation of God.

411–12 **book of lif:** Cf. *Apocalypse* 3.5.

414–15 **hadden or lassen:** See *Deuteronomy* 12.32. Mätzner (p.

235) quotes the Wycliffite version: "ne adde thow eny thing, ne lasse."

441 **heretage:** Salvation, here allegorically presented in terms of a deed or document giving one the right of ownership to property. Cf. George Herbert's seventeenth-century poem, "Redemption," which treats salvation in terms of rents and leases.

446–47 ***"Wo to hem . . . good"*****:** *Isaiah* 5.20.

454–56 **Adam . . . therof:** It was worse to attempt to conceal the transgression than to commit it in the first place.

465 **Ismael pleyide:** See *Genesis* 21.9ff, esp. verse 9 in the Vulgate rendering: "cumque vidisset Sarra filium Agar Aegyptiae ludentem [cum Isaac filio suo]. . . ." Clopper (p. 900) notes that "the relevance of the story to drama is obscure" and cites Nicholas of Lyra, who "interprets . . . 'playing' as idolatry, which he couples with lechery and lasciviousness, the consequence of which is death." However, Davis ("Milieu," pp. 128–30) traces an expository tradition originating with St. Augustine (see *Joannis Evangelium* XI.ii.12 [*PL*, XXXV, 1481–82]) and extending to John of Wales which allegorizes this biblical passage to condemn playing (*lusio*) as deception (*illusio*). Drawing also on St. Paul's epistle to the Galatians (4.22–23), John of Wales interpreted the episode in terms of fleshly malice (Ishmael) attempting to seduce and undermine the spiritual (Isaac) through deception (*Ioannis Valensis de regimine vite humane seu Margarita* [Lyons, 1511], Pt. 1, dist. 10, chap. 7, as cited by Davis, "Milieu," pp. 128–29).

472–73 **fleysh . . . spirit:** See *Galatians* 4.28–30: "For [soth], britheren, we ben sones of biheeste aftir Isaac; but now as this that was borun after the fleisch pursuede him that was aftir the spirit, so now. But what seith the scripture? Caste out the servaunt and hir sone, for the sone of the servaunt schal not be eir with the sone of the fre wijf" (*WB*); the quotation is from the later Wycliffite version in this instance. A Wycliffite epistle sermon on this passage presents a very different interpretation; see *English Wycliffite Sermons*, ed. Anne Hudson (Oxford: Clarendon Press, 1983–90), III, 558–59. Here the rejected woman and her son are identified allegorically with church ceremonies and the laws of Antichrist; the text insists, for example, that the "keping of thes cerymonies schulde not laste with the blis of hevene" (III, 558).

512–14 **ther is . . . men:** See *2 Corinthians* 6.14–16: "Sothly what partinge, or comuninge, of rightwisnesse with wickidnesse? or what felowschipe of light to derknessis? sothly what acordinge of Crist to Belial?" (*WB*).

539–41 **sithen religious . . . in dedis:** False show and covetousness are connected; cf. *The Lanterne of Light* for the complaint that false images, intended for deception, may be designed for the feeding of clerical covetousness—"why gedre ye prestis richesses by youre peintid images to make youre silf worldly riche in spoiling of the peple?" (p. 85). The *Tretise* insists on religious and charitable acts, not mere verbal or visual substitutes ("tokenes," "signes") which may be manipulated by a corrupt clergy.

543–44 **the apostasie of Lucifer . . . him:** As Lucifer drew many angels to follow him at the time of his fall, so apostate priests command the loyalty of a high percentage of the people (who indeed would insist that they are being properly loyal to the Church and devoted to its interests and to the divine commands). As hypocrites, such priests, like Lucifer, have much in common with stage players, who also outwardly pretend to be something that they are not. See the Chester playwright's Dominaciones, who tell Lucifer upon his rebellion that he has "begone a parlous playe" (*The Chester Mystery Cycle*, ed. Lumiansky and Mills, p. 8).

547–49 **the pleyinge . . . mo:** See *2 Kings* [*2 Samuel*] 2.14–31.

576–78 ***"The ende . . . sorowe":*** *Proverbs* 14.13, which Mätzner quotes in one Wycliffite version: "Lawghing schal be medlid with sorewe . . ." (p. 238).

587–91 **the children of Israel . . . men:** *Exodus* 32.6: "the puple sat to ete and to drinke, and arisen to pleye" (*WB*); this passage is quoted in *1 Corinthians* 10.7.

597–98 **as seith the apostele:** See *Colossians* 3.5, where the sins of "yvel coveitise, and averise" are associated with "mawmetis" and are condemned (*WB*); the citation is to the later Wycliffite version.

599 **spenden upon the pleyis:** Extant dramatic records collected by Records of Early English Drama show very substantial expenditures made in support of civic drama at such cities as Coventry, York, and Chester. At least some of the plays being criticized in the *Tretise* fall into the category of those to which contributions were made through some system of sponsorship; other plays, however, were presented with the goal of *raising* money (e.g., the saint plays at Braintree, Essex, which were produced in 1523–34 for the purpose of repairing the

church; see Clifford Davidson, "The Saint Play in England," in *The Saint Play in Medieval Europe*, ed. Clifford Davidson, Early Drama, Art, and Music, Monograph Ser., 8 [Kalamazoo: Medieval Institute Publications, 1986], pp. 35–36). For some suggestions with regard to the economic conditions which made lavish expenditures possible in the case of civic drama such as the Coventry plays, see Carolyn L. Wightman, "The Genesis and Function of the English Mystery Plays," *Studies in Medieval Culture*, 11 (1977), 133–36. There is no reason whatever to believe that the guilds at Coventry or York found the plays to be a financial burden except in periods of serious economic decline affecting either the individual guild or the entire community; see, for example, the Coventry mayor's petition in 1539 (*Coventry*, pp. 148–49) and the documents which John C. Coldewey mistakenly believes to be proof of "the recognition by all the guilds concerned that supporting the Corpus Christi plays was an onerous chore" ("Some Economic Aspects of the Late Medieval Drama," in *Contexts for Early English Drama*, ed. Marianne Briscoe and John C. Coldewey [Bloomington: Indiana Univ. Press, 1989], p. 86). No civic cycle lasting approximately two centuries could have survived so long without enthusiasm and fairly solid support from the guilds who were responsible for the actual production of the pageants.

607–08 **they bisien . . . selling:** The sponsors of civic drama were hardly able to separate spiritual profit from economic profit gained from the festivities which brought a large crowd of outsiders to the city on such occasions as Corpus Christi. At Coventry there was the added (and obviously non-spiritual) attraction of the Corpus Christi fair. The extant play texts show that there was clearly great difficulty experienced in distinguishing the sacred from the profane, for so thoroughly was the world sacralized through rite and image. The *Tretise*, however, sets out to make very clear distinctions between the secular and the profane on the one hand, and the sacred on the other; the first of these categories is associated with the flesh, the second with the spirit. In spite of natural weaknesses, men are to set their minds upon the sacred to the exclusion of all else; the plays are, as they would have been for Plato in ancient Greece, distractions which take the mind away from reality.

621–22 **"We witen . . . us":** *Exodus* 32.1.

628–33 **siche miraclis pleyinge . . . puple:** Perhaps an attack on the Franciscan view which, while valuing preaching highly, nevertheless saw playing as a more vivid kind of sermon; see David L. Jeffrey, "Franciscan Spirituality and the Rise of the Early English Drama," *Mosaic*, 8, No. 4 (1975), 25–34. See also Owst, *Literature and Pulpit*, pp. 471–547, Woolf, p. 367, and Briscoe, "Some Clerical Notions," pp. 1–13, for further discussion of the relation between drama and sermon material. As late as Philip Stubbes' *Anatomy of Abuses* the opinion that plays may "be as good as Sermons" is put forth only to be confuted as "blasphemie intollerable" (Hazlitt, p. 222). For Stubbes as for the writers of the *Tretise*, religious plays are to be regarded as much more offensive than secular productions (see ibid., p. 218).

638–40 **the golden calfe . . . licnesse of God:** For the golden calf see *Exodus* 32. While the defense of images in Canon 82 of the Council of 692 A.D. authorized realistic or at least anthropomorphic representations of the deity as opposed to the merely symbolic—it was held that the former had more educational value than the latter (Ernst

Kitzinger, "The Cult of Images in the Age before Iconoclasm," *Dumbarton Oaks Paper*, 8 [1954], 142)—the golden calf represents a class of idolatrous and therefore forbidden images. The golden calf is not an anthropomorphic image of God nor is it in any non-symbolic sense made in the "licnesse of God"; the writers of the *Tretise* are intent upon attacking the idea of the devotional image, and in so doing call attention to the most prominent example of Old Testament idolatry. The golden calf has also been frequently cited by iconoclasts as a biblical model of behavior toward idolatrous images. See Michael Camille, *The Gothic Idol: Ideology and Image-Making in Medieval Art* (Chicago: Univ. of Chicago Press, 1989), pp. 170–72, fig. 92.

646–47 **the word of God . . . don:** The "word" for the author of Part II of the *Tretise* is to be identified with the Word (*Logos*, *Verbum*) of *John* 1. This identification would also later be generally made by Protestants, especially the Puritan ministers of the late sixteenth and early seventeenth centuries who likewise saw the final result as the conversion of the soul through encounter with the Word in the course of hearing it preached; see, for example, John Cotton, *Gods Mercie Mixed with his Justice* (London, 1641), pp. 120–21. The devotional image, especially in drama where language is joined to spectacle, is therefore rejected as a source of conversion or of strengthening of the faith.

655–56 **"Alle thes thingis . . . hem":** Cf. *1 Corinthians* 10.11.

664–66 **childres pleyinge . . . pleyen:** See Kolve, pp. 28–29, and Philippe Ariés, *Centuries of Childhood*, trans. Robert Baldick (New York: Knopf, 1962), pp. 71–72. Ariés indicates, especially in his chapter on games and pastimes, how children tended to play adult games after the age of about five or six. There was, as he argues, tremendous pressure on the child to join the adult world. The writer of the *Tretise*, however, would deny to the older child as to the adult the activity of playing games, since it involves something other than sincere movement or action on the part of the players. *Jest* is to be replaced by *earnest* at the earliest possible age. Younger children's natural propensity for the illusions associated with *game* is thus seen as a sign of hereditary imperfection inherited from Adam.

676–80 **how whanne Helise . . . childre:** *4 Kings* [*2 Kings*] 2. 23–24; the wording in *WB* is "scorneden to him" (*AV*: "and mocked him"); however, the Vulgate reading "et inludebant ei" directly provided the source for the Wycliffite or Lollard writer. Elisha's curse brings from the wood two bears which killed forty-two boys.

681–82 **the balledness . . . of Crist:** Possibly from a play on words based on the Vulgate's word for baldness, for the text in Latin gives the children's jeers as "ascende calve, ascende calve" (*4 Kings* [*2 Kings*] 2.23); cf. R. E. Latham, *Revised Medieval Latin Word-List from British Sources* (London: Oxford Univ. Press, 1965), s.v. *calvaria* ("place of execution").

696 **"Cursid . . . yeer":** *Isaiah* 65.20.

697 **the world . . . at his ending:** The expectation of the *parousia* in apostolic times. A specific text is implied, but I have not been able to identify it with certainty. The authors of the *Tretise* believed that the end of history was imminent. This belief was shared with orthodoxy, and, as noted above, the extant Middle English cycles

and collections of plays dramatize Doomsday as an appropriate ending to their representation of salvation history. The general expectation was that the Doomsday plays were representations of scenes to be enacted *in the near future* as, without warning, the human race was to be called to account and history was to come to a close.

701–02 **venjaunce at the day of dome:** Doomsday as described in *Matthew* 25 with its emphasis on the Corporal Acts of Mercy is ultimately a very important matter for the *Tretise* since the biblical text provides a rationale for urgency in avoiding idleness and frivolity: the General Judgment will be a serious matter and will determine whether one will spend eternity in bliss or in punishment. On the final day of history the sheep (those worthy of salvation) will be separated from the goats (the damned). This culminating event of history is also the crucial event of each person's life.

708–13 **"right as it was . . . dome":** See *Matthew* 24.38–39: "For as in the days bifore the gret flood, they weren etinge and drinkinge, weddinge and takinge to weddinge, til into that day, in the whiche Noe entride into the shippe; and they knewen nat, til that the grete flood came, and toke alle men, so shal be the cumming of mannes sone" (*WB*). Typologically, the flood was regarded as foreshadowing the Last Day, when those more concerned with eating and drinking and with the other "things of the flesh" would again be destroyed. The ark, therefore, is usually seen as a representation of the Church, an institution which would provide sufficient safety for those who are on board—a point that is implied in the Noah pageants in the English cycle plays (see, for example, Clifford Davidson, *From Creation to Doom: The York Cycle of Mystery Plays* [New York:

AMS Press, 1984], pp. 50–52). At this point in the *Tretise*, the Lollard or Wycliffite writer, who rejects the view that the Church as an institution will give protection, extends a sharp warning to those who would separate the sign from the reality in play, for thus they would make themselves subject to God's vengeance and divide themselves from the safety afforded by true belief and charitable actions.

720–22 **strokis of þan hamer . . . dome:** Compare the visual depictions of warnings against swearing and sabbath breaking in which the crucified Christ is shown surrounded by various tools and instruments, as in the fifteenth-century wall painting at Breage, Cornwall; see A. Caiger-Smith, *English Medieval Mural Paintings* (Oxford: Clarendon Press, 1963), pp. 55–56, Pl. XX.

727–33 **"The Lord . . . aperen":** *2 Kings* [*2 Samuel*] 6.21–22: "And David seide to Michol, 'The Lord liveth, for I shal pleye before the Lord, that hath chosen me rather than thy fader, and than al the hows of him, and he hath comaundid to me, that I were a ledere upon the puple of the Lord of Israel; and I shal pleye, and fowlere I shal be maad more than I am maad, and I shal be meke in min eyen, and with hoond wymmen, of the whiche thou hast spoken, more glorious I shal apere'" (*WB*). Undoubtedly misled by the Vulgate text, the translator did not realize that the Hebrew writer was describing David's dancing, not the music-making with which he was frequently identified in iconography. According to Barish, this example as used by the author of the *Tretise* "completely undermines his own case" (p. 74). David's harping is normally used as a *defense* of the recreative arts and music; see *Dives and Pauper*, ed. Priscilla Heath Barnum, EETS, 275 (1976), I, Pt. 1, 297–98. However,

Clopper, citing Hugh of St.-Cher's commentary on the story of Isaac and Ishmael (*Opera omnia*, I, 27), notes a different interpretation which focuses not on David's "playing" but upon his response to Michal's reprimand. "Like Hugh," Clopper writes, "the *Tretise* writer describes Davidic playing as a penitential life of firm belief and patient suffering of persecution" (p. 901).

734–49 **So this pleyinge hath thre parcelis . . . Amen:** Clopper usefully paraphrases: "First, people should behold how many things God has given through his grace and thank him by fulfilling his will and trusting in him when they are reproved by enemies. Second, they should be steadfast in devotion and foul and reprovable to the world as Christ and his apostles were and as David said he ought to be. The third point is that we should be even more humble in our own eyes than in outward appearance because we are aware that we have committed more sins than are known by others" (p. 901).

Appendix: The Description of the Classical Theater in the *Troy Book* of Lydgate

From the end of antiquity to the Early Modern period knowledge about the conditions of performance in the classical theater of ancient Greece and Rome was available only through traditions descending from writings such as the *Etymologies* of Isidore of Seville, the remains of actual Roman theaters and amphitheaters, and manuscripts containing the texts of classical Latin plays, mainly the tragedies of Seneca and the comedies of Plautus and Terence. Isidore had identified the theater as a semicircular structure and as a place where the audience could stand about and watch the spectacle.[1] His notes on classical drama in the *Etymologies*, including misleading information about the structure of the stage, would be repeated over and over again until the sixteenth century.[2] The remains of Roman theaters seemed to corroborate some aspects of the iconography. John Capgrave commented on the roundness of the stages of East Anglia and identified them as locations where individuals "stand to se pleyis or westlinge."[3] While his report concerning English theaters[4] may have referred merely to contemporary playing places like the outdoor game place at Walsham-le-Willows,[5] Roman remains were visible on the Continent—in some cases, as in the instance of the theater near Viterbo in Italy, even providing well preserved examples of the Roman stage that have survived up to the present time.

Manuscripts containing the plays of Terence were especially copied for use in education—and the plays were imitated, most notably by the canoness Hrotsvita of Gandersheim. Miniatures in earlier Terence manuscripts were used as models for later copies such as the famous St. Albans Terence (MS. Auct. F.2.13) now in the Bodleian Library at Oxford. The latter manuscript is especially noted for its remarkable masks worn by the actors.[6]

Nicholas Trevet's statement concerning the structure of the classical theater and the relationship between actors and reciter may be regarded as fairly typical:

> The *theatrum* was a semi-circular open space, in the middle of which was a small house called the *scena*, in which there was a platform on which the poet stood to recite his works. Outside the house were the *mimi* who performed bodily movements while the pieces were being recited, by adapting themselves to whatever character the poet was speaking of.[7]

Trevet, an English Dominican who was active in the late thirteenth and early fourteenth centuries, derived his view of the stage from Isidore and others and thus repeated the idea that the poet took an active part in the recitation of the play while masked mimes acted out the gestures.[8] The identification of the *scena* as a "house" from which the poet read is, to be sure, most curious; a continental writer had previously described such "houses" as "like merchants' stalls covered with poles and hangings."[9]

When John Lydgate in his *Troy Book*—a work based on Guido della Colonne's *Historia Destructionis Troiae*, which was available to him in the library of the monastery at Bury St. Edmunds[10]—reported theatrical activity at Troy at the time of the Trojan War, he repeated a number of commonplaces about the classical stage. His description of the stage is contained in Book II, lines 842–926, of the *Troy Book*, a long work which appears in a number of manuscripts, including British Library MS. Cotton Augustus A.iv and MS. Arundel 99, and also was published in the sixteenth century.[11] It is an imaginary picture of the theater of antiquity, but there is useful evidence concerning the ways in which the theory and practice of the theatrical activity of the classical past were envisioned in the late Middle Ages in England:

And first also I rede that in Troye
Were songe and rad lusty fressh comedyes
And othir ditees that callid been tragedies.
And to declare so shortly in sentence
Of bothe two the ffinal difference:
A comedie hath in his ginning
At prime face a maneer compleining
And afftirward endith in gladnesse,
And it the dedis oonly dooth expresse
Of swich as been in povert plongid lowe.
But tragedye, who so list to knowe,
It beginneth in prosperitee
And endith also by adversitee.
And it also dooth the conquest trete
Of riche kinges and of lordis grete:
Of mighty men and oolde conqueroures
Which by frawde of fortunes sodeine shoures
Been ovircast and whelmyd from her glorye.
And whilom thus was halowyd the memorie
Of tragedies, as bookys make minde,
Whan they were rad or songyn, as I ffinde.

In the theatre ther was a smal awter
Amiddis satt that was half circuleer,
Whiche into the Eest of custom was direct
Upon the whiche a pulpet was erect,
And therinne stood an auncien poete
For to reherse by rethorikes swete
The noble dedys that were historial
Of kinges [and] princes for a memorial.
And of this oolde wourthy Emperoures,
The greet Emprise eek of conqueroures.
And how they gat in Martis hih honoure,
The lawrer grene for fin of her laboure—
The palme of knighthood disservid by old date
Or Parchas made hem passen into ffate.

And aftir that with cheer and face pale

With style enclined gan to tourne his tale
And for to singe aftir al hir loos,
Full mortally the strook of Antropoos:
And tells also for al her wourthy heed,
The sodeyn breking of her lives threed.
How pitously they made her mortal ende
Thorugh fals ffortune that al the world wol shende,
And how the ffin of al her wourthinesse
Endid in sorwe and in hih tristesse.
By compassing of ffraude or fals treson,
By sodeyn mordre or vengeaunce of poison,
Or conspiring of freting fals envye
How unwarly that they did die
And how her renoun and her hih ffame
Was of hatrede sodeinly maad lame;
And how her honour drough unto declin,
And the mischieef of her unhappy fin;
And how fortune was to hem unswete,
Al this was toold and rad of the poete.
And whil that he in the pulpeet stood
With deedly face al devoide of blood
Singing his ditees with muses al to rent
Amid the theatre shrowdid in a tent,
There cam out men gastful of her cheres,
Disfigured her facis with viseres,
Pleyinge by signes in the peplis seighte.
That the poete songon hath on heighte
So that ther was no maneer discordaunce
Atwen his ditees and her contenaunce.
Forlike as he aloffte did expresse
Woordis of joye or of hevinesse,
Meving and chere benethe of hem pleying,
From point to point was alwey answering.
Now trist, now glad, now hevy, and now light
And face chaunged with a sodein sight.
So craftily they koude hem transfigure,
Conforming hem to the chaunte plure.
Now to singe and sodeynely to wepe.

So wel they kowde her observaunces kepe,
And this [was] doon in Aprille and in May
Whan blosmys newe bothe on bussh and hay
And floures fressh ginne for to springe,
And the birdes in the woode singe
With lust supprised of the somyr sonne
Whan thise playes in Troye were begonne
And in the theatre halowyd and yholde.
And thus the [rites] of tragedies olde
Pryamus [the worthy] king began—
Of this matere no more telle I kan.

We can be sure that Lydgate's account is not a direct description in any sense of the actual medieval stage, but as a poet who had been retained to produce mummings for the court and city he certainly was familiar enough with contemporary practice.[12] It is therefore likely that at least some aspects of the medieval theater would have found their reflection in his remarks. The use of masks ("viseres") is well documented elsewhere in the dramatic records of the time,[13] though we may wonder if Lydgate might not in fact rather have been thinking of the masks in such manuscripts as the St. Albans Terence. Interestingly, one of the points that Lydgate emphasizes is the ability of the reciter, like the player in *Hamlet* II.ii who recites the famous speech describing the death of Priam, to project strong emotions. Hamlet's player likewise, through feigned emotion, became wan of visage and otherwise fitted his actions to the words of the fiction of the scene.

NOTES

1. Isidore of Seville, *Etymologiae* 18.42, as quoted by Joseph R. Jones, "Isidore and the Theater," *Comparative Drama*, 16 (1982), 33–34.

2. Ibid., pp. 31–44.

3. John Capgrave, *Ye Solace of Pilgrimes*, ed. C. A. Mills (London: Oxford Univ. Press, 1911), pp. 17–18.

4. Ibid., pp. 17–18.

5. Kenneth M. Dodd, "Another Elizabethan Theater in the Round," *Shakespeare Quarterly*, 21 (1970), 125–56; Clifford Davidson, *Illustrations of the Stage and Acting in England to 1580*, Early Drama, Art, and Music, Monograph Ser., 16 (Kalamazoo: Medieval Institute Publications, 1991), pp. 40–41.

6. See Davidson, *Illustrations of the Stage and Acting*, pp. 50–55; Leslie Webber Jones and C. R. Morey, *The Miniatures of the Manuscripts of Terence Prior to the Thirteenth Century* (Princeton: Princeton Univ. Press, n.d.), *passim*.

7. Nicholas Trevet, *Commentary on Boethius' 'De Consolatione Philosophiae'*; I quote the translation of this passage in William Tydeman, *The Theatre in the Middle Ages* (Cambridge: Cambridge Univ. Press, 1978), pp. 48–49; for the Latin text, see Mary H. Marshall, "Theatre in the Middle Ages: Evidence from Dictionaries and Glosses," *Symposium*, 4 (1950), 26.

8. For illustrations showing the poet reading in a booth in the center of a circular theater while masked mimes act out roles, see especially the miniatures in Paris, Bibliothèque Nationale Cod. Lat. Ars. 664 and Cod. Lat. 7907a; these illustrations are reproduced by Allardyce Nicoll, *Masks, Mimes, and Miracles* (London: Harrap, 1931), figs. 102–03. See also the woodcut in the Lyons, 1493, edition of Terence printed by Trechsel (cited in the Introduction, above, pp. 7, 39).

9. Hugutius (Uguccione) of Pisa, *Magnae Derivationes*, as quoted in translation by Tydeman, *The Theatre in the Middle Ages*, p. 48; for Latin text, see Marshall, "Theatre in the Middle Ages," p. 25, who quotes from MS. Laud 78, fols. 164^v–165^r, in the Bodleian Library.

10. Derek Pearsall, *John Lydgate* (London: Routledge and Kegan Paul, 1970), pp. 124–25; N. R. Ker, *Medieval Libraries of Great Britain*, 2nd ed.

(London: Royal Historical Society, 1964), p. 21.

11. See John Lydgate, *Troy Book*, ed. Henry Bergen, EETS, e.s. 97 (London, 1906), I, ix–x; for the sixteenth-century published version containing this episode, see *The Auncient Historie and Onely Trewe Cronicle of the Warres* (London, 1555), sig. F8^{r}–F8^{v} (*STC* 5580). In my transcription of the text I have generally followed MS. Arundel 99, fols. 30^{v}–31^{v}, with some emendations (in brackets) from MS. Cotton Augustus A.iv, fol. 29^{r}–29^{v}, and the sixteenth-century printed text.

12. See Rudolf Brotanek, *Die Englishen Maskenspiele* (1902; rpt. New York: Johnson Reprint, 1964), pp. 305–25.

13. See especially Meg Twycross and Sarah Carpenter, "Masks in Medieval English Theatre," *Medieval English Theatre*, 3 (1981), 7–44, and *The Staging of Religious Drama in Europe in the Later Middle Ages*, ed. Peter Meredith and John E. Tailby, Early Drama, Art, and Music, Monograph Ser., 4 (Kalamazoo: Medieval Institute Publications, 1982), *passim*. For the construction of masks of the type used in the early theater, see Meg Twycross and Sarah Carpenter, "Materials and Methods of Mask-Making," *Medieval English Theatre*, 4 (1982), 28–47.

Glossary

Complete lexicological information has not been included in this Glossary. The spelling reflects usage as presented in the text of the *Tretise* in this edition and in the quoted passages from Middle English in the Introduction, Notes, and Appendix. The letter *y* has been treated as *i* alphabetically when it is indicative of a vowel and not a consonant.

abide, abiden, *abide, persevere;* abidith, *abides, perseveres*
ablith, *enables, prepares the way*
abstene, *abstain;* absteneden, abstenyde, *abstained*
acording, acordinge, *in accord (with), agreeing*
agen, agens, agenys, agenus, *(prep.) against, in opposition to; toward*
agenward, *back again*
algate, *(adv.) always; at all events*
al maner, *all kinds of*
amis, *amiss, wrongly*
anentis, *(prep.) concerning*
Antropoos, Atropos, *one of three Fates of Greek mythology*
apere, aperen, *appear*
apostata, *(n.) apostate, person abandoning his religious belief;* apostatas, *(n., pl.) apostates*
apostasie, apostasye, *apostasy, abandonment of religious belief*
apostel, apostele, aposteyl, apostil, *apostle;* apostelis, *(n., pl.) apostles*
aray, *(n.) an arrangement in order; clothing or costume*
arisen, *rose up*
arn, *are*
assayen, *attempt*
assoile, *grant absolution*
atwene, *between*
auctorite, *authority*
aughten, awghte, *ought*
Austin, *St. Augustine*
avauntage, *advantage, benefit*
avoutrere, *adulterer;* avoutreris, avowtreris, *(n., pl.) adulterers (including in the religious sense, i.e., heretics)*
avoutrie, *(n.) adultery*
awghte, *see* aughten
awter, *altar*
axen, *ask*

ballard, *bald person*

balledness, *baldness*
be, *(prep.) by*
be, been, ben, *(v.) be; are; is*
beden, *(v.) bid, command;* biddith, *bids, commands;* bad, badde, *commanded;* beden, bedyn, bodyn, *bidden, commanded;* bidding, *(pr.p.) bidding, commanding*
before, beforn, byfor, byfore, biforn, biforne, *(prep.) before*
beforn, byfore, biforn, byforn, byforne, *(adv.) before, previously*
befornhond, biforehand, byforhond, byfornhond, *previously*
begiled, beguiled, *cheated*
begone, *begun*
beholden, beholdith, *observe, see*
beleve, bileve, byleve, *(n.) belief, creed*
beleve, *(v.) believe;* byleven, *believe, as expression of faith*
benemeth, bynimmeth, *takes away from;* bynomen, *taken away from;* bynimminge, *(pr.p.) taking away*
benfets, *(n., pl.) benefits, things well done*
beren, boren, *(v.) bear, carry*
bethenking us, *considering, keeping in mind*
betokeneth, *foreshadowed (as a type)*
bidding, *bidding, command;* biddingis, *biddings, commands*
biddith, *see* beden
bye, bien, *(v.) buy, purchase;* byinge, *(pr.p.) purchasing*
byfall, *happen*
bifore, biforn, *see* before, beforn
bygilen, *beguile, deceive;* begilid, *beguiled, deceived*
biheeste, *covenant, promise*
byhinde, *behind, aside;* put byhinde, *rejected*
byinge, *buying*
bileven, *(v.) believe, expression of faith*
bymoornyden, *see* morning
bynimminge, *see* benemeth
bishrewed, *see* shrewyn
bisien, bysien, *busy, make (themselves) active*
bisily, *(adv.) solicitously*
bisinesse, *(n.) effort, solicitude*
blasfeme, *(n.) blasphemy*
blasfemely, *(adv.) with blasphemy*
ble, *color*
bledes, *(v.) bleeds*
blode, *(n.) blood*
blonder, *confusion*
blosmes, blossemes, *blossoms*
bobbiden, *struck (with fists), insulted*
bodyn, *see* beden
bok, boke, booc, book, booke, *book; bible;* bokes, bokis, bookis, *(n., pl.) books*
boost, *(n.) boast*
bore, born, borun, *born*
bores, *(n.pl.) bears*

bot, *but*
bourde, *(n.) jest, joke, game, sport, amusement;* bourdys, *(n., pl.)* games, jests, amusements
bourden, *(v.) jest, joke, play;* bourdith, *jests, jokes, plays;* bourdinge *(pr.p.) jesting*
bourdfully, *(adv.) jestingly, playfully*
bowen, *bow, incline (away)*
brekere, *breaker, violator, as in* spouse brekere, *adulterer*
brent, *(v.) burned*
brynninge, *(adj.) burning (with emotion)*

cacchen, *catch; ensnare; get possession of, obtain*
can, *(v.) am able; know*
cardyn, *card (wool)*
carpe, *(v.) speak, complain*
cast, caste, *cast; expell*
certis, *(adv.) certainly*
chaunte, *chant, song;* chaunte plure, *song of lamentation, sung by poet*
charite, *charity, love*
chastite, *chastity*
cherche, chirche, chyrch, *(n.) church building; the Church;* cherch yard, *churchyard*
cheres, *faces*
cherl, *churl, bondsman, servant*
childre, children, *children;* childres, *(n., pl. gen.) children's*
clene, *clean, pure*
clepen, *call;* clepith, *calls;* clepiden, *called*
colowrably, *vividly, persuasively*
come, comen, comyn, *come*
comenden, *recommend*
comynte, *community, association*
comune, *common*
comunely, *commonly*
comuning, comuninge, *communing, having in common, sharing*
condempne, *condemn*
continaunse, *continence, self-restraint, esp. with regard to sexual control*
contrarious, *contrary, opposite*
contrarite, contrarity, *opposition*
contunuely, *(adv.) continually, without interruption*
coveytide, *coveted*
coveitise, coveytise, *covetousness*
covenable, *suitable, appropriate*
crede, *(n.) statement of faith, usually indicating the Apostles' Creed or Nicene Creed*
credence, credense, *credence; credibility*
cristen, cristene, *(adj.) Christian*
Cristemesse, *Christmas*
cristendam, *Christendom; Christianity*
croys, cros, *cross*
cure, *spiritual charge or office*
curious, *elaborate, expensively wrought*
custom, custome, *custom;* custumes, *customs*

damme, *mother (possibly contemptuous)*
dampnable, *(adj.) subject to damnation*
dampnacioun, *damnation (of unjust)*
dampne, dampnen, *(v.) condemn;* dampneth, *condemns;* dampnyd, *condemned*; dampning, *(pr.p.) condemning (to hell)*
dampnyd, *(adj.) damned, condemned*
dar, *dare;* darst, *dare*
deade, deed, *(adj.) dead*
deadely, deadly, *(adv.) deadly, mortal*
debate, *strife, quarreling;* debatis, *(n., pl.)* quarrels
decre, *decretal, decree*
dede, deede, *deed; actuality;* dedes, dedis, deedis, *(n.pl.) deeds; achievements*
defaute, *defect, insufficiency*
defendyd, *forbidden*
degyse, *disguise, i.e., costume wearing*
deliten, *(v.) delight, please (themselves);* delitith, *delights;* dilitid, *delighted;* diliting, *(pr.p.) pleasing*
denien, *contradict (as untrue), refuse, reject*
dere, *dear*
derre, *dearer*
derthe, *shortages, famine*
deth, dethe, *death*
dette, *debt*
devel, devil, devul, devvel, dyvul, *devil;* develis, *(n., gen.) devil's*
develiche, *devilish, evil*
dew, *due*
dilitid, diliting, *see* deliten
dylivering, *delivering, rescuing*
directe, *directed*
disceive, *deceive*
disciplin, discipline, dissipline, *system of moral conduct; penance, mortification;* disciplining, *disciplining, mortifying*
dishonouren, *(v.) dishonor, implying desecration*
disiren, *desire*
dispise, dispisen, *despise;* dispisith, *despises;* dispisid, dispiside, *despised;* dispising, *despising, having a low opinion of*
dispising, *(n.) contempt*
dispitouse, *cruel*
disservith, *deserves;* disserved, disservyde, *deserved*
distroy, distroye, distroyen, *destroy;* distruyith, *destroys*
ditees, *literary compositions, poems or dramas*
do, don, donn, doun, *(v.) do;* doith, doth, *does;* dide, diden, dude, *did;* don, done, *done; placed (in the sense of crucified);* doying, doyinge, doing, *(pr.p.) acting; doing; making*
dom, dome, *doom, judgment*
doughter, *daughter*

doun, *(adv.) down*
doute, dowte, *doubt;* no doute, no dowte, *no doubt, undoubtedly*
douting, *doubting, expressing scepticism*
doutouse, dowtous, *uncertain, doubtful*
drede, *(n.) dread, fear*
drede, dreden, dredyn, *(v.) fear*
droowgh, *(v.) drew*
dude, *see* don
duke, *governor*

eche, *each*
eek, *also*
eest, *east*
eetyn, *ate;* eting, etinge, *(pr.p.) eating*
efte, *after*
eyen, eyghen, iyen, *eyes*
eir, *heir*
eld, *(adj.) old;* eld time, *former times*
eldere, *older*
ellis, *else, otherwise*
elliswhere, elluswhere, *elsewhere*
emprise, *undertaking*
enemies, enmys, *enemies; persons opposed to God or to Christian doctrine*
enhauncyn, henhaunce, *comfort (spiritually), advance to a state of bliss, raise up*
eny, *any*
ensaumplide, *(v.) displayed, set forth as examples (to be followed)*
ententive, *heedful, eager*
enterly, *wholeheartedly, heartily; devoutly*
entirlodies, *interludes, plays, entertainments*
entride, *entered*
equite, *fairness, equity*
er, *ere*
ernest, *earnest, serious, opposed to play and game;* in ernest, *with seriousness, opposed to play and game*
ernestful, *serious, opposed to playful*
ernestfully, ernystfully, *with serious intent*
ernestly, *seriously*
erren, *err, stray, sin;* errith, *errs, strays from correct belief*
erringe, *straying*
Estryn, *Easter*
evel, *evil; see also* ivel, yvel
everlastande, everelastinge, *everlasting, eternal*
expresse, *(v.) express, speak*
expresse, *(adv.) specifically*
exsaumplen, *show by example;* exsaumplide, exsawmpplid, *displayed, set forth as examples (to be followed)*

fadir, fadre, fadur, *father;* fader, *(n., s. gen.) father's;* fadirs, *(n., pl. gen.) fathers'*
fautours, fawtours, *patrons, persons who encourage (especi-*

ally to do something reprehensible)
feding, fedinge, *feeding, indulging*
feerely, ferely, *(adv.) altogether, commonly (in a group)*
feerful, ferful, *fearful, horrible*
feigned, feined, feinyd, *false, feigned*
feith, *faith, implying trust and loyalty*
felawchip, felawchipe, felawschipe, *fellowship*
fellen, *fell*
fer, *far; much*
festnyd, *fastened, attached*
figure, *(n.) type, prefiguring*
figuren, *(v.) prefigure, foreshadow;* figurid, *prefigured, foreshadowed*
figuride, *in typological interpretation, that which is foreshadowed*
fine, *end (reward)*
fle, fleen, *(v.) flee, escape;* fleyinge, *(pr.p.) fleeing, escaping*
fleisch, fleysh, fleyssh, fleyshe, fleysche, flesche, fleyss, flessh, *flesh, the body, as opposed to the spirit*
fleyshly, fleysly, fleschely, *fleshly, as opposed to spiritual*
flode, *flood;* flodis, *(n., pl.) floods;* gret flood, *Noah's Flood*
folc, *people*
foly, folye, *folly, foolishness, without sense or rationality*
folily, *foolishly*
foolis, *(n., gen. pl.) fools'*
forbede, *forbid;* forbeden, forbedyn, forbedun, forbode, *forbidden, prohibited*
forseid, *aforesaid*
forsothe, *(as intensive) truly*
fortune, ffortune, *fortune, Fortuna, goddess of luck;* fortunes, *(n., gen.) Fortune's*
fre, *freeborn*
frely, *(adv.) freely*
frend, frynde, *friend*
frenschip, *friendship*
frer, frere, *friar;* freris, *friars;* frer minours, *friars minor, Franciscans*
frynde, *see* frend
furthe, *fourth*

gabben, *(v.) chatter*
gadering, *gathering, people in a group*
gamen, *game, including play acting;* somergame, *summer game*
gastful, *aghast, terrified*
geten, *get, obtain;* gat, *got, received*
gideren, *(v.) gather*
gife, gifen, give, given, giveth, *give;* givis, *gives;* gaf, *gave;* given, goven, *given;* giving, *giving*
gin, ginne, *trap;* ginnys, *(n., pl.)*

snares, enticements
ginne, *(v.) begin;* gan, *began*
ginninge, *beginning*
gladen, *become glad, happy*
gode, good, *good; morally strong; opposed to evil*
go, gon, *go*
gostly, *spiritual*
goun, *gown*
goven, *see* gife
great, greet, gret, grete, grette, *(adj.) great;* grettere, *greater*
greve, *grieve; afflict with pangs of conscience*
grevys, *thickets*
groundyd, *grounded, firmly based*
grucche, grucchen, *complain, grumble*

haat, *see* haten
hadden, *(v.) had; add, increase*
halowyn, *honor (as holy)*
halowyd, *(adj.) hallowed, consecrated*
ham, *them*
hamer, *hammer*
han, *have*
han, *(art.) an*
handwymmen, hoond wymmen, *handwomen, (female) servants*
harke, *ark (of the covenant)*
haten, haat, *(v.) hate;* hatedist, *hated*
hauteyn, *(adj.) haughty*
hay, *grass*
hede, hide, *heed*
heer, heere, here, *here*
heie, hegh, hih, *(adj.) high; great*
Helise, Helisee, *Elisha*
helpely, *helpful, affording help*
hem, *(pron.) them;* hemself, hemsilf, *themselves*
henhaunce, *see* enhaunce
hennys, *hence*
her, here, *their*
herby, *hereby, thus*
herbyforn, *previously*
here, heeren, heren, hern, herith, *(v.) hear;* herith, *hears;* herd, *heard;* heringe, *(pr.p.) hearing*
heringe, heryinge, *praising, worshipping*
herisie, *heresy, impermissible belief*
Heroudis, *Herod*
hert, *heart*
hest, heste, heest, heeste, *(n.) command;* hestis, *(n., pl.) commands*
hethene, *(adj.) heathen, non-Christian, implying Islamic*
heved, hevyd, *head*
hevene, *heaven*
hevy, *heavy (of mood), sorrowful*
hevinesse, *sorrow*
hyand, *see* hyinge
hide, *see* heed
hidous, hidouse, *terrible, dreadful*
hih, *see* heie
hyinge, hyand, *(pr.p.) hurrying,*

hastening
hir, hyr, *her*
hise, *these*
hit, *it*
hog-hyerd, *swineherd*
holde, holden, *hold; embrace; maintain; agree;* holdith, *holds, entertains;* holde, holden, holdun, yholde, *held*
holiy, *holy*
holy writt, *holy writings, bible*
homely, *(adv.) familiarly*
hond, *hand;* hondis, *(n., pl.) hands*
honoryn, *(v.) honor, venerate;* honouriden, *worshipped*
hool, *(adj.) whole*
hoole, *(n.) whole*
hooly, *(adv.) entirely*
hopiden, hopide, *(v.) hoped;* hopinge, *(pr.p.) hoping*
horedom, *whoredom*
hou, hough, *how*
houre, *(pron.) their*
hous, hows, *house*

idil, *idle; giving in to sloth*
idilnesse, idlenesse, *slothfulness;* idilnessis *(n., pl.)*
idilschip, *idleness, sloth*
yif, *if*
ypocrisie, *hypocrisy, pretending to be that which one is not*
ypocritis, *hypocrites*
irene, *iron*
Isidre, *Isidore (of Seville)*
ivel, yvel, yvele, yvil, *(adj.) evil, sinful*
yvel, yvele, yvil, *(n.) evil, wrongdoing, sinful*
iyen, *see* eyen

japen, japun, *(v.) jest, mock; trick (sometimes with the sense of seduce)*
japeris, *(n., pl.) scoffers, tricksters; jesters*
japing, japinge, *joking, mocking (possibly ribaldry)*
japinge stikke, *laughing stock; fool stick (figurative)*
japis, *(n., pl.) tricks, ribaldry, fraud*

kindam, *kingdom, e.g., heaven*
kinde, *(n.) nature*
kinde, *(adj.) kind, solicitous*
knowlechist, *(v.) have knowledge, awareness*
kunning, *knowledge, learning, wisdom*

lakking, lakkinge, *(pr.p.) lacking*
lasse, *(adj.) less*
lassen, *(v.) subtract, decrease*
lawying, lawghing, *(pr.p.) laughing*
lawrer, *laurel, prize for accomplishment*
leaute, leute, *(n.) faith*
lecchour, *adulterer*
ledere, *(n.) leader*
ledyn, *(v.) lead*
leesith, *loses*

leeve, leeven, leevyn, leven, *cease, reject, abandon, discontinue;* leevinge, leving, *(pr.p.) rejecting, turning aside from; failing*
leful, leveful, leeveful, *(adj.) allowable, lawful*
lefully, *(adv.) allowably*
lesing, lesinge, leesing, *lie, untruth;* lesingis, *lies*
lest, leste, *least*
lettris, *letters*
lewed, lewid, *unlearned*
licnesse, lickenesse, *likeness, appearance*
lie, lyen, liyn, *lie, deceive;* lieth, lyith, *lies, deceives;* lyinge, *(pr.p.) lying, deceiving*
lieris, *(n., pl.) liars*
light, *(adj.) easy, joyful*
lighte, *(v.) alighted, entered*
lightly, *(adv.) easily, casually*
liyn, *see* lie, lyen
liking, likinge, *pleasure;* likingis, *pleasures, sinful feelings*
liste, *desires*
lond, *land*
loose, *loss*
lovelich, *(adj.) beautiful, implying kind*
loven, lovyn, *love, worship;* lovyth, *loves, worships;* lovyd, *loved*
lowen, lowyn, *(v.) laugh*
loweth, *descends*
lust, *desire;* lustis, lustus, *(n., pl.) desires*
maad, *made*
Mahoun, *Mohammed (pejorative)*
mainteyned, meintenyd, *persevered in; sustained, supported*
maintenours, *supporters, patrons, with a suggestion of abetting those who do wrong*
maister, *master;* maistris, *(n., gen.) master's*
maner, maneer, *manner; sort*
maners, *customs*
manhode, *(Christ's) human nature*
mannes sonne, *Son of Man, Christ*
mannisch, mannische, *(adj.) human*
Martis, *(gen.) Mars'*
maumetre, maumetrie, maumetree, maumetrye, *idolatry*
maundement, *commandment*
mawmete, *idol;* mawmetis, *(n., pl.) idols*
mede, *(n.) reward*
medeful, *meriting reward*
medelid, medelyd, medlid, *(v.) mingled, mixed*
meke, *meek, humble, opposite of pride, which is chief of Seven Deadly Sins*
mekely, *(adv.) humbly*
mekenesse, *humility*
mekid, *made meek, humbled*
mene, *means, way of achieving (a particular end);* menes, *means, ways of achieving (an end)*

mengde, mingid, *(v.) mingled, mixed;* menging, *mixing (in a confused way)*
mengid, *(adj.) mixed, mingled; confused*
menis, *(n., pl.) men;* menis, mennes, mennis, mennus, *(n., pl. gen.) men's*
meste, *most, greatest*
mervelous, mervelouse, *marvelous*
mete, *food*
miche, myche, *much*
middes, *midst; middle*
mind, minde, *remembrance, memory; thought; mind*
ministre, ministren, *administer*
miracle, *(n.) miracle (of Christ or his saints);* miraclis, *(n., pl.)* miracles (of Christ or of saints)
myracles, miraclis, miriclis, *(n., pl.) plays (see also Introduction, above);* miraclis, *(n., pl. gen.) miracles'*
mirthe, merthe, *joy, pleasure;* mirthes, mirthis, *pleasures*
misbileve, *erroneous belief*
mistryst, *distrust*
mistristing, *distrusting, lacking in confidence in*
misusith, *distorts*
mo, *more*
moche, mochel, *(adj.) great*
modir, modre, *mother*
morning, mourninge, *mourning;* bymoornyden, *mourned*
mot, moot, moten, *must*
moven, *entice, encourage;* movyd, *moved, influenced; affected*
mowen, *may, might*
murdre, mordre, *murder*

nakid, nakyd, *naked, plain and unadorned*
namely, *particularly, especially*
nat, *not*
ne, *nor*
nede, nedith, *(v.) need*
nedeful, *necessary*
nedis, *(n., pl.) needs (requiring charity)*
neibore, neiebore, *neighbor;* neighboris, negheboris, neghyeboris, neieburs, *neighbors*
neighen, *(v.) draw near, approach;* neghing, *(pr.p.) approaching, drawing near*
never the latere, *nevertheless*
nyle, *do not (contraction of* ne wile*)*
Noe, Noye, *Noah*
noon, *(adj.) no*
noten, *notice*
nou, *now*
nouther . . . ne, *neither . . . nor*

obeschaunce, *obeisance, obedience, submission, compliance*
ocupien, *(v.) engage;* ocuped, ocupied, ocupiede, *engaged;* ocupyinge, *engaging*
ony, *any*

onys, *once*
on live, *alive*
oo, oon, *one*
opynly, *(adv.) openly, manifestly, publicly*
othere while, *sometimes*
oune, *own*
outher . . . outher, *either . . . or*
overveinliche, *utterly in vain*
owith, *ought, is obligated to*

pacience, paciencie, *patience*
parcel, *part;* parcelis, perselis, *(n., pl.) parts, portions or segments*
parceners, *see* percener
Parchas, *Fates in Greek mythology*
parlous, *dangerous*
party, partie, partye, *(n.) part, share*; partis, *(n., pl.) parts*
passid, *past*
Paternoster, *Lord's Prayer*
peyen, *pay;* payid, *paid, pleased*
pecible, *peaceable*
peintid, *(adj.) painted*
peintinge, *painting*
peintour, *painter, artist*
peinture, *paintings*
pens, *pence*
peple, puple, *people, especially in a group or associated with a particular place;* peples, *(n., pl. gen.) people's*
peraventur, peraventure, *(adv.) perhaps (by chance)*
percener, *partner, partaker, sharer;* parceners, perceneris, *(n., pl.) partners, sharers*
pere, *equal (in the social order)*
perilis, *(n., pl.) dangers*
persin, person, persone, *person*
player, playere, *(n.) player, actor;* pleyeris, *actors, but also participants in a game; musicians*
pley, *(n.) drama (as enacted); also game, sport;* pleyes, pleyis, pleyys, *(n., pl.) plays, games*
pley, pleye, pleyen, pleyin, pleyn, pleyne, *(v.) play, acting or recreation; play a musical instrument;* pleyith, *plays;* pleyed, pleyide, pleyiden, *played*; pleying, pleyinge, pleynge, *playing (in theatricals or games)*
plesaunt, *pleasing (to God)*
plesauntly, *pleasingly (with respect to God)*
plesen, plesyn, *please, satisfy;* plesid, *satisfied*
plesingly, *(adv.) acceptably (for the sake of God's pleasure)*
plonged, *descended*
pore, *plain*
povert, povertie, *poverty, condition of economic deprivation*
preche, prechen, *preach;* prechid, *preached*
preyere, *prayer;* preyeris, *(n., pl.) prayers*

preyen, *(v.) pray;* preinge, preying, *praying*
preisith, *praises;* preiseden, preisiden, *praised*
prest, prist, *priest;* prestis, pristis, priestis, *(n., pl.) priests*
Priamus, *Priam, king of Troy*
pris, *(n.) price, value*
prist, *see* prest
pristhode, *priesthood, ordination*
provyn, *prove, demonstrate;* proveth, *proves*
Psauter book, *psalter, book of psalms*
puple, *see* peple
pursuede, suede, *pursued, followed*
put, puttun, *put;* puttith, *puts*

quen, *queen*
quick, quik, quike, *living, opposed to dead*

rebaudye, ribaudye, *ribaldry, immorality, immodest jesting*
rede, reden, riden, *(v.) read; recognize*
regnyde, *ruled*
rehersid, *remembered, repeated, recited, narrated*
rein, *rain*
rekeninge, *reckoning, judgment*
religious, *clergy*
repref, *(n.) reproof*
reprovable, reprowable, *reprehensible, shameful*
reprovyd, reprovyde, *reproved, rebuked;* reproving, *rebuking*
reson, resoun, resun, *reason*
revers, reverse, *(n.) the opposite*
reversen, reversyn, *(v.) invert or turn upside down, contradict;* reversith, *reverses, inverts, turns upside down;* reversiden, *reversed;* reversing, *(pr.p.) contradicting, reversing*
riden, *see* reden
right, *(adj.) right; correct*
right, riht, rit, *(adv.) hence*
rightwise, *(adj.) righteous, legitimate*
ritwesnes, rightwessnesse, *righteousness, rectitude*
ros, *rose (in resurrection);* risen, *rose*
rude, *uneducated, unlearned*

savacion, *salvation*
sche, *she*
scheding, *shedding*
schewen, *show, demonstrate;* schewid, *shown, revealed;* schewiden, shewiden, *showed, demonstrated*
schort, *short*
schuld, schulde, shulde, schulden, shulden, schuldest, shuldest, schuldist, shuldist, *should*
se, seen, seyen, *(v.) see;* seen, seyn, *seen;* seeing, seeinge, seing, seinge, *(pr.p.) seeing*
sechen, *seek;* seckith, sekith,

seeks
seelde, *seldom, rarely*
seemely, *seemly, attractive in appearance*
seye, seyn, seyen, seist, *say;* seith, *says;* seiden, *said;* seying, seyinge, *(pr.p.) saying*
sein, seint, *saint;* seintes, seintis, *(n., pl.) saints*
seme, semen, *seem, appear;* semys, semyth, *seems, appears;* seming, *seeming;* in seming, *as if*
sentense, *(allegedly) authoritative opinion*
seremonies, *ceremonies*
serve, serven, *serve*
service, servise, *religious service, office*
seside, *ceased*
sett, sette, *set, establish;* settith, *sets, establishes;* setteden, *set;* settinge, *setting, placing*
shende, *disgrace*
shent, *disgraced*
shew, showe, *show, appearance*
shoures, *showers*
shrewe, *(n.) rogue, villain*
shrewidenesse, shrewidnesse, *wickedness, maliciousness*
shrewyn, *(v.) scold or curse;* bishrewed, *cursed;* shrewinge, *(pr.p.) scolding or cursing*
shul, *shall*
siche, *such*
sight, sighte, *sight, spectacle;* sightes, sightis, *sights, spectacles*
sight, sighte, *sight, ability to see*
signe, *sign;* signes, signis, singnis, singnys, *(n., pl.) signs*
siker, sikir, *(adv.) surely, credibly*
silf, *self*
sites, *sees*
sith, sithe, sithen, sithis, *since, because*
skilful, *(adj.) reasonable, rational*
sle, *(v.) slay, kill;* sleeth, *slays, kills;* sleyn, *slain*
slidir, *(adj.) slippery, treacherous*
smite, *hit;* smiten, *driven, smitten*
sodayne, sodein, sodeine, sodeyn, *sudden*
sodaynly, sodeinly, sodeynely, *(adv.) suddenly*
sofisen, *see* suffise
somyr, *summer*
sonder, *sunder, break apart*
sone, *(n.) son;* sones, *(n., pl.) sons*
sone, sonne, *(n.) sun*
sone, *(adv.) soon, quickly*
songe, *(v.) sung*
sorewe, sorowe, *sorrow, unhappiness*
sorwinge, *sorrowing*
sothely, sothly, *(adv.) truly*
souner, *sooner*
soure, *sore, bitter*
spedely, *quickly*

speeke, *speak;* spekyth, *speaks;* spac, spak, *spake*
spinnyn, *(v.) spin (wool)*
spirit, spirite, *spirit; soul, as distinguished from body;* spiritus, *(n., gen.) spirit's*
spoiling, *(pr.p.) despoiling, robbing*
stant, *consists*
statys, *conditions*
steyen, *(v.) rise;* steyede, *went (up);* steye, *(imper.) go up*
steracle, *dramatic spectacle*; steracles, *(n., pl.)*
steryn, stiren, *(v.) stimulate;* stiring, *(pr.p.) encouraging, stimulating*
styinge, *rising, i.e., climbing*
suede, *see* pursuede
suerte, *certainty*
suffere, *suffer;* suffrith, *suffers, endures;* suffred, *endured*
suffice, suffisen, sofisen, *suffice;* suffisith, *is sufficient*
suffraunce, *long suffering, endurance*
suffring, *enduring*
supprised, *?surprised*
swerd, *sword*
swering, sweringe, *swearing, cursing*
swete, *sweet, pleasant*
swetnesse, *sweetness, delight*
swich, swyche, *such*

take, takun, *take; receive;* takith, *takes;* taken, takyn, takun, *taken;* toke, tooc, *took;* taking, takinge, *taking, removing;* tac, take, *(imper.) take*
tarriere, *(n.) lingerer; one who holds back*
tastiden, *tasted*
teche, *teach;* techith, *teaches, informs;* teching, *(pr.p.) teaching*
teching, *(n.) teaching, doctrine*
tenyd, *(v.) grieved*
teris, *tears*
thenken, *(v.) think, consider;* thenkes, thenkith, *thinks, considers;* thenkinge, *considering; remembering*
than, thanne, *(adv.) then*
the, *(pron.) thee*
ther, *(pron.) their*
tho, *(pron.) those*
thof, *though*
thrall, *bondservant*
threed, *thread;* lives threed, *thread of life*
thretith, *(v.) threaten;* threting, *(pr.p.) threatening*
thridde, *third*
throwyn, *lay (upon), throw;* throwen, thrown, *cast out;* throwinge, *throwing, laying (upon)*
thurgh, *(prep.) through*
tide, *time*
to, *too*
tobrokun, *broken, disobeyed*
togidere, togydere, *together, at*

the same time
tokne, *token, sign;* tokenes, *(n., pl.) (outward) signs*
ton, *one*
tooc, *see* take
toon, *the one*
tother, *the other*
totoren, *torn apart*
toun, *town*
tourne, *turn, fashion*
travele, traveile, *(n.) labor (sometimes oppressive); effort; troubles*
travelinge, traveilinge, *(pr.p.) laboring, troubling*
travelous, *oppressive, wearisome*
trete, treytyn, *take, handle*
treuthe, trewth, trewthe, trowe, trowthe, trwthe, *truth;* trewthis, *truths*
trew, trewe, trwe, *(adj.) true*
trewly, *truly*
triste, *sorrowful of mood*
tristesse, *(n.) sorrow*
tristus, *trusts, has confidence in;* tristenede, *trusted;* tristing, *(pr.p.) trusting*
tunge, *speech, language*
turne, *turn, transform;* turneth, *turns, converts;* turnyd, turnyde, *turned;* turning, turninge, *turning, converting, transforming*
two so myche, *twice as much*

undisposith, *makes (one) undisposed*
unkinde, *against nature*
unkindely, *unnaturally; ungratefully*
unkindenesse, *unnaturalness*
unknowing, *not knowing, ignorant*
unleful, *prohibited, unlawful*
unsckilfuly, *unreasonably, to an unreasonable extent*
unswete, *unsweet, unpleasant*
untrewe, *false*
unwarely, *without taking heed*

vaniteis, *(n., pl.) vanities*
vein, veine, *vain, lacking in value*
veleinye, *see* vilenye
venjaunce, venjaunse, *vengeance, retribution*
verely, verily, verreyly, verrily, werrily, *(adv.) actually*
verry, verre, verrey, verry, werre, werrey, werry, *(adj.) actual, true*
vertu, vertue, *virtue, moral strength*
vetailis, *(n., pl.) victuals*
vicis, *vices*
vilenye, veleinye, *villainy, indignity, dishonor, malice*
viseres, *masks*
visiting, *visitation, as when God comes to comfort one*
voice, vois, *voice*

waiteris, *(n., gen. pl.) those who wait*

waitinge, *attending*
wantes, *(v.) is lacking*
wantown, *wanton, unrestrained*
wastid, *(v.) laid waste, destroyed*
watte, *(imper.) know*
waxen, *grow;* waxith, *grows;* waxen, *grown*
wede, *(v.) become insane*
weye, *way;* weies, weyys, *ways, paths where persons might pass*
weilen, *lament;* weiliden, *lamented*
wenen, *(v.) think*
wepe, wepen, wepyn, *(v.) weep;* wepten, *wept;* weping, wepinge, *(pr.p.) weeping*
weren, wern, *were*
wery, *weary*
weryen, *(v.) tire;* weryinge, *(pr. p.) tiring, referring to those who have become weary*
werinesse, *weariness*
werkis, *(n., pl.) works*
werre, werry, werrey, *see* verre *(adj.)*
werrily, *see* verely *(adv.)*
werse, *worse*
whanne, *when*
whelmed, *overwhelmed*
wherthoru, *by means of which*
whil, while, *while, time*
whilom, *formerly*
wicke, *wicked*
wickidnesse, *wickedness, sinfulness, evil*
wyenges, *wings*
wyilde, *wild*
wijf, *wife*
wil, wile, wilen, willen, wilt, *(v.) will*
will, wille, *(n.) will, volition*
wymmen, *(n., pl.) women*
wis, wise, *intelligent, wise*
wise, *manner, as in "the same wise"*
wite, *(n.) sense, mind;* wittis, *(n., pl.) wits*
witen, wote, *(v.) know;* woost, *(2sg. pres. ind.) know*
withinneforthe, *within, inwardly*
withouteforth, withoutforthe, *outwardly*
wode, *wood, forest*
wolde, wolden, woldest, wolen, wolt, *would*
wonninges, *(n., pl.) dwellings*
woost, *see* witen
worchen, worschen, *(v.) work;* worchith, *works;* worching, *(pr.p.) working*
worschip, worschipe, *(n.) worship, honor*
worschipen, *(v.) worship, honor;* worschipith, *worships, honors;* worschipid, *worshipped, honored;* worschipiden, *worshipped, honored;* worschiping, *worshipping, honoring*
wote, *see* witen
wrathen, *(v.) rage (against), resist*
wrooth, *(n.) unwilling (to the point of anger), hating*

yerd, yerde, yird, *rod*
yhe, *yea*
yif, *(prep.) if*
yilding, *giving up*
yole, *Yule, Christmas*

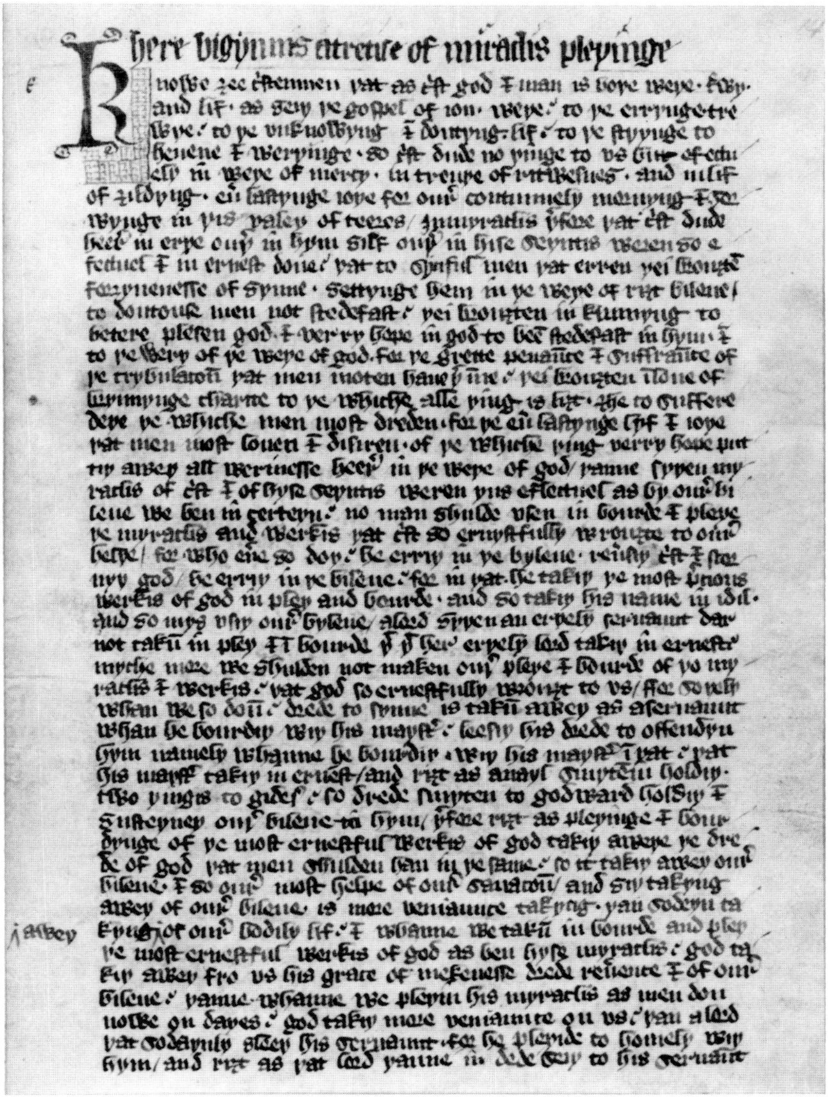

Here bigynnis a tretise of miraclis pleyinge

Knowe ȝee cristen men þat as crist god & man is boþe weye · trewþe
and lif · as seiþ þe gospel of ion · weye to þe erringe trew
þe to þe unkunnynge & doutynge lif · to þe styinge to
hevene & weryinge · so crist dude noþinge to us but effectu
ely in weye of mercy · in treuþe of ritwesnes · and in lif
of ȝildyng · everlastinge ioye for oure continuely mornyng & sor
wynge in þis valey of teeres / miraclis þerfore þat crist dude
heere in erþe outher in hym silf outher in hise seyntis weren so e
ffectuel & in ernest done · þat to synful men þat erren þei brouȝten
forȝyvenesse of synne · settynge hem in þe weye of riȝt bileve /
to doutouse men not stedefast · þei brouȝten in kunnyng to
betere plesen god & verry hope in god to been stedefast in hym · &
to þe wery of þe weye of god · for þe grette penaunce & suffraunce of
þe tribulacioun þat men moten have þerinne · þei brouȝten in þe love of
brennynge charite to þe whiche alle þing is liȝt · ȝhe to suffere
deþe þe whiche men most dreden · for þe everlastynge lif & ioye
þat men most loven & disiren · of þe whiche þing verry hope put
tiþ awey all werinesse heere in þe weye of god / þanne syþen my
raclis of crist & of hyse seyntis weren þus effectuel as by oure bi
leve we ben in certeyn · no man shulde usen in bourde & pleye
þe myraclis and werkis þat crist so ernystfully wrouȝte to oure
helþe / for who ever so doþ · he erriþ in þe byleve · reversiþ crist & scor
niþ god / he erriþ in þe bileve · for in þat he takiþ þe most precious
werkis of god in pley and bourde · and so takiþ his name in idil ·
and so mysusiþ oure byleve / a lord syþen an erþely servaunt dar
not takun in pley & in bourde þat þat his erþely lord takiþ in ernest ·
myche more we shulden not maken oure pleye & bourde of þo my
raclis & werkis þat god so ernestfully wrouȝt to us / for soþely
whan we so doun drede to synne is takun awey as a servaunt
whan he bourdiþ wiþ his mayster leesiþ his drede to offendyn
hym namely whanne he bourdiþ wiþ his mayster in þat þat
his mayster takiþ in ernest / and riȝt as a nayl smyten in holdiþ
two þingis togidere so drede smyten to godward holdiþ &
susteyneþ oure bileve to hym / þerfore riȝt as pleyinge & bour
dynge of þe most ernestful werkis of god takiþ aweye þe dre
de of god þat men shulden han in þe same · so it takiþ awey oure
bileve & so oure most helpe of oure savacioun / and siþ takyng
awey of oure bileve is more venjaunce takyng · þan sodeyn ta
kyng awey of oure bodily lif · & whanne we takun in bourde and pley
þe most ernestful werkis of god as ben hyse myraclis · god ta
kiþ awey fro us his grace of mekenesse drede reverence & of oure
bileve · þanne whanne we pleyen his myraclis as men don
nowe on dayes · god takiþ more venjaunce on us · þan a lord
þat sodaynly sleeþ his servaunt for he pleyide to homely wiþ
hym / and riȝt as þat lord þanne in dede seiþ to his servaunt

1. British Library, Add. MS. 24,202, fol. 14[r].

2. British Library, Add. MS. 24,202, fol. 14v.

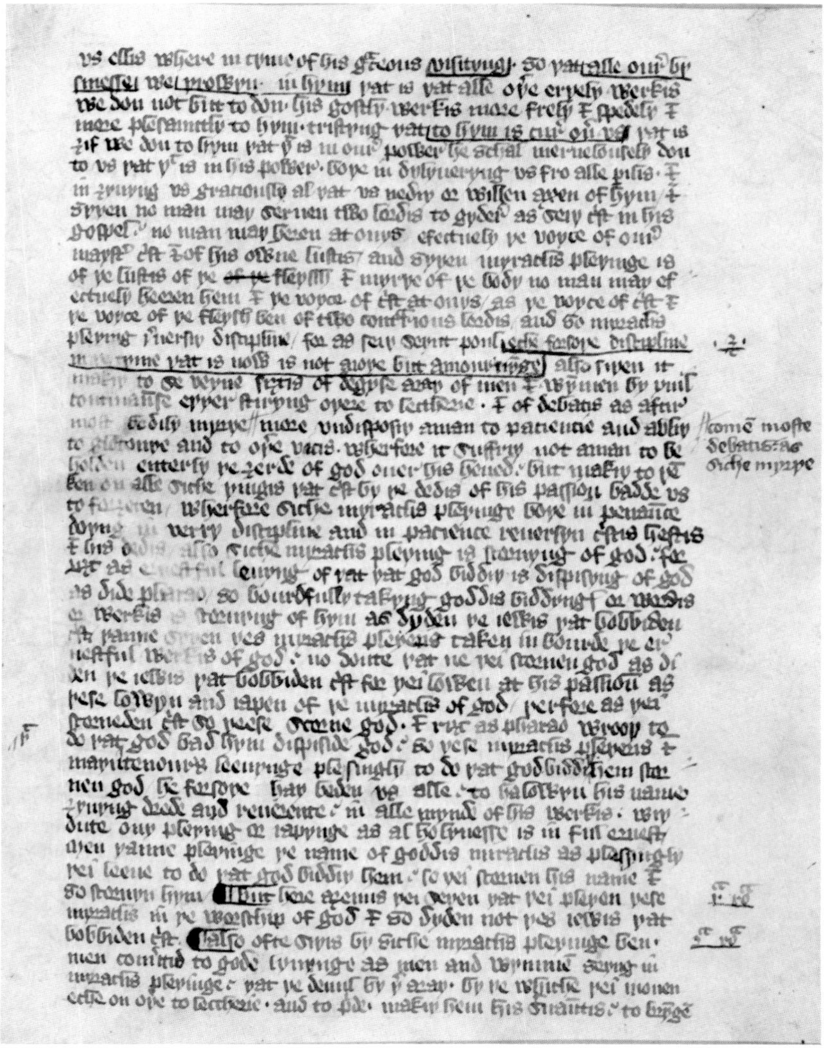

vs ellis where in tyme of his gracious visityng. so þat alle oure bi-
synesse we moven in hym þat is þat alle oþer erþely werkis
we don not but to don his gostly werkis more frely & spedely &
more plesauntly to hym. tristyng þat to hym is cure of vs/ þat is
ȝif we don to hym þat þat is in oure power he schal merveylously don
to vs þat þat is in his power. boþe in delyueryng vs fro alle perils. &
in ȝyuyng vs graciously al þat vs nedyþ or willen axen of hym/ &
syþen no man may serven two lordis to gyder as seiþ crist in his
gospel. no man may heren at onys efectuely þe voyce of oure
maystir crist & of his owne lustis/ and syþen myraclis pleyinge is
of þe lustis of þe ~~of þe~~ fleysh & myrþe of þe body no man may ef-
fectuely heeren hem & þe voyce of crist at onys/ as þe voyce of crist &
þe voyce of þe fleysh ben of two contrarious lordis. and so myraclis
pleyinge reversiþ discipline/ for as seiþ seint poul eche forsoþe discipline .2.
in þe tyme þat is now is not of ioye but of mourninge/ also siþen it
makiþ to se veyne siȝtis of degyse aray of men & wymmen by yuil
continaunse eyþer stiryng oþere to leccherie. & of debatis as aftir
most bodily myrþe/ more vndisposiþ a man to pacience and ablith | come moste
to glotonye and to oþer vicis. wherfore it suffriþ not a man to be- | debatis as
holden enterly þe ȝerd of god over his heued. but makiþ to for- | siche myrþe
ȝeten alle suche þingis þat crist by þe dedis of his passion badde vs
to þenken. wherfore suche myraclis pleyinge boþe in penaunce
doyng in verry discipline and in pacience reversyn cristis hestis
& his dedis. also suche myraclis pleying is scornyng of god. for
riȝt as ernestful leeuyng of þat þat god biddiþ is dispisyng of god
as dide pharao. so bourdfully takyng goddis biddyngis or wordis
or werkis is scornyng of hym as diden þe iewis þat bobbiden
crist þanne syþen þes myraclis pleyeris taken in bourde þe ernestful werkis of god. no doute þat ne þei scornen god as diden þe iewis þat bobbiden crist for þei lowen at his passion as
þese lowyn and iapen of þe myraclis of god/ þerfore as þei
scorneden crist so þese scornen god. & riȝt as pharao wroþ to
do þat god bad hym dispiside god. so þese myraclis pleyeris &
maynteneris leevinge plesingly to do þat god biddiþ hem scornen god. he forsoþe hath beden vs alle. to halowen his name
ȝyuyng drede and reuerence in alle mynde of his werkis. wiþoute ony pleyinge or iapynge as al holynesse is in ful ernestful men þanne pleyinge þe name of goddis miraclis as plesingly
þei leeue to do þat god biddiþ hem so þei scornen his name &
so scornyn hym. but here aȝenus þei seyen þat þei pleyen þese
myraclis in þe worschip of god & so diden not þes iewis þat
bobbiden crist. also ofte sythis by siche myraclis pleyinge ben
men converted to gode lyvynge as men and wymmen seyng in
myraclis pleyinge þat þe devul by her aray by þe whiche þei moven
eche on oþer to leccherie and to pride makiþ hem his servauntis to bringe

3. British Library, Add. MS. 24,202, fol. 15r.

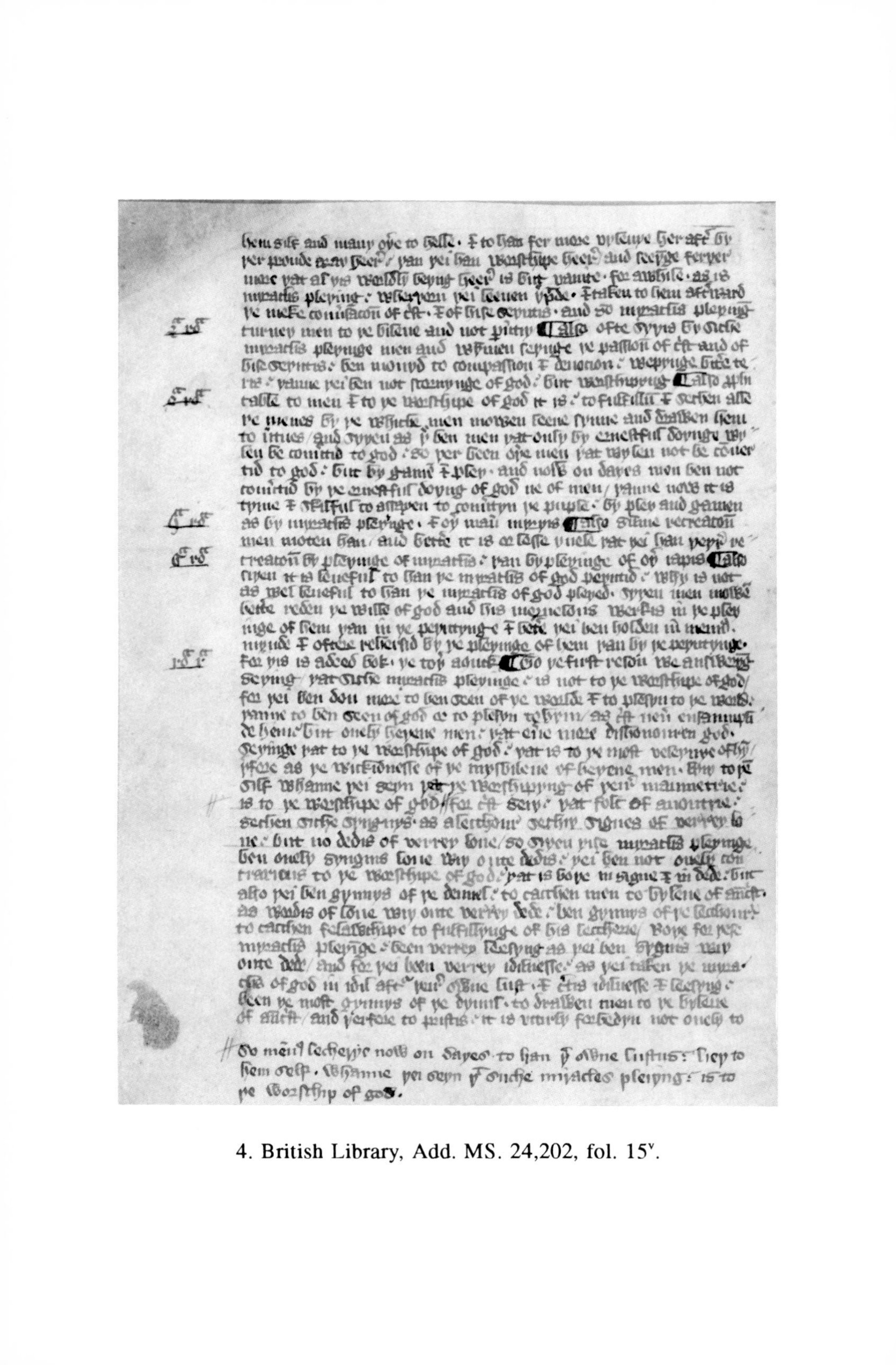

4. British Library, Add. MS. 24,202, fol. 15v.

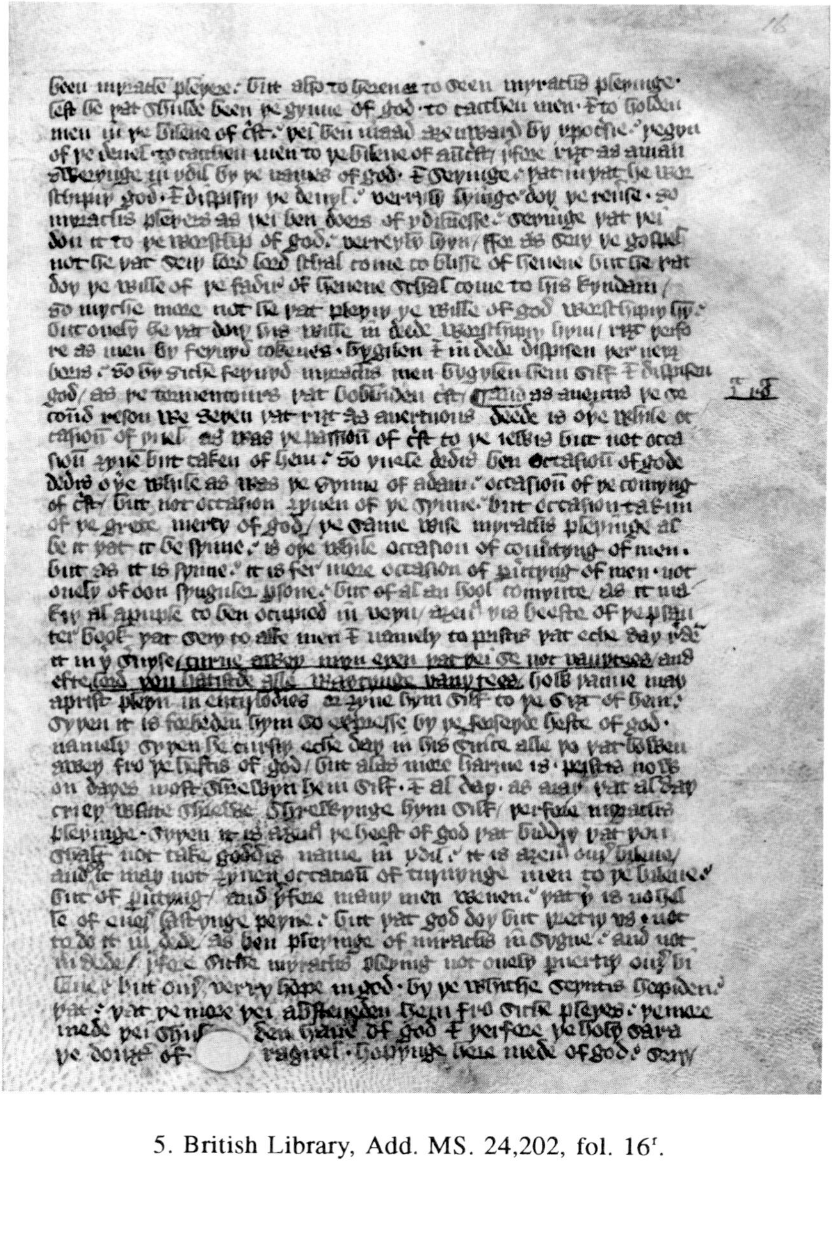

been myraclis pleyere. but also to bileeve to seen myraclis pleyinge·
lest he þat shulde been þe gynne of god· to cacchen men· & to holden
men in þe bileve of crist. þei ben maad [illegible] by ypocrisie. þe gyn
of þe devel· to cacchen men to þe bileve of anticrist / þerfore riȝt as a man
swerynge in veyn by þe names of god· & seyinge þat in þat he wor-
shipiþ god· & dispisiþ þe devel. verily lyinge doþ þe reverse· so
myraclis pleyers as þei ben doers of ydilnesse. seyinge þat þei
don it to þe worschip of god. verreyly lyen / for as seiþ þe gospel
not he þat seiþ lord lord shal come to blisse of hevene but he þat
doþ þe wille of þe fadir of hevene shal come to his kyngdam /
so myche more not he þat pleyiþ þe wille of god worschipiþ hym.
but onely he þat doþ his wille in dede worschipiþ hym / riȝt þerfore as men by feyned tokenes· bygilen & in dede dispisen her neiȝ-
bours. so by siche feyned myraclis men bygilen hem silf & dispisen
god / as þe tormentours þat bobbiden crist / [illegible] as auctours þe se- [illegible]
cond reson we seyen þat riȝt as ernestful dede is oþer while oc-
casion of perel as was þe passion of crist to þe iewis but not occasion ȝyven but taken of hem. so yvele dedis ben occasion of gode
dedis oþer while as was þe synne of adam. occasion of þe comyng
of crist / but not occasion ȝyven of þe synne· but occasion takun
of þe grete mercy of god / þe same wise myraclis pleyinge al
be it þat it be synne. is oþer while occasion of convertyng of men.
but as it is synne. it is fer more occasion of pervertyng of men· not
onely of oon singuler persone. but of al an hool comynte as it makiþ al a puple to ben ocupied in veyn / aȝenus þis heeste of þe sau-
ter book þat seiþ to alle men & namely to prestis þat eche day reden
it in her servyse / turne awey myn eyen þat þei se not vanytees / and
efte / lord þou hatidist alle waytynge vanytees. how þanne may
a prest pleyn in entirlodies or ȝyve hym silf to þe siȝt of hem.
syþen it is forbeden hym so expresse by þe forseyde heste of god·
namely syþen he cursiþ eche day in his servise alle þo þat bowen
awey fro þe hestis of god / but alas more harme is· prestis now
on dayes most shrewen hem silf· & al day· as a man þat al day
crieþ [illegible] shrewynge hym silf / þerfore myraclis
pleyinge· syþen it is aȝenus þe heest of god þat biddiþ þat þou
shalt not take goddis name in ydil. it is aȝenus oure bileve /
and it may not ȝyven occasioun of turnynge men to þe bileve.
but of pervertyng / and þerfore many men wenen. þat þer is no helle of everlastinge peyne. but þat god doþ but þretiþ us & not
to do it in dede / as ben pleyinge of myraclis in signe. and not
in dede / þerfore siche myraclis pleyinge not onely perverteþ oure bileve but oure verry hope in god· by þe whiche seyntis hopiden.
þat [illegible] þat þe more þei absteneden hem fro siche pleyes. þe more
mede þei shul[illegible] ben have of god & þerfore þe holy sara
þe douȝter of [illegible] raguel· hopynge here mede of god. seiþ/

5. British Library, Add. MS. 24,202, fol. 16r.

tobie 3o

seid þou woost þat neuere I coueitide man & clene I haue kept my
soule fro alle lustis / neuer wiþ pleyeris I myngid me my silf
and by þis trewe confessioun to god as sche hopide sche
hadde hir preyeris herd & grete mede of god / and syþen a
3onge womman of þe olde testament for kepyng of hir
bodily vertue of chastite & for to worþily take þe sacrament of
i man — matrimonye whanne hir tyme shulde come abstenyde hir
fro al ydil pleying & fro al cumpany of idil pleyeris myche
more a prist of þe newe testament þat is passid þe tyme of
childehod & þat not onely shulde kepe chastite but alle oþer
vertues ne onely mynystren þe sacrament of matrimonye but alle
oþer sacramentis & namely syþen hym owiþ to mynystre to
alle þe puple þe precious body of crist awghte to abstene hym
fro al ydil pleying boþe of myraclis & ellis / for certis syþen
þe quen of saba as seiþ crist in þe gospel schal dampne þe
iewis þat wolden not resseyve þe wisdom of crist myche more þis
holy womman sara at þe day of dom schal dampnen þe pristis
of þe newe testament þat 3yvis hem to pleyes reversen hir
holy maners aprouyd by god & by al holy chirche / þerfore sore
auwten pristis to be aschamyd þat reversen þis gode holy wo
man & þe precious body of crist þat þei treytyn in þer hondis.
þe whiche body neuer 3af hym to pley but to alle siche þing
as is most contrarious to pley / as is penaunce & suffryng of
persecucioun / and so þes myraclis pleyinge not onely reversiþ
feiþ & hope but verry charite by þe whiche a man shulde
weylen for his owne synne & for his neyeburs & namely
pristis for it withdrawiþ not onely oon persone but alle þe puple
fro dedis of charite & of penaunce in to dedis of lustis & likyn
gis & of feding of houre wittis / so þanne þes men þat seyen
pley we a pley of anticrist & of þe day of dome þat sum man
may be conuertid þerby fallen in to þe heresie of hem þat reuersyng
ad ro. 20 — þe apostele seyden do we yuel þingis þat þer comyn gode
þingis / of whom as seiþ þe same apostele dampnyng is riht
wise ¶ By þis we answeren to þe þridde resoun seyinge þat
siche myraclis pleyinge 3yuen occasioun of werpyng (wepyng) &
wepynge & medeful / but þe wepyng þat fallis to men & wy
men by þe si3te of siche myraclis pleyinge as þei ben not
principaly for þeire oune synnes ne of þeire gode feiþ wiþ in
forþe but more of þeir si3t wiþoute is not alowable
byfore god but more reprouable / for syþen crist hym silf re
prouyde þe wymmen þat wepten up on hym in his passioun myche
more þei ben reprouable þat wepen for þe pley of cristis
passioun leevynge to wepen for þe synnes of hem silf & of þeire
wepten — children / as crist bad þe wymmen þat [illegible] hym ¶ & by
þis we answeren to þe ferþe resoun seyinge [illegible] inge / þat no

6. British Library, Add. MS. 24,202, fol. 16v.

man may be convertid to god: but onely by þe ernestful doynge of
god & by noon veyn pleying. for þat þat þe word of god worchiþ not
ne his sacramentis: how shulde pleyinge worchen þat is of no vertue.
but ful of defaute. þerfore riȝt as þe weping þat men wepen ofte
in siche pley: comunely is fals wittnessinge: þat þei lovyn mo
re þe likyng of þeir body & of prosperite of þe world: þan likynge
in god & prosperite of vertu in þe soule and þerfore havyng more co
passion of peyne: þan of synne. þei falsly wepyn: for lakkynge
of bodily prosperite: more þan for lakkyng of gostly as don dampnyd
men in helle. riȝt so ofte sithis þe convertynge þat men semen
to ben convertid by siche pleyinge: is but feynyd holynesse: worse
þan is oþer synne biforehande. for ȝif he were verryly convertid:
he shulde haten to seen alle siche vanytes, as biddiþ þe hestis of
god. al be it: þat of siche pley he take occasion: by þe grace of
god to fle synne & to folowe vertu. and ȝif men seyn heere. þat
ȝif þis pleyinge of myraclis were synne: whi while god convertiþ
men: by þe occasion of siche pleyinge. heereto we seyen þat god
doþ so: for to comenden his mercy to us. þat we þenken en-
tierly: hou good god is to us: þat wiþil we ben þenkynge aȝeinis
him doynge wickidnesse & wrongly seyinge him: he þenkiþ upon
us good & sendynge us his grace: to fleen alle siche vanyte.
and for þer shulde no þinge be more swete to us þan siche maner
mercy of god: þe psalter book clepiþ þat mercy: blessynge of swetnesse ~~[illegible]~~ where he seiþ: þou cam bifore him in blessyngis
of swetnesse. þe whiche swetnesse al be it þat it be likynge
to þe spirit: it is while we ben here: ful traveilous to þe body.
whan it is verry as þe flesh and þe spirit: ben contrarious.
þerfore þis swetnesse in god in ..: wil not been verely had:
while a man is ocupied in seyinge of pleyis. þerfore þe prestis þat
seyn hem silf holy & bysien hem aboute siche pleyis: ben verry ypocritis and lieris. And herby we answeren to þe fifte resoun:
seyinge þat verry recreacion is leveful ocupyinge in lasse werkis: to more ardently werchen grettere werkis. and þerfore siche myraclis pleyinge ne þe sighte of hem is no verrey recreacion: but fals & worldly. as provyn þe dedis of þe fautouris
of siche pleyis þat ȝit nevere tastiden verely swetnesse in god
traveilynge so myche þerinne: þat þeir body wolde not sof-
fisen: to beren siche traveyle of þe spirite. but as man
goþ fro vertue into vertue: so þei gon fro lust into lust
þat þei more stedefastly dwellen in hem. and þerfore as þis
feynyd recreacion of pleyinge of myraclis is fals cunte: so it is
double shrewidnesse. worse þan þou þei pleyiden pure vanytees.
for now þe puple ȝyveþ credence to many mengid lesyngis
for oþer mengid truþis & maken wenen to been gode:
þat is ful yvel: & so ofte sithis lasse yvele it were: to pleyin

7. British Library, Add. MS. 24,202, fol. 17r.

8. British Library, Add. MS. 24,202, fol. 17v.

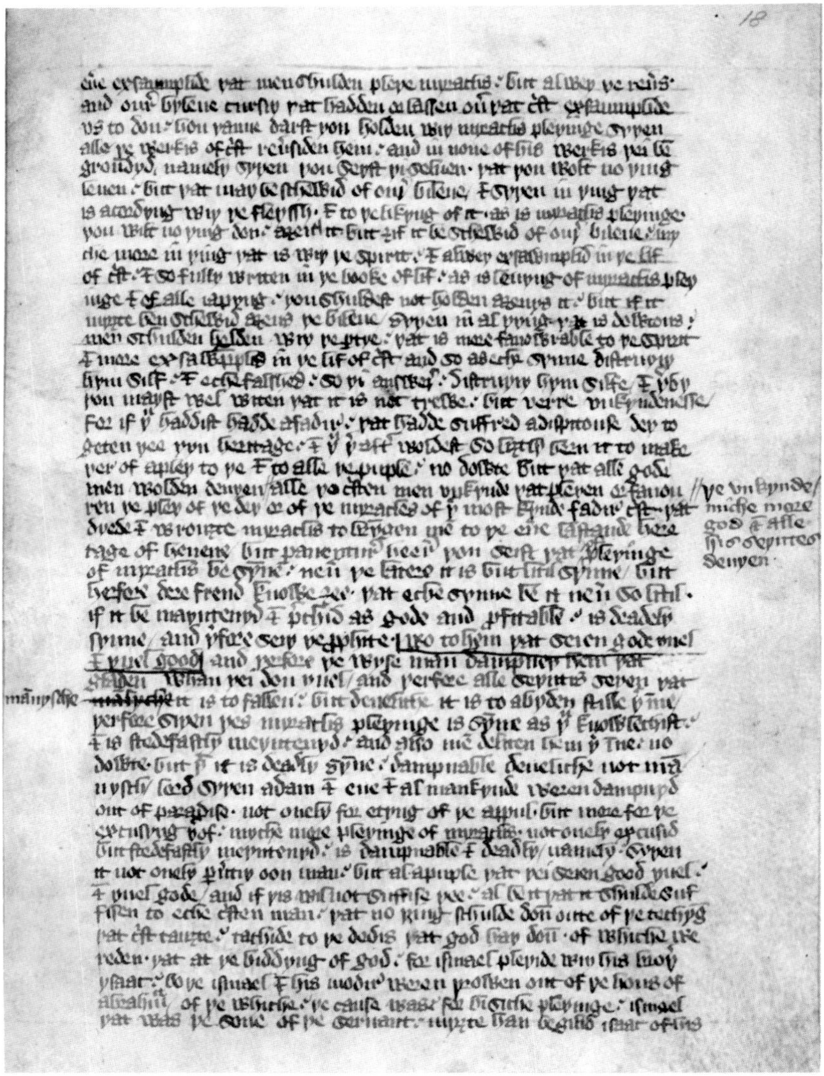
cue ensaumplide þat men shulden pleye myraclis. but also þe reneied
and oure bileue cursly þat hadden chasten oure þat crist ensaumplide
vs to don. hou þanne darst þou holden wiþ myraclis pleyinge syþen
alle þe werkis of crist reuersiden hem. and in none of his werkis þei be
groundyd. namely syþen þou seyst þi seluen þat þou wost no þing
leuen. but þat may be shewid of oure bileue. and syþen in þing þat
is acordyng wiþ þe fleyssh. and to þe likyng of it. as is myraclis pleyinge
þou wilt no þing don azenus it but ȝif it be shewid of oure bileue. mych
the more in þing þat is wiþ þe spirit. and alwey ensaumplid in þe lif
of crist. and so fully writen in þe booke of lif. as is leuyng of myraclis pley
inge and of alle lapyng. þou shuldest not holden azenus it. but if it
myȝte ben shewid azenus þe bileue. syþen in al þing þat is doutous.
men shulden holden wiþ þe partye. þat is more fauorable to þe spirit
and more ensaumplid in þe lif of crist and so as eche synne distruyeþ
hym silf. and eche falshed. so þi answere distruyeþ hym silfe. and by
þou mayst wel witen þat it is not trewe. but verre vnkyndenesse
For if þou haddist hadde a fadir. þat hadde suffred ascharnouse deþ to
geten þee þin heritage. and þou þerafter woldist so liȝtly beren it to make
þer of a pley to þe and to alle þe puple. no doute but þat alle gode
men wolden demen alle þo cristen men vnkynde þat pleyen or fauou // þe vnkynde
ren þe pley of þe deþ or of þe myraclis of þe most kynde fadir crist. þat — miche more
diede and wrouzte myraclis to bryngen vs to þe euerlastande here — god and alle
tage of heuene. but parauenture here þou seist þat pleyinge — his seyntes
of myraclis be synne. neuerþeles it is but litil synne. but — demen.
herfore dere frend knowe ȝee þat eche synne be it neuer so litil.
if it be mayntened and preisid as gode and profitable. is deadly
synne. and þerfore seiþ þe prophete. wo to hym þat seien gode euel
and euel good. and þerfore þe wyse man dampneþ hem þat
gladen whan þei don euel. and þerfore alle seyntis seyen þat
manysshe [struck] it is to fallen. but deuelishe it is to abyden stille þerinne
þerfore syþen þes myraclis pleyinge is synne as þou knowlechist.
and is stedefastly meyntened. and also men deliten hem in þerinne. no
doute but þat it is deadly synne. dampnable deuelishe not man
nyshly. seed syþen adam and eue and al mankynde weren dampnyd
out of paradise. not onely for etyng of þe appul. but more for þe
excusing þerof. myche more pleyinge of myraclis not onely excusid
but stedefastly meyntened. is dampnable and deadly. namely syþen
it not onely peruertiþ oon man. but al þe puple þat þei seien good euel.
and euel gode. and if þis wil not suffise þee. al be it þat it shulde suf
fisen to eche cristen man. þat no þing shulde don oute of þe techyng
þat crist tauzte. nameliche to þe dedis þat god hath don. of whiche we
reden. þat at þe bidding of god. for ismael pleyide wiþ his broþer
ysaac. bobe ismael and his modir weren prolben out of þe hous of
abraham of þe whiche þe cause was for bitirli pleyinge. ismael
þat was þe sone of þe seruaunt. myȝte han begilid ysaac of his

9. British Library, Add. MS. 24,202, fol. 18r.

10. British Library, Add. MS. 24,202, fol. 18v.

11. British Library, Add. MS. 24,202, fol. 19r.

bysynde. & mennis lustis bifore & so mennis wil to ben maad þan bi
his owne wille: no wondir þof he sende oure vengaunce þ aft.
as be moost nede for his grete riȝtwisnesse & mercy/ and siþen
it is þat þe wise man seiþ/ þe ende of myrþis is sorowe/ & aftir
pu. 14. oure lawȝyng schal be medelid wiþ sorowe/ and þerfore as
experience puteþ ensaumplen þat suche men apostasie in þe
puple & schide neiȝ þe vengaunce of god upon vs outher of pesti-
lence outher of debate outher of flodis or of derþe & of many oþer
and comunely whan men be most vnskilfuly merye: sone
aftir falliþ sorowe/ siþen suche myraclis pleyinge now on day
es. witnessiþ þre þingis/ first is grete synne bifore/ þe se
cound it witnessiþ grete foly in þe doinge/ and þe þridde gre
et vengaunce aftir/ for riȝt as þe children of israel whan
moyses was in þe hil bisily preyinge for hem þei mystristing
to hym worschipiden a calf of gold & afterward eten & drinken
& risen to pleyn & afterward weren slayn of hem þre & twen
Exod. 32. ty thousend of men/ so þanne as þis pleyinge witnesside þe
synne of þ maumetrie bifore & her mystrist to moyses. whan
ne þei schulde most han tristened to hym: and aft. þ foly in þ
pleyinge/ and þe þridde vengaunce þat cam aft.: so þis mira
of men. clis pleyinge is verre witnesse of auerice & coveytise bifore þat
is maumetrie as seiþ þe apostele/ for þat þat þei schulden spenden
upon þe nedis of þ neiȝboris: þei spenden upon þe pleyis.
& to peyen þ rente & þer dette þei wolen grucche: and spende þ to
two so myche upon þ pley þei wolen no þinge grucchen/ also
to gideren men to gidere to bien þe derre þer vetailis & to sti
ren men to glotonye & to pride & boost þei pleyn þes myraclis.
and also to han wherof to spenden on þese myraclis. & to holde
felawschipe of glotenye & lecherie in suche dayes of myraclis
pleyinge: þei bisien hem before to more gredily bigilen þ neiȝbors
in byinge & in sellyng/ and so þis pleyinge of myraclis now
on dayes: is verre witnesse of hidous coveytise þat is mau
metrie/ and riȝt as moyses was þ tyme in þe hil most preiynge
aboute þe puple: so now is crist in hevene wiþ his fader most
bisily preiynge for þe puple/ and neiȝ þe same as þe children
of israel diden þat tyme þat in hem was in þ pleyinge of þ
maumetrie most folily to distroien þe grete travele of moy
ses: so men now on dayes aft. þer hidouse maumetrie of
coveytise in þ pleying of myraclis þei don þat in hem is
to distroie þe continuel preyer of crist in hevene for hem/ and
so þ myraclis pleyinge witnessiþ þ most folye in þ doinge/
and siþen as vnkyndely seiden to aaron þe children of israel
moyses beinge in þe hil. we witen neuer what is of moyses.
make siþen goddis þat gon bifore us: so vnkyndeli seyen

12. British Library, Add. MS. 24,202, fol. 19v.

men nowe on dayes · crist doþ now no myraclis for us: þerfore we
pleyen þe olde · addyng many lesyngis þerto so colourably: þat
þe puple ȝyve as myche credense to hem as to þe trewþe / and
so þei forȝeten to ben bysie of þe weyes of crist for þe mawmetrye þat men don to siche myraclis pleyinge / mawmetrye
[illegible]: for siche pleyinge men as myche honouren or more:
þan þe word of god whanne it is prechid / and þerfore blasfeme
þei seyen þat siche pleyinge doþ more good: þan þe word
of god whanne it is prechid to þe puple / alas what more blas-
femie is ageinst þee · þan to seyen to don þe ~~biddyng~~ þi biddyng.
as is to prechen þe word of god: doþ fer lasse good: þan to don þat
þat is bodyn onely by man & not by god · as is myraclis pleyinge
but forsoþe as þe liknesse of myraclis we clepen myraclis: riȝt
so þe golden calfe þe children of israel clepiden it god / not for it was
in itsilf · but for þei maden it to liknesse of god · in þe whiche
þei hadden mynde of þe olde myraclis of god bifore · & for þat
liknesse þei worschipiden & preysiden as þei worschipiden & preysiden god in þe dede of his myraclis to hem / and þerfore þei diden [illegible] mawmetrye / so siche now on dayes myche of
þe puple worschipen & preysen onely þe liknesse of myraclis þe
of god as myche as þe word of god in þe precious moþ by
þe whiche alle myraclis be don: no doute þat ne þe puple doþ
more mawmetrie now in siche myraclis pleyinge: þan dide
þat tyme þe puple of israel þat in pleyinge of þe calf · in as myche as
þe lesyngis & lustis of myraclis pleyinge þat men worschipen in hem is more contrarious to god · & more acordynge wiþ
þe devel þan was þat golden calf þat þe puple worschipid / and
þerfore þe mawmetrie þe þat tyme was but figure & liknesse
of mennus mawmetrye now / and þerfore seiþ þe postel alle
þes þingis in figure fellen to hem and þerfore in siche myraclis [illegible]
pleyinge þe devel is most plesid · as þe devel is best payed to
disceyve men in þe liknesse of þat þing · in whiche by god [illegible]
weren comfortid byforhond · and in whiche þe devel was [illegible]
[illegible] byforhond / þerfore oute of doute siche myraclis pleyinge:
[illegible] myche more vengaunce þan dide þe pleyinge of þe children
of israel after þe pleyinge of þe calf / as þis pleyinge [illegible] but
[illegible] grettere & mo benefetis of god / alas [illegible] children
pleyinge witnessiþ þer fadris synnes before hem & þe owne
original synnes bifore · & þe owne defaute of wisdom whanne
þei pleyen · & þer chastisyng afterward schal more greve
hem: so myche more þis myraclis pleyinge witnessiþ [illegible]
[illegible] synnes beforehond · & þe forȝetyng of þe mayster
crist · and þe owne folye · & þe folye of [illegible] passinge þe folye
of children · & þat þis is grete vengaunce to comyn to hem

13. British Library, Add. MS. 24,202, fol. 20r.

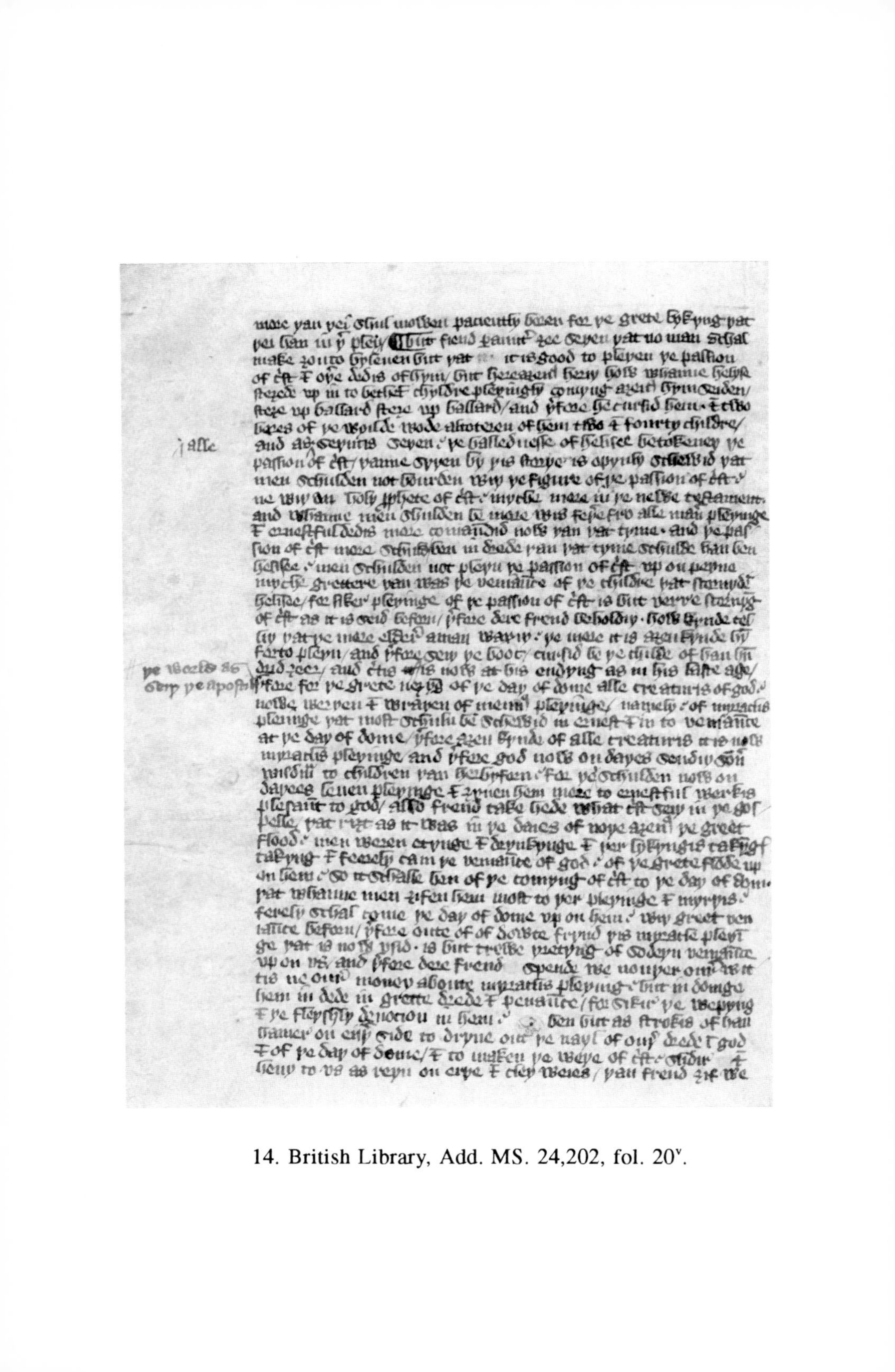

14. British Library, Add. MS. 24,202, fol. 20ᵛ.

15. British Library, Add. MS. 24,202, fol. 21[r].